The
PHOTOGUIDE
to
Low Light
Photograph

GW01606948

THE ⓕ PHOTOGUIDES

THE PHOTOGUIDE TO THE 35 mm SINGLE LENS REFLEX	Leonard Gaunt
THE PHOTOGUIDE TO HOME PROCESSING	R E Jacobson
THE PHOTOGUIDE TO ENLARGING	Günter Spitzing
THE PHOTOGUIDE TO PORTRAITS	Günter Spitzing
THE PHOTOGUIDE TO FLASH	Günter Spitzing
THE PHOTOGUIDE TO EFFECTS AND TRICKS	Günter Spitzing
THE PHOTOGUIDE TO MOVIEMAKING	Paul Petzold
THE PHOTOGUIDE TO 35 mm	Leonard Gaunt
THE PHOTOGUIDE TO COLOUR	David Lynch
THE PHOTOGUIDE TO FILTERS	Clyde Reynolds
THE PHOTOGUIDE TO COLOUR PRINTING	Jack Coote
THE PHOTOGUIDE TO LOW LIGHT PHOTOGRAPHY	Paul Petzold

This book is sold subject to the Standard Conditions of Sale of Net Books and may not be re-sold in the UK below the net price

The PHOTOGUIDE to Low Light Photography

Paul Petzold

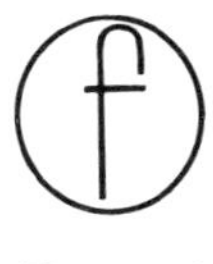

Focal Press
London & New York

© Focal Press Limited 1976

All rights reserved. No part of this publication may be reproduced, stored in a retrieval system, or transmitted in any form or by any means, electronic, mechanical, photocopying, recording or otherwise, without the prior permission of the Copyright owner.

ISBN 0 240 50922 6

Text set in 10/12 pt. Photon Univers, printed by photolithography, and bound in Great Britain at The Pitman Press, Bath

Contents

What is Low Light?

Low light is any light that is lower in power than we are normally accustomed to when taking photographs. It includes the light that we see and live by much of the time. It might be the light from a window, from a table lamp, from a fire or candle, a streetlamp or a neon sign – or any other light source that happens to be there.

Because it occurs naturally, and is not deliberately put there for photography it is very often called 'existing' or 'available' light. Modern cameras with fast lenses can take pictures by this light without much difficulty. But many people still do not realize that and consequently never attempt it. They tend to be prejudiced by old wives' tales that anything but broad daylight is "too dark."

In fact, some kind of existing light has been used since the beginning of photography. Victorians used daylight through the large windows of their glass-house studios although their films were very slow.

Today, we use window light not because we have to but because we want to. It has a character all its own and some people consider it the best light source for portraiture.

Advantages

Existing light has the practical advantages of cheapness and convenience. There are no special lamps, no cables, no search for a power source, no bulbs to blow or be replaced and no batteries to charge or change. There is no problem with setting up stands or finding conveniently placed supports for lamps and so there is nothing to be knocked over or tripped over.

Existing light also allows you to take pictures without disturbing the subject – indeed he may not even be aware that you are taking a picture at all. You can take pictures where flash would be unwelcome or even forbidden. You can also make your pictures look more natural than those taken with flash or lamps, because the light is coming from the right place and in the right way. That does not mean, of course, that the film in your camera sees a scene in the same way as your eye. But what existing light photography does avoid is the very deliberate and artificial effect of carefully placed lighting – something one never sees in real life.

Working by existing light frees you from the problem of maintaining the right distance from the flashgun or lamps to the subject.

You have more freedom to move about and concentrate on getting good pictures. It offers great variety of lighting character. Any effects gained are always in tune with the situation in which they are found because they are the actual lighting in the scene. Window light in particular offers great scope for variations and is more controllable than you might think.

But existing light is also capable of giving you effects in their own right. It all depends how you tackle the particular situation you find. You can get curious highlights or lighting angles which entirely transform the appearance of a subject. You can get silhouettes, subjects outlined in light, grotesque toplighting – all from sources which, treated another way, also serve for very straightforward photography. It is a similar game to playing with photographic lights but the rules are different and it depends far more on keeping your eyes open and taking notice of the effects that are all around you.

Shortcomings

Of course existing light photography also has shortcomings. Certain light sources place a restriction on what you can do. They may not be powerful enough to allow you to get the particular type of picture you envisaged. Or they may be the wrong colour so that your pictures have an unpleasant tinge.

Existing light does not offer the control of the individually movable light. Nevertheless it often provides more interesting pictures because photographic lamps are really quite difficult to use skilfully and it is only too easy to fall back on standard lighting set-ups.

But it is quite wrong to assume that existing light offers no scope for control. It is a different kind of control. Although you may not be able to manipulate the light source you can often move the subject to gain more or less the same ends. In some cases you may be able to extinguish a light or use a reflector or shader of some sort to add light or take it away. You could also combine available light with a photographic lamp in a main or support role.

In this book we are concerned with existing light mainly as a prime source.

Taking successful pictures by existing light is largely a question of knowing how to use it and make the most of it. The important thing to avoid is trying to force something out of it that it cannot give. You should not work against it but go along with it. The following chapters tell you how to experiment and discover for yourself the joys and excitement of working with light that is already in the scene – however weak that light may be.

The Limits of Picture Taking

It is safe to say that most subjects you can see, you can photograph – with only a few reservations. The question of how weak the light can be for a picture depends to a large extent on what you hope to achieve. If you have a weak light source and you are aiming to secure some detail in the shadow areas of a subject lit by it, you clearly have more of a problem than if you are going to content yourself with a subject in deep shadow and "drawn" only in a few highlights.

The problem is one of exposure – the amount of light that is received by the film. This is governed by the brightness of the light reflected by the subject, the aperture set on the lens and the length of time the light is allowed to act on the film. Films of different sensitivities, or speeds, require differing amounts of light to give the same effect. For situations in which little light is available you have a greater need to use films of higher speed than normal, whether you shoot in black and white or colour.

The camera

Any camera with a lens of reasonably wide maximum aperture, say *f*2.8 or larger, that you can set normally, is suitable for available light photography.

Almost the only type of camera which is either inconvenient or impossible for the job is the fully automatic type which sets its own exposures according to a reading obtained by a built-in exposure meter but does not allow you to "override" the system and set exposures manually. It is possible, even with some of these cameras, to control the exposure settings to some extent by adjusting the film speed setting ring. This misleads the meter into thinking the camera is loaded with a film of a different speed from that which is actually inside. But the camera must have a meter which indicates the exposure setting in some way, otherwise you will not be able to tell what aperture you have, in fact, set.

As some fully automatic cameras are designed for working only at normal light levels you may encounter other snags. The meter may not be sensitive enough to read low light levels. On some cameras if the meter does not obtain a reading the shutter release is automatically locked and the camera cannot be used at all. A fully

automatic camera whose meter *is* sensitive enough may give you a reading and automatically set an aperture or exposure combination which still does not give you the effect you were after.
As a general rule then, the best camera for available light photography is the one that gives you enough control over exposure to cope with all the situations you will meet – and this fortunately is so in the great majority of cameras.

Exposure

Assuming that you have a camera which does allow manual control of exposure you can use this in various ways according to the subject. You may be able to set the maximum aperture and, having taken a reading which indicates the shutter speed you can use, hold the camera in the hand while you take the picture. If the shutter speed indicated is lower than 1/30 sec you should set the camera on a tripod or some other solid support to gain sufficient steadiness during the exposure. Few people can hand-hold a camera rigidly enough to obtain really sharp pictures at 1/15 sec settings. However, once you have opted for a tripod or other support in a particular situation you have also given up some of the freedom of movement you would enjoy with the camera held in the hand. Depending on the subject, this may or may not be a loss. With active subjects such as children or animals the tripod may put you at a disadvantage. At shutter speeds as low as 1/15 sec you have little chance of getting critically sharp results with a moving subject anyway. But a tripod deprives you of mobility; it slows you down because it takes longer to move from one position to another and line up the camera on the subject again. Also the tripod shots all tend to be at the same height, unless you adjust for this.
Provided your subject does not move, a tripod may allow you to take time exposures (see page 42). You may then be able to set smaller aperture than the maximum and so increase the available depth of field.
Depth of field is the distance range in front of and behind the point focused on by a camera, within which the subject still appears acceptably sharp. Subjects closer than, or beyond these two limits appear

out of focus. The further outside the depth of field the subject is placed the more out of focus it appears. The maximum lens aperture so often necessary for available light situations unfortunately offers the least depth of field so unless you focus accurately there is a greater risk of the subject appearing unsharp. If the situation allows you to stop down the lens to a smaller aperture you gain more depth of field. Depth of field always extends somewhat farther behind the focused point than in front.

The apertures and the shutter speeds on a camera are directly interrelated in terms of exposure value. They work together controlling the amount of light reaching the film (how much and for how long), in equal steps. A change of one aperture stop (or *f* number) is worth as much as a change to the next shutter speed. So, if you want to get more light to the film you can open the aperture by one, or two stops, say. This has the same effect as reducing the shutter speed by two steps.

The standard aperture series is *f* 1.4, 2, 2.8, 4, 5.6, 8, 11, 16. The smallest figures represent the largest apertures and are the settings you are most likely to need in existing light photography. From the smallest aperture, *f* 16, each of these figures represents a doubling of the effective exposure, so that *f* 11 gives double the exposure of *f* 16, *f* 8 gives double that of *f* 11 and four times that of *f* 16 and so on.

Working in conjunction with these the standard range of shutter speeds controlling the period in seconds for which the light is allowed to reach the film is as follows:

1, 1/8 1/15 1/30 1/60 1/125 1/250 1/500 1/1000

It will be noticed that some figures have been rounded off for convenience.

Choice of shutter speeds

The settings likely to be most useful in available light photography are the slower speeds, 1/30 and 1/15, mainly for shots where the camera is hand held or partially supported. When on a tripod or other solid object which is being used to support the camera, exposures of 1/8–1 sec are possible or even time exposures. For time exposures the shutter is held open for periods longer than one second and this is

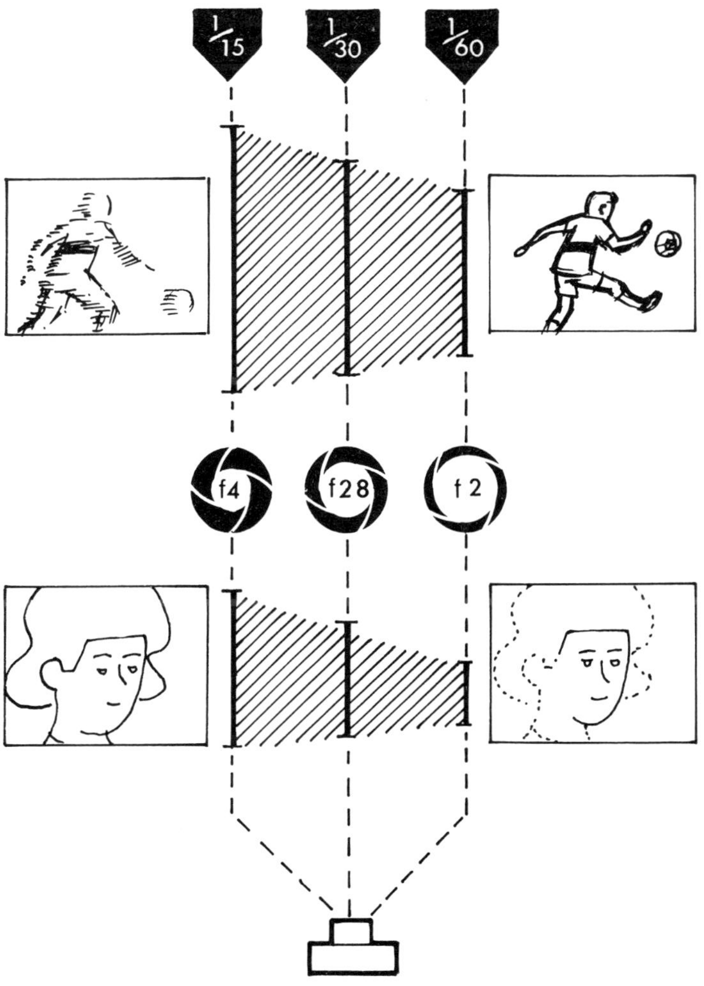

Shutter speeds and apertures in low light. Different combinations to give the same exposure have different uses. A slow shutter speed with a small aperture can not arrest action but gives greater depth of field. A faster speed stops action but the wider aperture needed gives little depth and makes focusing more critical.

made possible by the "B" setting provided on most cameras. Normally such exposures, and indeed all these below 1/15 sec can only be successful where there is absolutely no movement in the picture.

Now, suppose that your exposure meter indicates a setting of *f*4 at 1/15 sec for a low light situation. Because there is nothing handy to rest the camera on, you might feel that 1/15 sec is rather risky for a hand held shot. Any slight camera movement at such a slow shutter speed might make the whole picture slightly unsharp. Or maybe the subject itself is not quite stationary. You may well decide that you have a better chance of a good result if you reset the shutter to the next faster speed, 1/30 sec. This gives the film less exposure. But if you can compensate for that by also resetting the aperture to the next largest stop, *f*2.8, the film gets the same amount of light – a shorter burst of light but more of it.

You could go one step further if you really felt the need. Suppose the subject is an animal that is moving about quite a bit. You are more likely to be moving the camera to follow it. There is now less chance of the camera or subject being quite still for the exposure. So to be on the safe side you move up to the next faster speed – 1/30 sec. You again compensate for this reduction in exposure by opening the aperture further, to *f*2, if the camera can do it. Again, for this shot the film receives the same amount of light. And you can shoot with reasonable confidence of there being no blur from camera or subject movement. You do, however, have the problem that you now have even less depth of field so your subject is more likely to pass out of focus if you do not maintain the same camera/subject distance, or make quick adjustments of focus on the camera lens when necessary to keep the subject sharp. When shooting by available light, where you are often working on the critical end of the exposure scale, success largely depends on balancing these two factors, shutter speed and aperture, in a way that suits the situation, yet allows the film enough light to give a proper image.

Choice of aperture

Now let us look at a case where the aperture setting would be the main priority. Here, you use the shutter speed to regulate the exposure and make it agree with the recommendation given by the meter for the aperture you have chosen.

The chief advantage of using smaller apertures is the gain in depth of field. This is particularly important when the camera is focused on a subject at close range, but the importance also depends on the kind of subject you are photographing. If the subject has great depth dimensionally and you want the furthest and nearest parts as sharp as possible, a small aperture setting is indicated. With many low light situations that would probably mean that you would have to settle for a time exposure – especially if you were determined to use the smallest apertures, which allow very little light to pass. A time exposure means putting the camera on a tripod or rigid support and having an immobile subject. If the subject is not deep dimensionally but is likely to move about, a small aperture helps. But the necessary slow shutter speed may then record some subject movement as a blur. So it may be more practicable to use a wider aperture and be prepared to refocus or move with the subject.

If you are fairly close to your subject you may need more depth than usual to get it all sharp. But the further away your camera, the greater, in effect, is the depth of sharpness. So a mobile subject in existing light is easier to photograph from a distance – with the smallest aperture that allows a reasonably practical shutter speed.

If a subject is bulky, and you are taking pictures from nearby, it may not be essential to have the whole of it sharp. For a start you need hardly worry about the background. In existing light pictures you expect that to be out of focus almost as a rule. The best principle to follow if you have little depth of field at your disposal and want to place the plane of sharp focus in the best place is to focus on the most prominent part of the subject. This may be the nearest part or the most brightly lit but it is always the centre of interest – the place to which the eye is drawn for the meaning in the picture. In the case of human subjects this is invariably the eyes (unless they are not in the picture). It does not matter too much if the rest of the head, in front and behind is out of focus as long as the eyes are sharp. But what you should try to aim for with portraits in low light is that the face – eyes, nose and mouth – is all sharp. The hair, ears, clothes, etc do not matter nearly so much.

There are cases where you deliberately select a wide aperture to make sure that some features in front of the subject, or in the background are thrown well out of focus. But with most low light situations this would probably happen anyway. A wider aperture, if possible, would be used only to exaggerate that effect. Inevitably there are occasions when your existing light subject is two-dimensional or very nearly so. Because the subject has no depth you have no need to worry about depth of field. So you can use a wide aperture. But you *must* focus accurately. If, however, you are photographing a painting or drawing or copying a photograph you are not likely to use a wide aperture. You are after the best image quality you can get, so you generally put the camera on a tripod and use a very small aperture and a long exposure.

Lens performance

Stopping down to a smaller aperture does in the majority of cases improve the performance of the lens. Few camera lenses give their best sharpness, resolution and contrast at or near full aperture. However, low light work is one of those areas in photography where actual lens performance often seems to matter less than usual. You are often taking pictures of subjects which are inherently full of contrast – window-light portraits for example. In a picture, this contrast in lighting gives the illusion of sharpness even if the picture is not really sharp. In many existing light situations much of the subject may be in shadow. Here again, lens performance is not critical as any lack of sharpness in the image is lost in the darkness. Certain forms of domestic lighting tend to destroy the impression of sharpness in a picture taken by them. Lens performance becomes insignificant by comparison and hardly detracts from the picture if it is not quite up to standard. So in most of your pictures you really do not have to worry too much about lens performance when working at wide apertures.

Adding a stop or two

In any given situation your meter tells you what exposure to give. You may be content to take this advice and shoot accordingly. But what does an exposure reading mean? With certain kinds of existing light subject, exposure estimation can be a hit and miss affair. If the subject is full of contrast – bright highlights and large areas of shadow – the meter may take an average reading of all it can see and tell you to give an exposure which may not give you the exposure you wanted. There may be far too much detail in the shadow. More often your results show just the reverse of this. You have lost most of the interest of your picture in deep shadows. (Only occasionally there may be the odd case when all you wanted was a bright outline of highlights with very deep shadow elsewhere.) Occasionally you can partially remedy this with the aperture control.

An exposure meter treats every subject as if it consists mainly of mid-tones. This description tallies with the majority of scenes taken under normal outdoor conditions. But existing light subjects are often nothing like that at all. You may have very high contrast in the picture and you would like to expose the film in such a way as to favour either the highlights or the shadow areas. A person seated by a window may be very brightly lit on the face but their attractive clothes fade away into darkness. When you take your reading the meter is strongly influenced by the bright face and the strong light coming in through a part of the window also seen in the picture. It adds up all these bright and dark areas and gives you a reading which will make the *average* of them come out as a mid-tone on the film. If the average is a low, shadowy level you will get some shadow detail, but the highlights may be overexposed. If the average is a brighter tone, which is more likely to be the case, you will get correctly exposed highlights but no details in the shadows. So an interesting dress completely disappears.

Film cannot cope with as great a range of contrast as can our eyes. Sometimes, therefore, it helps to bias the "correct" exposure in such a way as to favour either one area or another. In the case of a scene which you feel is too full of shadow you could try opening up the aperture by a stop or two, without touching the shutter setting. This would give you twice or four times more exposure than that indicated by the meter. You will certainly gain some detail in the shadows. But you may "clog up" details in the brighter areas by overexposure. The features in a person's face which are shown by small variations in tone may be lost and the whole face may simply become a white blob.

Meanwhile light from the window may now be so overexposed that it causes some flare in the picture. Those are the dangers of playing with exposure. Still, it is worth a try if it is done with moderation. There is less risk if you reduce exposure in order to deepen the shadows except that you may lose too much of the subject in darkness and make the picture rather lifeless by allowing the highlights only a dull tone.

In black and white photography you can modify the effect to some extent in printing. But you should still aim to produce the negative that is capable of giving you the print without trouble. Remedies applied in printing rarely result in a first class print. With colour, particularly transparencies, you must aim for exactly the effect you want. If you wish to bias your exposure a stop or two under or over to try and improve the picture, it is safest to take a shot at the recommended exposure as well. This may be the best one!

Not enough light

The best policy where your meter tells you that there is not enough light, and if there is nothing else you can do, is to shoot anyway and chance it. Your results may not be quite what you wished but at least you will have a picture. You may even be pleasantly surprised. As we have seen, meters can be rather pessimistic sometimes and expect everything before them to be in a convenient range of normal tones.

If there is insufficient light and you have no hope of using any of the remedies previously suggested there are two remaining courses of action. Use a faster film, or try to get some more light on the subject.

Faster film

It might be said that if you are going to do low light photography you should start by loading your camera with a fast film. But you may not realize when you load the camera that you will be taking existing light pictures. This is a familiar problem. As familiar, in fact, as the reverse case – you load for low light pictures, then suddenly find that you need to take some outdoor shots in bright sunshine. That may be dif-

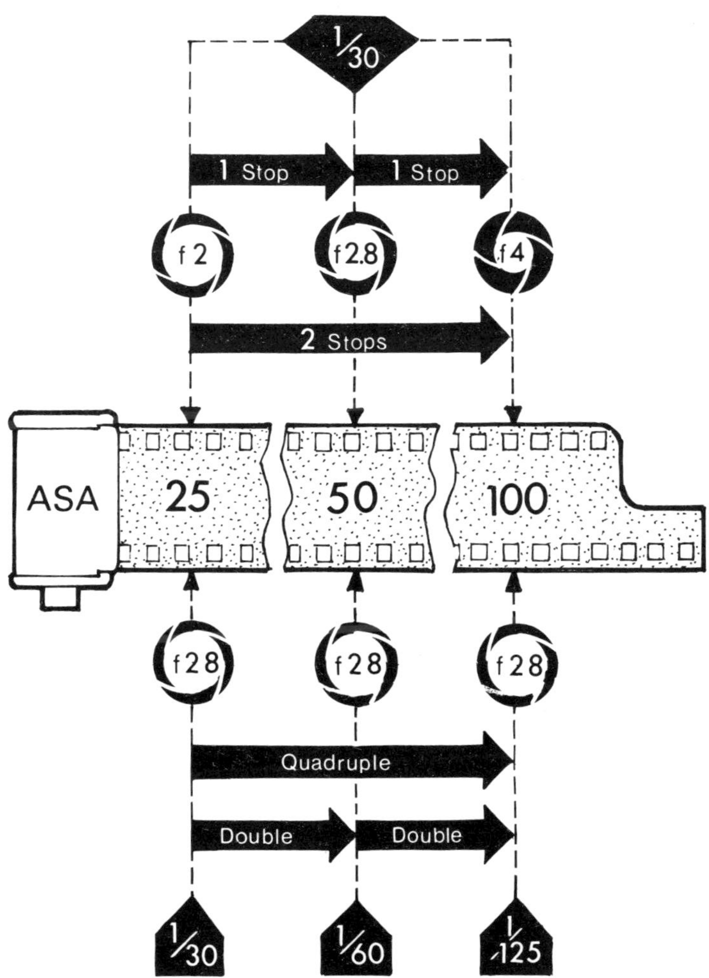

The speed or sensitivity of the film you choose governs the shutter speed and aperture you can set in a given low light situation. If you use a film of double the speed you can set the aperture at one whole stop smaller for the same shutter speed or set the shutter to give half the exposure time at the same aperture. Using a film four times as fast gains you another stop, or half the exposure time again.

ficult with fast film. The final solution is, of course, to have two cameras, one loaded with film of normal speed and another with fast film for existing light photography. But if you work in colour *and* black and white you need *four* cameras to cover all eventualities! What advantages or disadvantages, if any, are there in using a faster film?

The great advantage of a faster film is that it needs less exposure to yield the same result as an ordinary film. Whereas a normal colour film may have a speed of 64 ASA, you can use a fast film of 160 ASA – nearly three times the speed.

The ASA speed rating given to a film is the effective sensitivity as stated by the manufacturer. The letters ASA stand for the once so-called American Standards Association. Their system of speed rating is the most commonly used and, together with the German DIN system is recognized internationally. Although these two systems are different they can be translated across with a conversion table. Many films, in fact, have the speed in both systems marked on the film package.

The speed given to a film is one calculated by the maker when testing the material under certain fixed laboratory conditions. It is the speed *recommended* for setting on the camera meter so that it estimates the exposure in each case bearing the film in mind. This speed rating is not, however, inviolable. Several factors can affect the speed of a film – the quality of the light source, the kind of processing the film receives, whether any filter is used on the camera (see page 182). Where a film is processed commercially, the laboratory assumes that it has been exposed at the recommended rating. For the purposes of existing light photography it is possible to "up-rate" a film, ie by setting the meter at a higher ASA figure than that recommended for the film. In that case the film must be push-processed (see page 204) to make up for the loss in exposure and the laboratory informed accordingly. Obviously, there are limits to how far this forcing of speed can be taken.

At present we will assume that all films are to be exposed at the recommended ASA settings. The ASA ratings are directly proportional to one another – a film of 100 ASA is double the speed of one of 50 ASA and four times as fast as one rated at 25 ASA. Each doubling of the ASA speed represents one whole stop difference in exposure. (The equivalent DIN figure advances by 3 for every doubling of the

ASA number, thus: 18, 21, 24 DIN equals 25, 50 and 100 ASA.) This, of course, also represents one shutter speed difference.

A "medium" speed black and white film is likely to be rated at 125 ASA or around that figure. Fast film, of the kind you might use for available light photography, might be 320 ASA. Colour films are still generally given a lower speed rating. So you would reckon in terms of 64 ASA for a medium speed material whereas 160 ASA is a fast colour film.

What effect will this extra speed have in a typical case where you are working with existing light? Your exposure meter says you should be exposing at an aperture of *f*2.8, which might be the maximum on your camera, and a shutter setting of 1/8 sec where the camera needs to be on a tripod or other solid object and the subject must be absolutely still. With a film of three times the speed you could be using a shutter speed of 1/30 sec. That would allow you to hand-hold the camera and photograph movement – say, an average amount of human or animal activity – with a fair certainty of having most of your pictures free from blur.

On some cameras, where the meter, by locking the shutter release, does not allow you to take a picture, it may change its mind if your camera is loaded with a faster film.

A camera that has no speeds below 1/30 sec may operate with fast film using the slowest available speed whereas this would have been too short an exposure for an ordinary film. A certain picture which has only a marginal chance of coming out successfully with standard speed film may be well within the reach of your camera if you shoot with a faster material.

The main disadvantage of using a fast film is that it has a more prominent grain structure. This is less likely to be noticeable on projected transparencies than in prints made from negatives – depending on the degree of enlargement. Prominent grain generally tends to show up most strongly in mid-tones. It is far less obvious in shadow or highlight areas. In many kinds of existing-light picture the contrasts are strong and most of the picture is in deep shadow. For these there may be less reason for avoiding the fastest films. Provided the subject is kept large in the picture area and therefore you are not enlarging from only a small portion of the negative, and the film is processed according to instructions, grain is not likely to be a great problem. Some people actually like grain in their pictures. If you are one of them, you are fortunate. The means by which you force it to appear are very beneficial to shooting at low light levels.

If you are shooting colour transparencies there are really no shortcomings with using a faster film. You have only the problem of whether the material is too fast for general work as well and this applies to all fast film. In all your general work you will probably find that you have to set the higher shutter speeds and smallest apertures for virtually every shot. This may be a snag if you want to use speeds and apertures for creative purposes. In bright scenes you may find that even with the smallest aperture and fastest shutter speed on your camera the film is still overexposed. You can fit a neutral density (ND) filter over the lens to reduce the brightness of all colours proportionally. ND filters are available in various strengths, but they are usually quite expensive.

Another attribute of the fast film favours its choice for shooting colour transparencies. It allows a greater margin of error in exposure before the picture becomes unacceptably under- or over-exposed. As the projected film is the actual film used in the camera, there is no scope for correcting errors in exposure after processing.

Adding light

There are many ways, depending on the situation, in which you can increase light on your subject without resorting to flash or photo lamps.

You could try moving your subject to a position that takes advantage of any areas where the light is stronger – light pools around domestic lights, windows, fires, etc. The light could possibly be reinforced with extra light from the existing lamps by moving them closer or switching on any lights that have been overlooked. Normally a single domestic light does not add much to what you can see in a setting already lit by several others, unless the extra light is close by.

If the main source is daylight through a window, you could move up a table lamp to put some extra light in to the shadow side of the subject. A very effective alternative with window light is to pick up light with a suitable reflector positioned facing the window but on the shady side

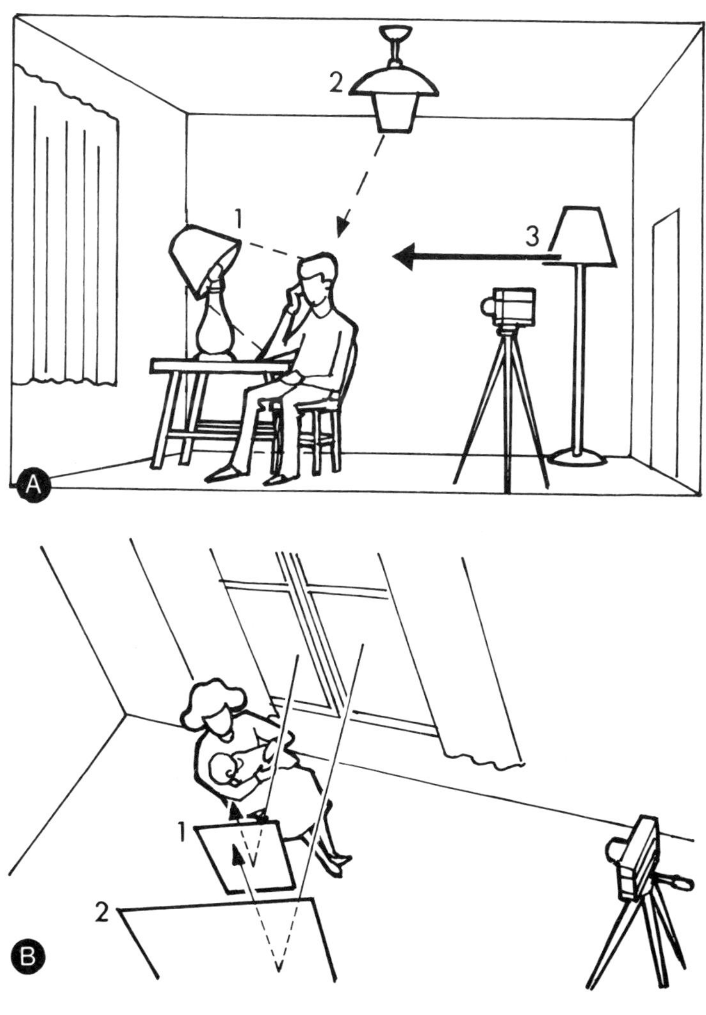

Increasing the light on the subject. A. You can (1) move the subject closer to the light source, (2) switch on the main source or other lights or (3) move the light closer to the subject. B. To lighten shadows on the opposite side of the main source use a small reflector for close up portraits, and a large reflector for a full figure.

of the subject. This light can be angled in to the shadow area and, provided the reflector is not too far away, it is amazingly strong. The strength can be adjusted with the distance of the reflector, according to the type of reflector used (see page 45).
Reflectors can also be used in some domestic light shots but are usually not so effective because the main light source is not nearly as powerful as daylight. Reflectors are useful in dim outdoor situations. Glimmering sky light can be reflected into the subject's face. A beam of sunlight in a dark woodland can be picked up with a reflector for the same purpose. Lights from shop windows, streetlamps, etc can all be controlled to a greater or lesser extent by this device.
Finally, if, despite all the foregoing measures, the light still eludes you, try making do with what there is. The effect might be rather interesting!

Where you can Take Low Light Pictures

If you want to take pictures by existing light you must be aware of the light. You need to take advantage of any light you can get, so it is as well to accustom yourself to looking out for it. It is surprising how many situations we take for granted without thinking too much about the light unless we are struck by a particularly remarkable effect. It might be a sunbeam in a forest, smoke clouds lit by a nearby lamp, or a really good rainbow. Occasionally our eyes are cheated by the light. We happen to catch it at an angle where it makes an object look unfamiliar or even sinister. We move the head slightly and the effect vanishes – it was just the light. But normally we hardly notice the light is there and just let it get on with its job. And we only use it to see what we are doing. With photography, however, we depend on the light much more. And if we do not take our own light with us, in the form of flash or lamps, we rely entirely on what we can find.

This is really only a matter of seeing, but seeing in a different way – or rather, two ways. You can make yourself more conscious of the light to weigh up whether or not there is enough to take a photograph – and whether it is right for what you want. You will notice how strong the light is, what colour quality it has, the angle it is coming from, and how well it illuminates the subject.

Another approach is to search for any effects the light might be giving.

Existing light sources often create more varied character and mood in scenes than the light you take with you. You may want to take a picture because the light strikes the subject in a particularly interesting way. Or you may go for an effect in the light itself – including the light source in the picture. Light effects are discussed in a later chapter, but it is worth pointing out at this stage that anything you can photograph is potentially of value, so you should not automatically dismiss what you see simply because it is not giving you what you had in mind.

The more you notice your surroundings the more use they can be to your picture taking. Try looking around you even if you do not have your camera with you. Notice where the light is coming from and where it falls. In which areas is it strongest? What does it do to the surroundings? Where are the shadows and what are they like? The habit of awareness develops quite quickly and you will probably wonder why you had never noticed such things before.

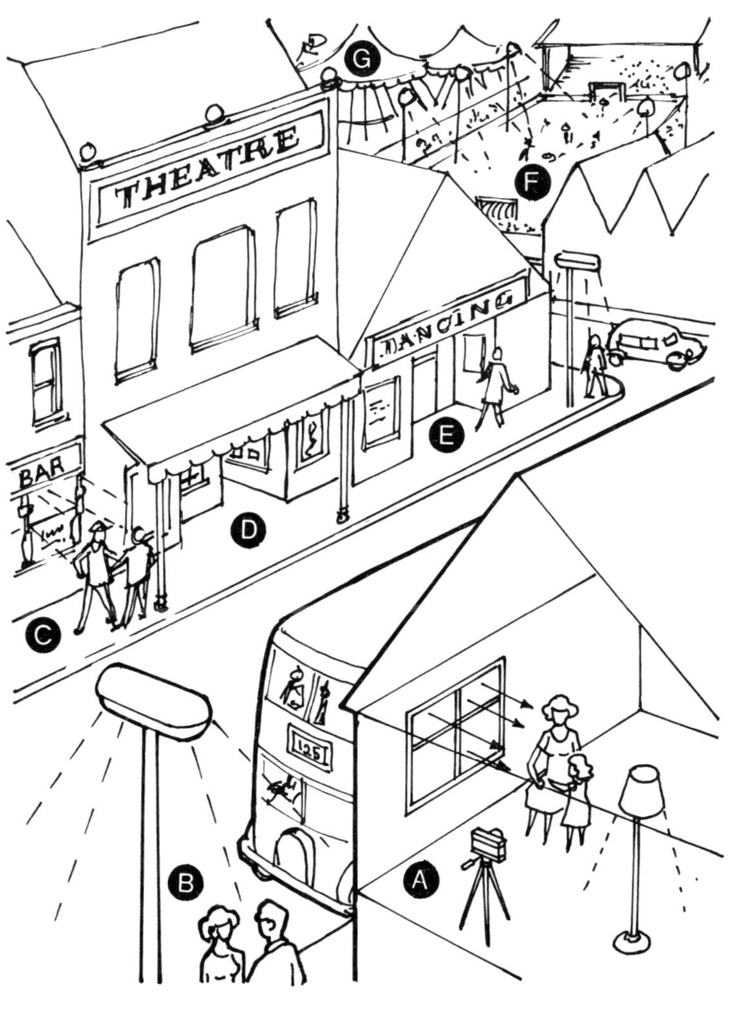

Where to look for low light pictures: (A) Indoors using window light or existing lamps (B) outdoors under street lights by shop windows etc. (C) in pubs, clubs and restaurants (D) theatres (E) dance halls (F) sportsgrounds and stadia (G) at circuses, funfairs and other events.

Where to look

You may take pictures by existing light because you have to – there is nothing else available. Or, you may deliberately seek such situations, for a special effect, mood or atmosphere, or just the challenge.
In either case you are confined to shooting in places where enough light is to be found to make a picture possible at all.
Outdoors you can take pictures by morning or evening light, including sunsets, in dull weather or in shady places. Night-time opportunities for existing light photography are provided by streets with strong overhead lighting, city lights or illuminations, floodlighting on buildings, shop windows, car headlamps, lamps in markets or town centres and reflections in streets from any of these sources, bonfires, fireworks, moonlight, the moon itself, the night sky, lightning, snow caught in strong light, and so on. The light may serve only as a means of illuminating your subject, or the source itself may be featured in the picture with or without the subject. Night photography can yield many attractive effects.
Indoors, you may take pictures at a club, cafe, pub, restaurant, church, museum or gallery where you do not want to use flash because you would make the subject aware of being photographed or you would spoil the atmosphere. In some places such as theatres or shows flash or lamps would be out of the question (if, indeed, photography is even permitted) because of the nuisance they cause. In a ballroom, dancehall or circus you would normally have to rely on available light. Wedding receptions, parties or other indoor meetings, musical gatherings, gaming establishments, auction rooms, railway stations and industrial works are all potentially existing light situations. At home or in other peoples' homes you would probably shoot by window light or ordinary domestic lamps.
There is no limit to the number of places you can find for available light photography.

Existing lamps and light pools

Daylight is all around us. Wherever we move we have more or less equal brightness. Even with relatively dim morning or evening light

which tends to come more strongly from the horizon than from above, there is still plenty of light from the sky around.
Artificial light nearly always comes from something nearer a point source. Unless many lights are involved, the light is very directional, shadows are deep and the contrast between light and shade in your pictures is quite strong. A relatively smaller portion of each picture contains mid-tones than pictures taken in ordinary daylight. Consequently, it is more difficult to get large areas of even colour, or smooth grey tones if the picture is monochrome. But the greatest problem with ordinary artificial lights is their power. If you are shooting with only one main light, it must be quite close to the subject to provide adequate lighting. Move it only a little further away and the light level reduces drastically.
There is a law which governs the intensity of light in relation to its distance from a point source. We may treat a single lamp as a point source, and the law applies well enough even if that lamp has a shade on it. According to this so-called inverse square law, the intensity of light reaching a subject is inversely proportional to the square of the distance between the lamp and the subject. This means that if you double its distance from the lamp, the subject receives only a quarter of the intensity of light that it had before. At three times the distance only one ninth of the light intensity falls on the subject. The reason for this is easily explained. The light from a lamp radiates in all directions. Therefore, if the lamp is placed further away the light is spread over a greater area and is therefore not so bright. This process is interfered with to some extent when a lamp is placed in a reflector. Some of the light that should be radiating in other directions is gathered up and redirected forward, focused over a narrower angle. In the case of domestic or display spotlights (or the light from a projector) the light is concentrated in an almost parallel beam. The intensity does not reduce much with distance and the inverse square law does not apply at all.
The law would apply most rigorously with small light sources placed in totally non-reflecting surroundings – a bright pinpoint in a void. A streetlamp at night might almost meet this requirement, or a bare light bulb hanging in a very dark room.
In practice ordinary domestic lights are in diffusers of one kind or another and a percentage of their light is reflected from light coloured

walls, the ceiling or furnishings. Some light fittings contain many lamps and often the room is lit by lights placed in various positions around it giving an all round diffused light with no strongly lit areas being apparent. But this can be very deceptive. If you were to take a photograph in such a room you might be surprised by what you got. Instead of an even, overall light level the room looks rather shadowy, with pools of light around the various lamps placed about the room.

Light pools are what you have to look for if you are short of light. Despite a high level of ambient light in any situation the inverse square law still holds good. As you bring your subject closer to the light source so the light increases. If he is at half the distance he receives four times as much light. This is an enormous difference in terms of exposure – two full stops. It can be the difference between getting a picture and not getting it. The ambient light may put some detail into the shadows but it will not light the subject.

The faster your film and the wider the maximum aperture you can use, the less dependent you are on the light pools. But the lighting on your subject may have less contrast. The depends how much ambient light there is. Where there is only a single light source the faster film or wider aperture allows you to work further away from it, which might give you more scope because the subject has more room to move. The faster film may enable you to work so far from the centre of the light pool that the subject begins to pick up light from a second light placed further off. The two-lamp lighting may be more pleasing – or it may not.

Indoors or out, you should always look out for light pools that will help you to take pictures that might otherwise be difficult, or impossible, to achieve.

How to Get the Picture

Taking a picture by existing light is often quite a straightforward matter. When you run into trouble it is usually because there is insufficient light on the subject.
Several basic techniques, none of them difficult to put into practice, will overcome your problems in the majority of cases. It is as well to understand these working methods before you attempt to apply or adapt them to the various subjects and situations discussed in later chapters.

Exposure problems and the meter

The meter in your camera is not basically designed for available light photography. It is intended for average situations where the illumination over the subject is fairly even and not exceptionally low – in other words, typical outdoor daylight scenes with or without sunlight. Many meters are simply not sensitive enough to give a reading for an existing light shot although the camera is quite capable of giving you the picture. Other meters give a reading but you must be quite sure what that reading means, as we shall see.
Exposure meters on most ordinary cameras are designed to give an exposure for the whole picture area seen by the camera lens. If the meter is built in but does not read through the camera lens it always reads the same area even if the camera allows lenses to be interchanged for others giving a wider or narrower view of the subject. Modern single lens reflex cameras often have the meter built in behind the lens in such a way that it takes its reading from the whole and/or part of the view seen through the lens (TTL). So-called spot meters read from only a limited part of the picture. The exact area varies from model to model. Meters that read from the entire view seen by the lens have that view adjusted automatically if the lens is changed for another of wider or narrower angle. Spot metering cameras have advantages in certain available light situations where you want to take your reading from only a part of the scene without going up to the subject.
An exposure meter may be built in to the camera or it may be a separate instrument that you hold in the hand. The latter allows you the freedom to walk about taking readings without having to move

the camera. This can be an advantage in low light situations where the camera has been placed on a tripod or carefully lined up on the subject beforehand and it would be inconvenient to move it. Otherwise, apart from the separate meter not being linked in any way with the camera exposure mechanism it does essentially the same job as a built-in meter. You take your reading and transfer the calculated settings to the camera shutter and aperture controls.

Some people like to use a separate meter although they already have one in the camera, because of its independence of the camera. For much available light photography that has advantages. You can go up to your subject and take a reading from nearby, pointing the meter only at the part or parts you are interested in and measuring the light levels there. You *can* do this with the built-in meter, moving the camera up to the subject, taking a reading and then moving back to the shooting position to take the picture. But with some cameras this is not possible because there is no means of either setting or "holding" this exposure reading before you take up the final shooting position.

Most older meters use selenium photocells. The light falls on a sensitive cell, generates a tiny current which passes to a galvanometer indicating the exposure. Built-in selenium meters sometimes move the aperture, automatically setting the required stop. The selenium meter often takes its readings from a wide view despite the inclusion of lenses or baffles designed to "blinker" it for a view equivalent to that of a camera lens. The small selenium meters built in to cameras (they are never TTL type meters) are less sensitive to light at the lower end than most larger hand-held meters.

The other type of meter in wide use (and for many years the standard meter fitted to cameras) is the cadmium sulphide (CdS) type. Instead of a cell, it uses a photo-conductor placed in a circuit supplied by a small battery. Light falling on the light-responsive element affects its electrical resistance and a galvanometer also placed in the circuit measures the consequent current variations and translates them to exposure readings or adjustments. The advantage of the CdS meter is that it can be made more sensitive to light than the selenium type and would therefore, on the face of it, seem more suitable for light measurement at low levels. Its small physical size allows it to be positioned behind the camera lens as a TTL meter, which a selenium type cannot. A disadvantage is that you occasionally need to change the battery.

Generally speaking, the separate hand-held meter, whether CdS or selenium, can be made more sensitive to light at lower levels because there is no need for it to be small enough to fit into a camera. A separate meter can have a large light sensitive cell area.

But the actual, or claimed sensitivity of a meter at low light levels can easily lead you astray when it comes to taking readings by existing light. The meter cannot automatically tell you in every situation exactly what exposure to give to get a correct result; it is only a guide, and it can be misled. The situation may make it easy for the meter to give a reading, or it may not. And the "correct" result largely depends on what you yourself want the picture to look like.

How to take a low light reading

Some low-light situations present few exposure reading difficulties. You are not likely to have much trouble if the scene or subject is evenly lit – there are few significant shadow areas and no particularly insistent highlight. If the light is strong enough to make the meter register you could just take a general reading and set that. Or you could take a close up reading of your subject and set this accordingly. Difficulties arise when your subject contains widely varying brightnesses as so many low light scenes do, of if the light is too low to get a reading.

Suppose your picture is a room lit only by one or two table lamps. From the camera viewpoint this scene has one or two bright highlights (the lamps) and small areas of mid tone (the light pools) around them. The rest is in shadow. It is a scene consisting of patches of light.

An exposure meter adds together all areas, bright or dark, and indicates the average of these areas as a mid tone. If you want a photograph properly exposed for the whole room, not merely the lamps and their light pools, you cannot simply point the meter at it and expect to get a dependable reading. You may be lucky. The chances are that you will not, because the reading taken in this way can be influenced by so many factors.

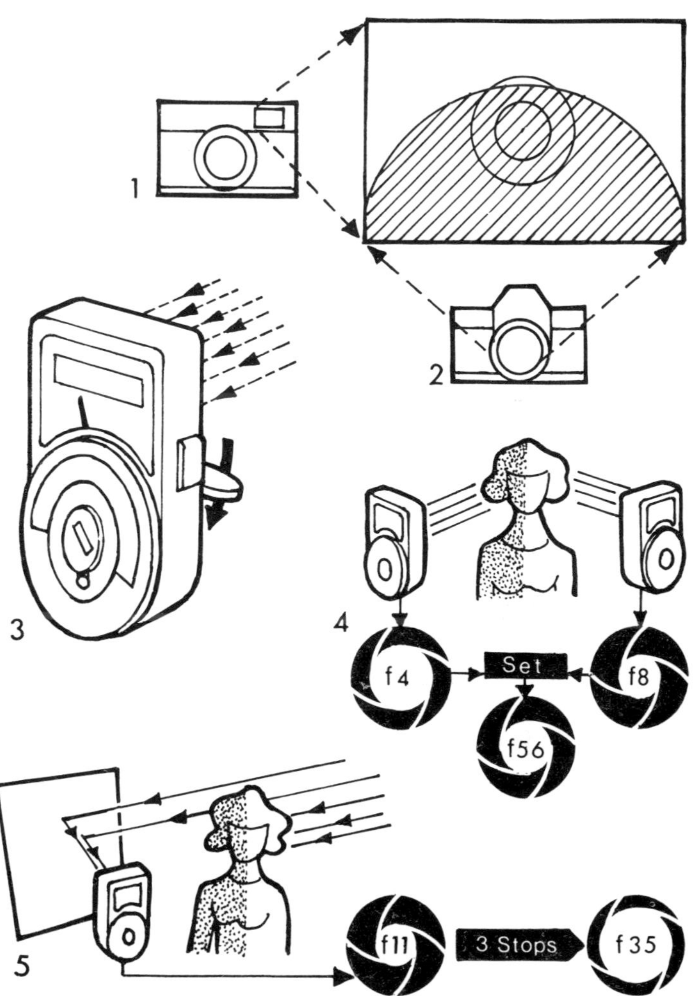

Taking low light exposure readings: (1) Selenium cell meters take their reading from the whole picture area or more (2) CdS and Silicon blue meters fitted to give readings through the taking lens are often 'centre weighted' and take more of the reading from a small area, where the main subject interest is, than from the rest of the picture. (3) Many separate hand exposure meters have a special sensitivity range for low light readings operated by a switch or by opening a baffle. (4) Hand held meters are convenient for taking averaging-readings from more than one part of the subject, or (5) standard grey or white card readings.

If, on the other hand, you walk into the scene and point the meter in to the shadow area you may not get a reading. If you do, you will have to reduce the exposure by a stop or so for that reading to be any use at all.

A reading which includes one or other of the lamps may at least make the meter react but it will indicate less exposure than you need – ie, an exposure which shows a lamp shade as a mid tone will render the rest of the room in deep shadow. So you would have to add to this exposure to lighten those shadows sufficiently.

You could try and find a mid tone in the scene – an object lit to a brightness level somewhere between the lightest and darkest areas. If you take a close up reading from that and set it you may be nearer the mark, but it depends on your ability to judge a mid tone. It may also be difficult to find a mid tone area large enough for even a close up reading. You may be mainly interested in a particular subject in the picture – a person's face for example. They may be in a light pool. The surroundings may not be too important. In that case you could simply take a close up reading off the face and set that. The remainder of the scene would be left to shift for itself. Remember, when taking readings that you do not hold the meter so close that you shade the reflecting surface. You must also take care not to obstruct the meter, or to allow strong oblique light to strike it. This would lead to a false reading. Another method is to take a reading of a highlight area, another of a shadow, and set the average.

A more reliable approach is the "artificial highlight" or white card method. This is most useful when working in such low light that the meter does not register at all. You point the meter at a sheet of white paper and take a reading. Even very low light situations can give sufficient brightness for such a reading so at least you have something to go by. You then give 2½–3 stops increase to the exposure indicated and you have a setting that should allow you ample shadow detail. What you have done is to provide an artificial highlight area large enough to allow a reading to be taken. This has a fixed relationship to the light levels in the scene that you cannot meter, so it should always be correct. It is best applied in scenes consisting of large areas of shadow and few highlights.

Each of these exposure reading methods can be useful in the right situation, but there is still some element of chance, especially if you

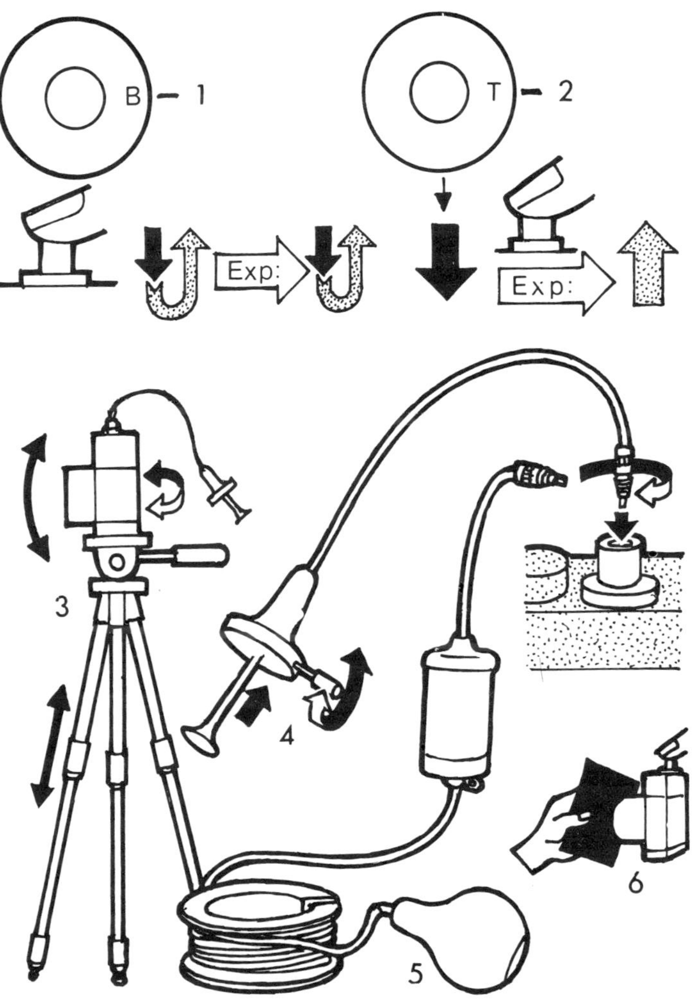

Making time exposures: (1) Set the camera on B, press the release, count off the time and let go of the release. (2) On old cameras with T setting, press once to open the shutter, count time, press again to close shutter. (3) A tripod is the ideal method of steadying the camera for time exposures, and a pan and tilt head allows precise adjustments to the framing. (4) A cable release allows time exposures without touching the camera; the plunger can be locked to hold the shutter open. (5) An air release can be used for remote controlled shooting. (6) To give repeated exposures to the same frame open the shutter and use a black card in front of the lens.

are shooting colour transparencies. To be on the safe side with scenes having a wide tone range you should take more than one picture at different exposures, "bracketing" your estimated reading by adding or reducing it accordingly. It is normally enough to add one stop (doubling the exposure) to gain significantly in shadow detail, or subtract one to reduce the highlights. But, as a generalization, rather than risk losing the subject in shadow it is better to overexpose the highlights, because they are usually a small part of the picture area.

Time exposures: how and when

Many cameras have provision on the shutter control for making exposures of up to one second duration. Exposures of longer than 2 seconds have to be made by opening and closing the shutter manually and counting the open period yourself. These are known as "time" exposures. For time exposures the shutter is set on the "B" position. On pressure of the release the shutter opens. The release is held down until the requisite exposure period has elapsed, and is then let go, when the shutter closes. On a few cameras, mainly those with electronic timing devices built in to the shutter (so called "electronic" shutters) exposures of greater than one second are timed by the camera mechanism.

When do you use them?

Time exposures are a last resort in photographing by existing light. You have to make such a long exposure because there is insufficient light to do otherwise even at full aperture and with a fast film. Occasionally you might choose a long exposure in preference to a shorter in order to be able to use a small aperture which gives greater depth of field. You might do this if you had focusing problems with a particular subject. Time exposures are quite common in night photography. They are not difficult to do but they do require more care in preparation than the ordinary shot.

To obtain a sharp image with a time exposure, both camera and subject must be absolutely stationary while the shutter is open. Any subject movement, or accidental jogging of the camera will result in an unsharp or blurred image. This, however, is occasionally done deliberately for the effect (see page 95).

With the camera held firmly against, or wedged into a solid object it is just possible to obtain sharp time exposures of a few seconds. But for reliable results the camera should, ideally, be placed on a tripod. It can, instead, be stood or rested on a solid object, but it can never be held in the hand. Even the steadiest pair of hands are far too unstable a support for exposures of more than one second, or indeed for exposures of greater than 1/15 sec.

With the camera set on a tripod, a cable release (a long one is best) should be screwed into the release socket. This avoids the need to touch the camera at all during the exposure. Sometimes the cable socket is separate from the release, but it is more often in the centre of the button. You should wind on the film before finally lining up the camera, and then check the scene again through the viewfinder just before pressing the release. You press the release firmly until you hear the shutter open, count the seconds and finally let the shutter close again. For very long exposures it is an advantage to be able to keep the shutter open without having to hold the release the whole time. Many cable releases are fitted with a locking screw to hold the plunger down during the exposure. If you let go of the cable release after locking it let it down gently, keeping it slack, to avoid any camera movement. With an air release, a plunger operated by a rubber bulb on the end of a long tube, you can stand well away from the camera while exposing. You cannot use the camera's delayed action release (self-timer) satisfactorily on the "B" setting.

Avoid walking about during time exposures unless the tripod or support is on a very solid floor. The slightest floorboard movement can take the sharpness off the picture by being transmitted as vibration up the tripod leg to the camera. It is always safest to keep still during time exposures.

It is sometimes useful to be able to take a time exposure in several "bursts" rather than in one long shot. You cannot close the shutter and open it again, as this would mean winding on the film, or at least touching the camera to re-cock the shutter. You can, however, block the camera lens with a piece of matt black card. This technique is virtually essential when making very long exposures in dark public interiors such as cathedrals when you cannot prevent people walking in to the picture (see p 191). Give yourself a long exposure time by deliberately selecting a small aperture (this will also give you greatest depth of field). If anyone walks into the shot while you are exposing you can quickly cover the camera lens. At that point you stop counting the exposure time. The unwanted person's intrusion in to the picture may occupy such a small part of the exposure time you have selected that they do not register at all on the film – provided they keep on the move. If they stop, you may be in trouble. So it is wise to block the lens and avoid that risk. When the view is again clear you can remove the card and continue counting or timing the exposure.

A more refined means of control using this black card, and one which takes a little more practice, can also be useful when taking time exposures in very dark and lofty interiors, or in other situations where the lighting is uneven. If one whole part of the scene is much darker than the rest you can use the card to shade the brighter part during the actual exposure. This is especially handy when shooting colour transparencies, which leave you without the extra means of control after taking the picture that you would have in printing from a negative. If your picture is a side aisle in a church you shade the bottom part of the picture for part of the exposure and so give extra time for the dark vault. You should watch what you are doing through the viewfinder before you take the picture, see where you have the card, and start the shot with the card in that position. Keep the card moving the whole time to avoid giving a hard edge to your shading. Use a large card and do not place it too close to the camera. You should experiment with different periods of shading if you want perfect results. You could start by shading for a third of the total exposure time but much depends on the circumstances. This technique, though simple, gives you transparencies or negatives to print from which are of the very best quality and the technique is the only way to get first class results without using extra lighting.

Focus problems in low light

The kind of situation where the subject is so dark that you need to use a time exposure can give you problems in trying to focus the camera.

Looking through the viewfinder you may be able to find a small highlight to focus on. Alternatively, you could hold a lamp or a burning match in the scene and focus on that. This might be adequate for focusing with coincident image, ground glass or microprism type rangefinders but would not be easy with the split image type, for which you need a larger area. So you would have to light a small area of the subject with the lamp. Failing this, set the distance manually on the focusing ring. In critical situations you might measure this distance with a tape measure.

Using reflectors and flash

A reflector is a cheap and efficient way of adding light to your picture. Provided there is enough light to pick up and reflect, it works very well. A reflector is normally used to add light to a part of the subject that is underlit. It may, however, provide the primary light source. A favourite example of this is the picture of a child reading a book by a window, where light is reflected from the open book into the child's face, which would otherwise have been in shadow. Another is where a person standing under a lamp post is illuminated by light reflected from the newspaper he is reading.

Besides objects such as books or newspapers that are deliberately placed in the scene to provide reflection, there are many existing natural reflectors – the walls in a home, objects around the room, a second person's face or the white shirt they are wearing, a polished table, a nearby mirror or drape may reflect a considerable quantity of light. If the subject is positioned correctly it is possible to use this as a key light. In another position it may provide a secondary source to fill the shaded side of the subject and avoid creating a picture full of heavy shadows.

You can use a reflector to change the quality of light. If the only available light is rather too harsh for a portrait, and would give inky shadows, you could reflect this light into the subject's face and in so doing, diffuse it.

Actual applications for reflectors are discussed later (see page 110) but it remains to itemize the various types of reflector and the light they give.

Reflectors may be categorized by the softness (diffuse quality) of light they reflect. The softest would be a white or coloured broken surface such as a crumpled newspaper. Coloured paper gives a reflection of coloured light but it is not a strong reflection unless the source is relatively powerful, such as a domestic spotlight. Even then, the reflection is soft and covers a wide area.

A harder reflector can be made by using the matt side of kitchen foil, crumpled perhaps. The reflection is quite strong but still diffused. It reflects light into a larger area than its own physical size.

A directional reflector giving hard strong light can be made by pasting aluminium foil shiny side upward on a rigid board. The board need not be large, but the area such a reflector can illuminate is little larger than the reflector itself.

The hardest, and most efficient reflector in those terms, is a mirror. This, essentially, reflects the same quality of light as that which is falling on to it. It forms, in effect, a second light source. If it reflects a spotlight, it becomes a second spotlight, if a table lamp, it is another, if window light it is like adding a second window. It reflects light in proportion to its size. A mirror the size of a window is as effective as a second window. A small mirror may not cover enough of the subject to show more than its own shape in light projected on to the subject. Mirrors must be used properly if they are to be used at all. Often, a more commonplace reflector will serve better.

Reflectors can be used to light still life objects, small areas in general scenes, to provide the odd highlight to be picked up by a shiny subject in the picture or, in the most popular role, portraiture – or pictures of people (see page 129).

The most convenient reflector to carry about is a large piece of aluminium foil folded up and stuffed in your pocket or gadget bag. It is amazing how useful such a simple accessory can be if you are taking pictures by existing light.

Flash

In theory, flash illumination has no place in a book about existing light. It eliminates the advantages of working with existing light – the naturalness, convenience, inconspicuousness, cheapness, and ease of operation. Its light is totally alien to the sort of effects that one hopes to get with the light that one finds.

Nevertheless, flash can be handy if relegated to a support role. In such a position it need not necessarily wreck the atmosphere of a scene. Cunningly used, especially as an indirect (ie, reflected) source it can surreptitiously make a contribution that gives a picture just that little extra light it may need. It should only really be necessary if all else fails, and even then only if you already have the equipment. The relevance of flash, of various levels of sophistication, in existing light photography is discussed in the final chapter (see page 214) on adding light.

Outdoor
Low Light
Pictures

If you do much photography outdoors there have probably been many times when, as evening begins to draw in and the light gradually fails, you take your last few pictures and put away your camera, dismissing the thought of any further picture-taking that day – only because the light level has dropped. Yet twilight, and morning light offer many opportunities for photography that do not exist during the hours of full daylight.

Morning and evening

Morning and evening light alters the appearance of things from what you normally see, giving prominence to objects that are otherwise unremarkable. A natural feature such as a tree, which in daylight seems quite innocuous, can grow into a sinister shape by the evening – outlined against the fading sky. You can shoot by the morning or evening light to capture the effect it has on the subject, or you can photograph the sky itself.

The daylight at the beginning and end of day is of quite a different colour from that around noon. The further it is towards evening the "warmer", or more reddish-yellow the light becomes. Likewise, in the early part of the morning. The sooner after sunrise the warmer is the colour of the light. This is because the sun is reaching us, in effect, through a thicker layer of atmosphere when it is nearer the horizon than when it is overhead. The blue wavelengths of light are scattered in the atmosphere whereas the red wavelengths penetrate it and reach us more easily. This is why the setting sun looks so orange. The further towards noon it is the "colder" or whiter the light becomes until the sun assumes its normal "white heat". Through the thinner atmospheric layer the blue and red wavelengths reach us more equally.

Colour film is even more aware of the colour of light than your eyes are. If you take a photograph in the evening hoping for midday colour quality you will be disappointed. Either you must accept that morning and evening light is going to make your subject look more yellow or orange (and this can be very pleasant) or you have to try and compensate for this colour. The sensible approach is to accept the way that nature arranges things. Evening light has its own character, after all. It is possible to compensate for the warmth of the light at the beginning and end of day by fitting a so-called morning and evening filter over the lens of your camera. This is a slightly blue-tinged filter which removes the yellowish light that you find objectionable. The filter also necessitates a slight increase in exposure to compensate for its absorption of light – which may not be too welcome when you are already shooting in weak light.

Morning and evening light is of course much weaker than full daylight and with certain subjects, particularly where movement is involved, problems with exposure can arise.

The most striking aspect of the light at these times of day is the direction it comes from, and thus, the character or mood it imparts to the scene. The sunlight, if the sun appears, is very near the horizon. There are long shadows and large unlit areas. All features that get any light receive it virtually from one side only, which can cause problems as well as advantages. One problem is that you may have great apparent contrast in the picture while at the same time you are concerned with very subtle differences in tone or colour. An advantage is that the low-angle light is very attractive and gives the picture the flavour of the time of day at which it was taken. Ordinary daylight pictures tend to lack any definite sense of time.

If the sun does not appear and, instead, you have a heavy mist, fog or cloud layer, the scene has a dull grey atmosphere overall, no shadows and little contrast. The light has no ability to draw out shapes or texture in the subject and there is little hope for very lively results.

A wide range of intermediates exist between these two kinds of sunrise or sunset. Only if the weather interferes do you get mornings or evenings showing no real evidence of the time of day.

Sunsets and twilight

Sooner or later everyone tries to get a picture of a sunset. Such a blaze of colour is an obvious subject for colour film. In fact, in black and white so much of the effect is lost that unless there are some very strong cloud formations or great foreground interest, the picture is hardly worth taking at all.

If you see a particularly beautiful sunset you have to work quickly to get it at its best. Sunsets do not last very long; the colours soon fade and darken, and the clouds, those castles in the air, soon move on. In a few moments the blaze of red and gold and feeling of other-worldliness has gone and it turns to a dismal purple grey. If you take your time all this may happen while you are still fiddling with your camera.

The best sunset pictures have an interesting foreground. An open landscape may be improved by the stark black shape of a tree in the foreground, or some other well defined features in the middle distance, such as a building, a fence or a human figure. You are even luckier if you can manoeuvre yourself quickly enough into a position that gives you reflections from the red sky on the surface of water, on rooftops or some other feature that catches the light. A brilliant sunset momentarily bathes the whole world in its glow. Colour film is particularly responsive to this red cast and even tends to exaggerate it a little. If your companion looks into the sunset, his face may be aglow with its fire, the leaves on the trees are tinged with colour, even the grass. You don't have long to forage for pictures like these, but it may be more worthwhile looking about for them than photographing the sunset itself.

A high viewpoint may have given you just the expansive foreground you wished for, or you may have just come up to an old bridge at the right moment. More likely, the foreground has rather dull subject matter and you have no time to find a better position. A sunset is, however, one of those rare cases for which you can plan a picture in advance. If you notice a good view near to where you live, a place where the evening sky gives attractive silhouettes and a fine foreground, you could wait for a good sunset and immediately go to take up your pre-planned position. In this sneaking way you are very likely to come up with an exceptional sunset picture. You must, of course, have noticed on previous evenings where the sun goes down, so that you don't arrive on the spot only to find that the sun has gone down in the wrong place.

With sunrise you want to try and retain in your pictures an impression of limpid suffusion of light through a moisture laden morning air. The sky may be rosy; it may be pale yellow. The beauty may not be in the sky but in the light falling on the things around you – the bedewed plants, the spiders web with its rows of glistening droplets, the light

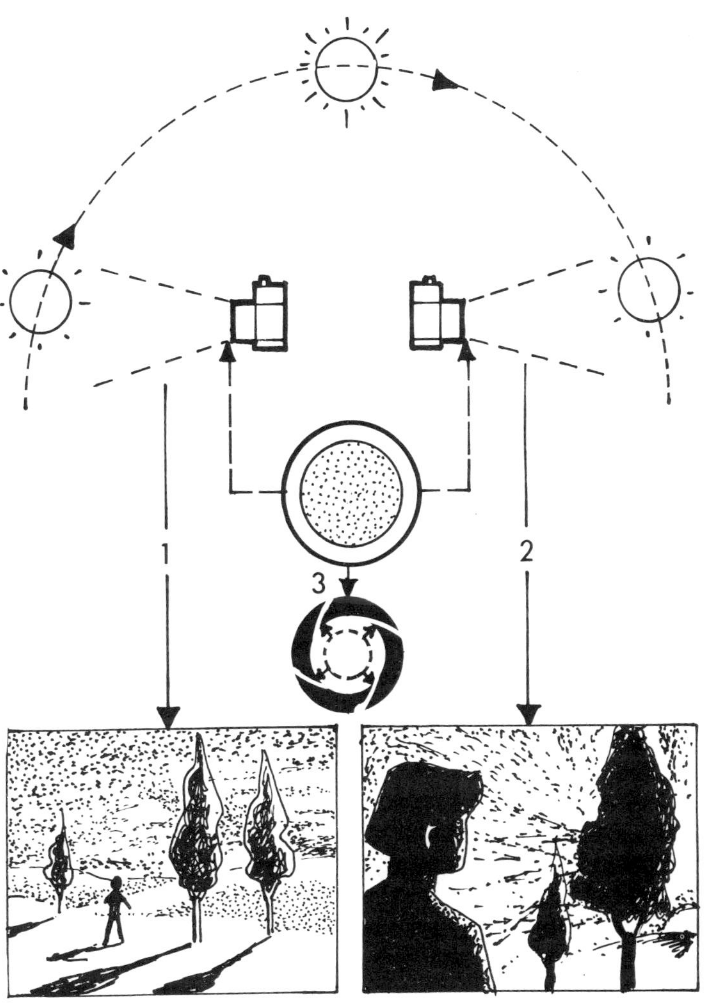

Sunrise and sunset. (1) The rising sun is weaker than at other times of day and casts long shadows which could be included in the picture to evoke the right mood. (2) Sunsets are most striking when shapes are silhouetted against them. (3) A morning or evening filter used after sunrise or before sunset to correct for warm colour requires a slight increase in exposure.

that makes the snow translucent and the frost luminescent. Low angle morning light softly diffused through the atmosphere gives a feeling of restfulness and calm. This mood will emerge in your pictures. Pictorially the light has great charm at this time of day.

The light is directional and the shadows long and rather deep but best results with morning and evening light come by keeping the exposure to a minimum, whether you are shooting in colour or black and white. You must try to preserve a feeling of lightness in the picture. (In black and white this would suggest a combination of low contrast film and soft working developer for the best results.) With colour, overexposure dilutes the vivid colours. In black and white, it spoils the subtle differentiation between tones. Bracketed exposures of, say, a stop either way are advisable for perfection. They should not, however, be necessary merely to secure a reasonable picture; an acceptable exposure is far easier to estimate than with many other forms of existing light. (For suggested exposures see tables.)

Twilight, or the deep shade of a wood or cavern, are conditions that offer only a particular quality of light for photography rather than any spectacular effects. Twilight can be made to serve as a sort of gentle backdrop for night scenes where there are lights in the picture. General views taken in thes conditions are often more detailed, colourful and interesting than those shot in deep night. This is because the twilight still allows some shadowy details to be seen in the picture, alongside those revealed by any lamps in the scene itself. After sunset, the sky (or its reflection in water) can be a quite intense blue. The exposure for twilight pictures with illuminations in the picture would just allow hand-held shots working at, or near, full aperture with normal speed colour films. But night photography, as such, is a matter for a later chapter (see page 74).

Deep shade

The deep shade found in heavily sheltered places outdoors, gives you the same trouble as you find in all cases where the existing light is less plentiful than you could wish. Moreover, it does not offer in compensation the appeal of any special character or dramatic effect. It is just dull.

You generally have to work at a fairly wide aperture even at the slowest safe shutter speeds for hand holding. This means that you must take more care with focusing because of the reduced depth of field that comes with shooting with the lens fairly wide open. Direct exposure readings of the subject indicate, as stated before, the exposure for the sum of tones to be registered as a mid tone. You may be tempted to reduce the exposure to correct this rendering for a particularly dark scene. However, with colour, the fact that you are giving a long exposure can result in underexposure (see reciprocity law failure, page 162) so you are advised to follow the meter reading. In black and white work you can make any such adjustments in printing and it is better to give a full exposure so that you have the shadow details if you want them.

With colour, especially transparencies, it is far more important to get the exposure right. Again, much depends on the individual situation and what kind of result you are hoping to get. But, as a rule, under- or over-exposure with colour film tends to disturb the colour balance as well as the density of the tones in your subject. If you overexpose a colour film on flesh tones you lose not only the modelling but the colour of the skin. Your subject looks pale and washed out. A deeper, richer effect, a dramatic though perhaps not true flesh tone, results from underexposure in colour. Slight overexposure weakens colours in the picture, slight underexposure intensifies the colour saturation.

You are very likely to find when shooting in the shade in daylight that the picture assumes a definite colour cast, usually blue or green. This tendency varies from one film to another. Some films have a weakness, as it were, for a certain colour whenever the exposure is not quite right. The actual cause of this is that the sandwich of three sensitive layers, each representing a subtractive primary colour, that make up the tripack colour film reacts in different ways to variations in exposure. This results in slight alterations in colour rendering of any, or all, of the layers. The bias or cast that appears is the net result of these separate colour layers behaving in different ways due to meeting exposure demands for which they were not designed, ie: lengthy exposure times, or under- or overexposure. The layers in different makes of colour film react differently. Consequently with low light work when you are expecting a fairly standard result you in fact obtain colour renderings which vary far more widely from one make of film to another than if those films had been exposed under normal full daylight conditions.

One tends to expect more accurate colour rendering in daylight, however dim, than in artifical light situations. Nevertheless, there *are* these problems. One way to minimize them is always to choose a wide aperture rather than a long exposure time because of the effects of long exposure times on colour rendering (see page 162).

Colour film is always likely to exaggerate any colour bias in the light falling on the subject. In certain cases you can prejudge the likely colour bias in a picture taken in low light outdoors. This can in some cases be corrected. We have already seen that with a morning and evening (pale blue) filter you can correct for the pinkishness of the daylight at these times of day.

If the subject is in deep shade and is mainly lit by blue skylight filtering through heavy foliage, for example, then the resulting picture will certainly assume a fairly strong blue cast. If the sky is overcast, this blueness is less pronounced. Nevertheless, the subject and surrounding colours have a rather cold appearance and skin tones may look pale and lifeless. The correction required here is in the opposite direction from that needed for morning and evening light

You can place a pale straw filter over the camera lens to correct for light from an overcast sky, and for blue skylight and all pictures of people use a medium straw filter. The extra exposure required for these weak filters is not really significant.

The colour bias in a low light outdoor picture may not be due to the skylight. Light reaching the subject can also be affected by coloured reflecting surfaces nearby. Colour picked up in this way is reflected on to the subject as in the childhood game of holding a buttercup under the chin as a test for liking butter. Thus, green grass, red brickwork or water (blue) can interfere with the colour rendering of the subject. You should be on guard for this and if necessary move the subject. Don't forget, colour film is far more susceptible to such influences than the human eye – so much so that one can be quite startled by the results!

Occasionally, if the surroundings are so dark that the subject contrasts are too strong, you can reflect some light in to the shadow parts of a small subject such as a human face by using a neutral reflector.

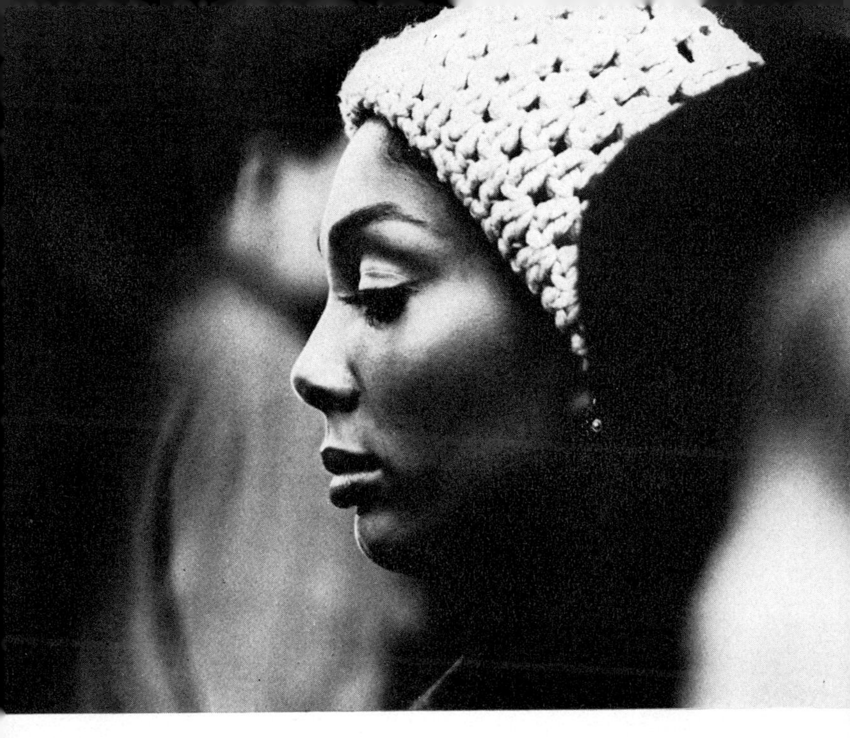

Face in the crowd. Often, when working in low light situations you have to use a very wide aperture which gives very reduced depth of field. But it also allows you to isolate nearby subjects from busy surroundings provided that you focus carefully and do not lose the outlines against backgrounds of a similar tone – *Geri Della Rocca de Candal.*

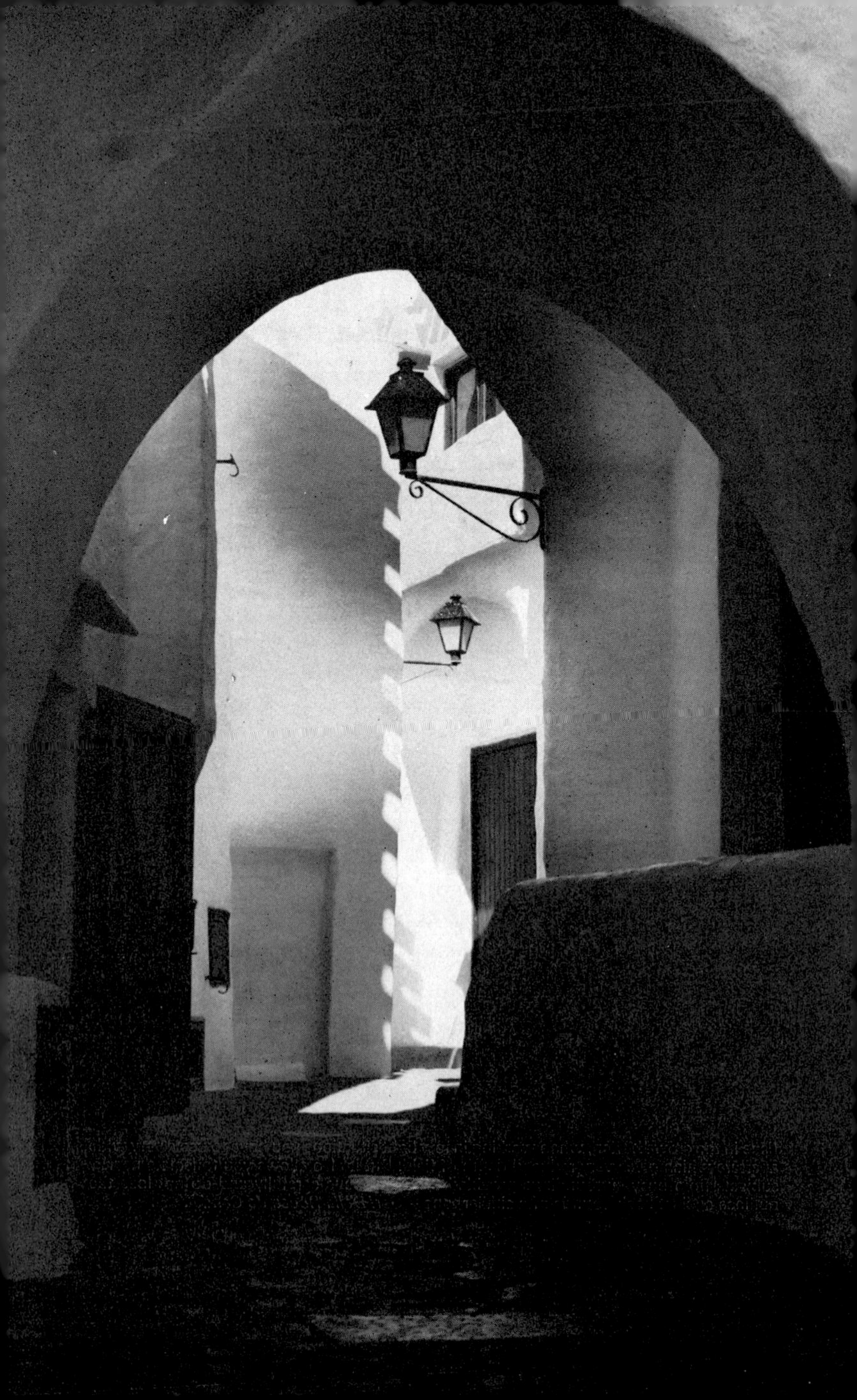

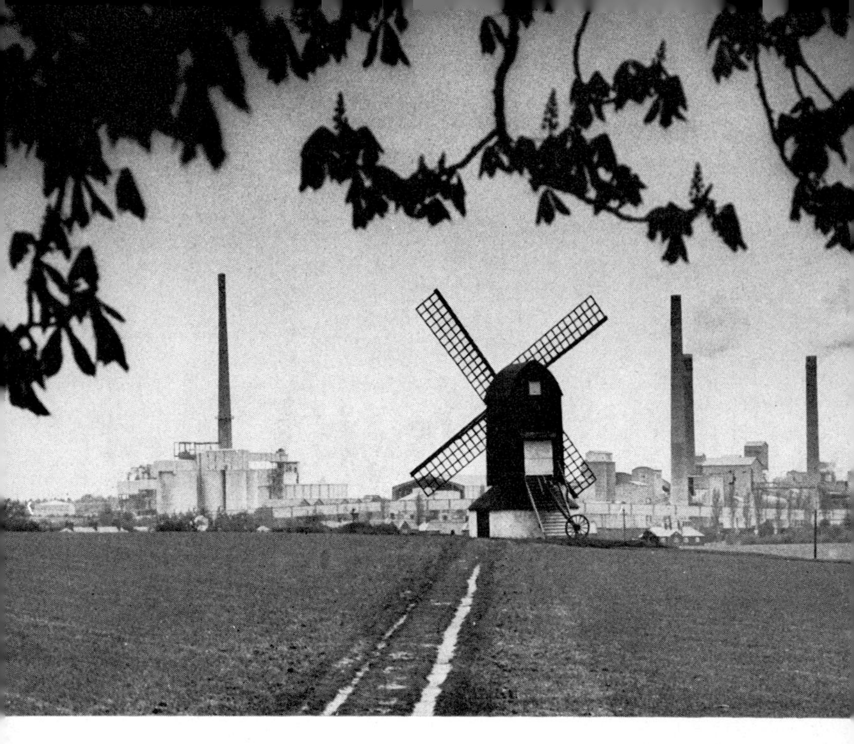

Dull weather. Industrial landscape, old and new in which a straightforward general exposure reading should be adequate, perhaps pointing the meter downwards a little to avoid taking in too much of the sky – *Raymond Lea.*

Opposite: Minorca. Splash of sunlight in dark corner; the shadow area forms the larger and more interesting part of the picture and exposure favours that. But do not overexpose so much that you distort the tone values and so lose the impression of shade – *Peter Rowe.*

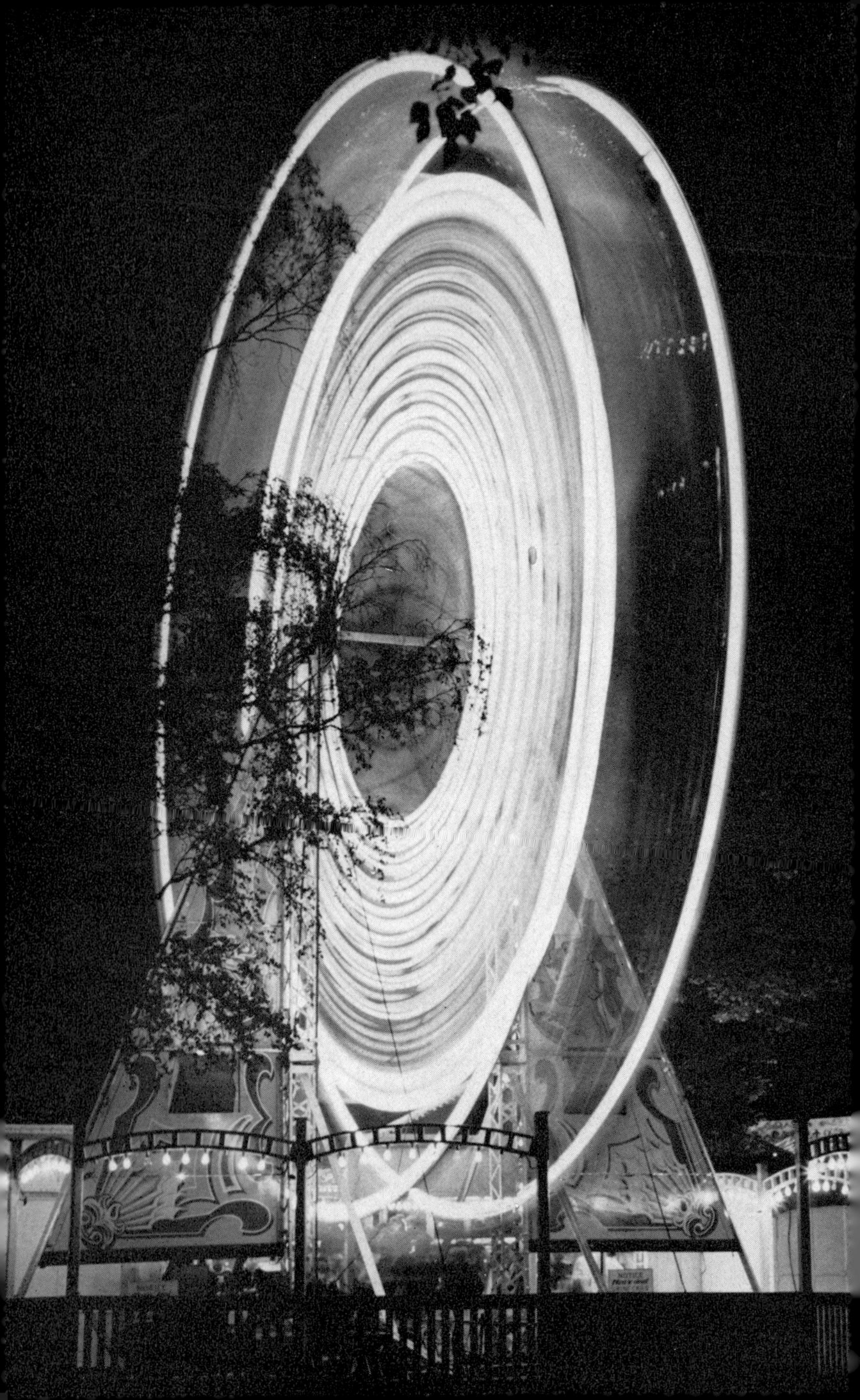

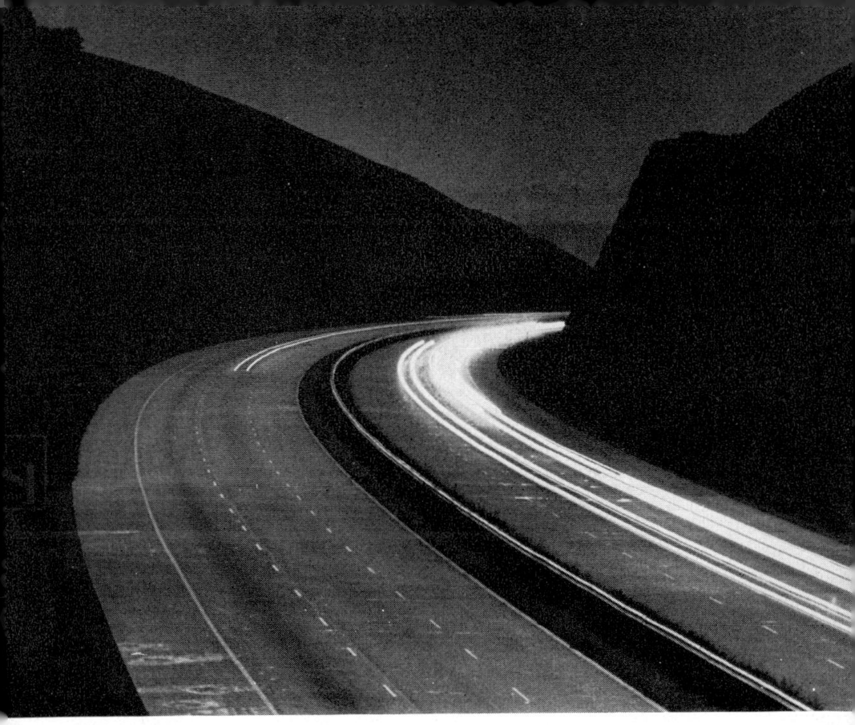

Motorway cutting through the Chiltern hills at night. A time exposure of, perhaps, half a minute can pick up light trails from passing traffic. Use a small stop to avoid brightening the scene generally – *Raymomd Lea.*

Opposite: Big wheel at night. Set a very small stop for an exposure long enough to allow say, one complete revolution, but not so long as to register the sky – *Peter Rowe.*

Page 62, top: Underexposure with evening light stresses the highlights and reduces shadow areas to a solid black – *Karl-Heinz Mers.*

Bottom: Houses of Parliament, London. Exposure for the sky, with its fine cloud formation, ensures that the spires and towers are seen in sharp silhouette – *Geri Della Rocca de Candal.*

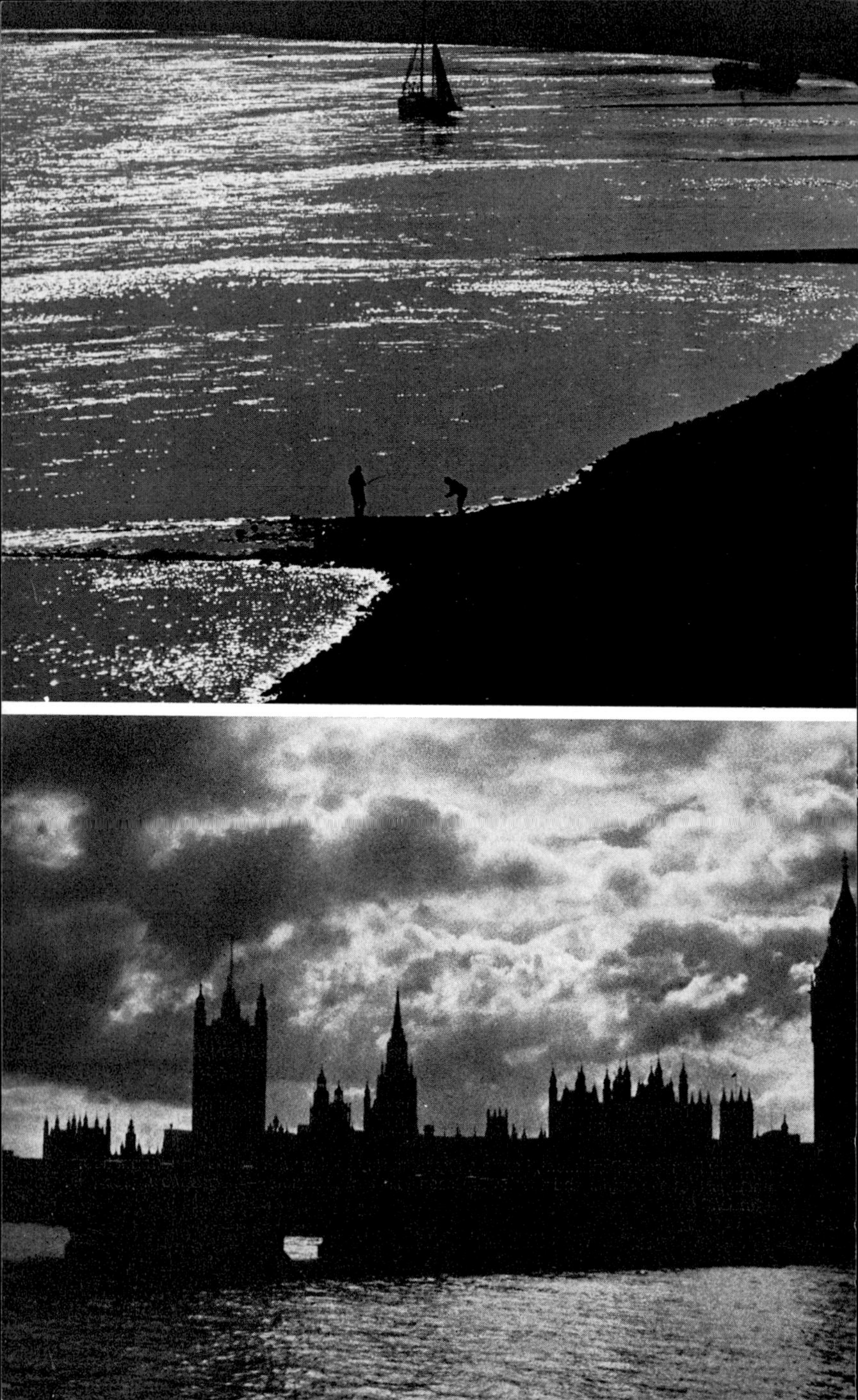

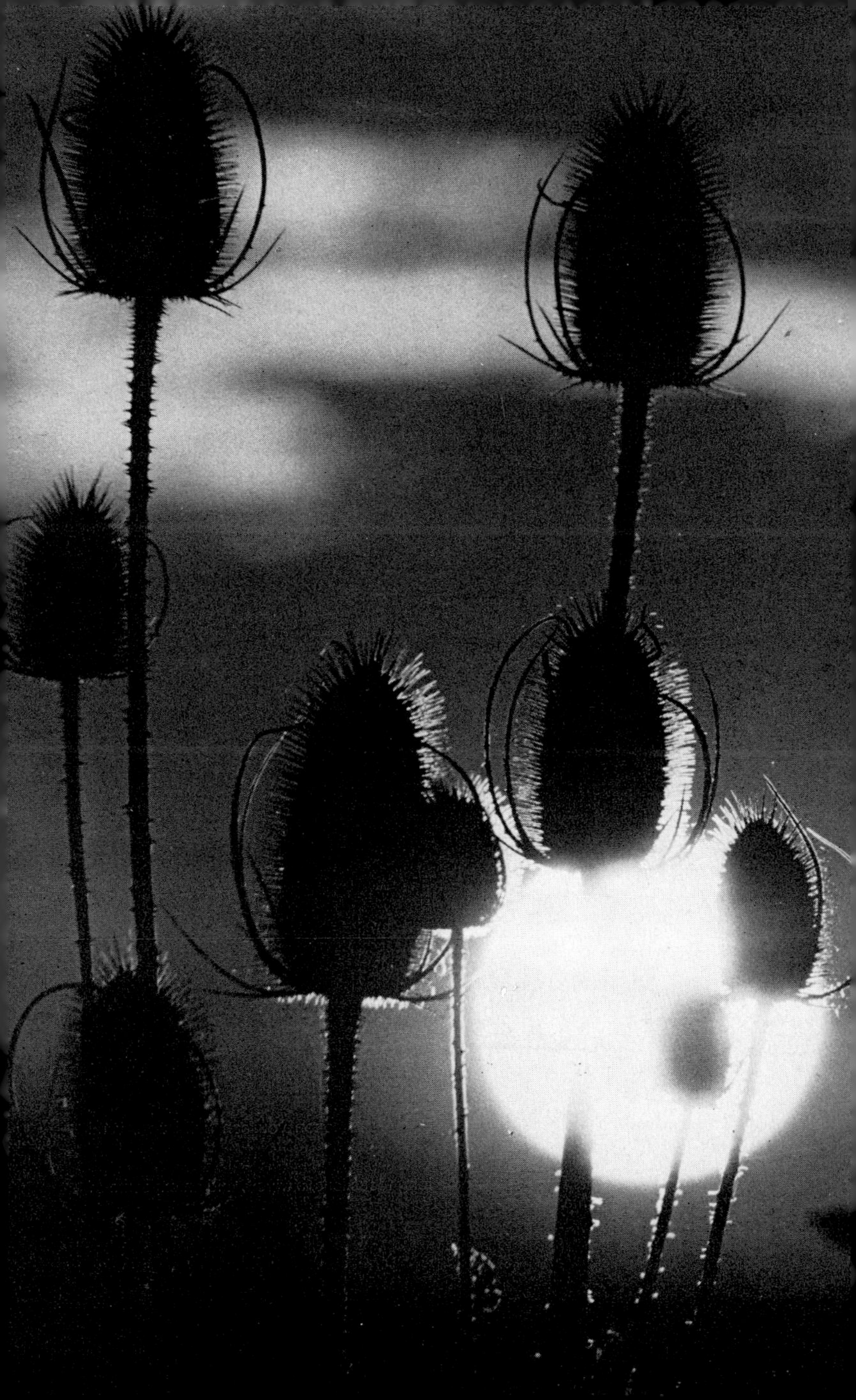

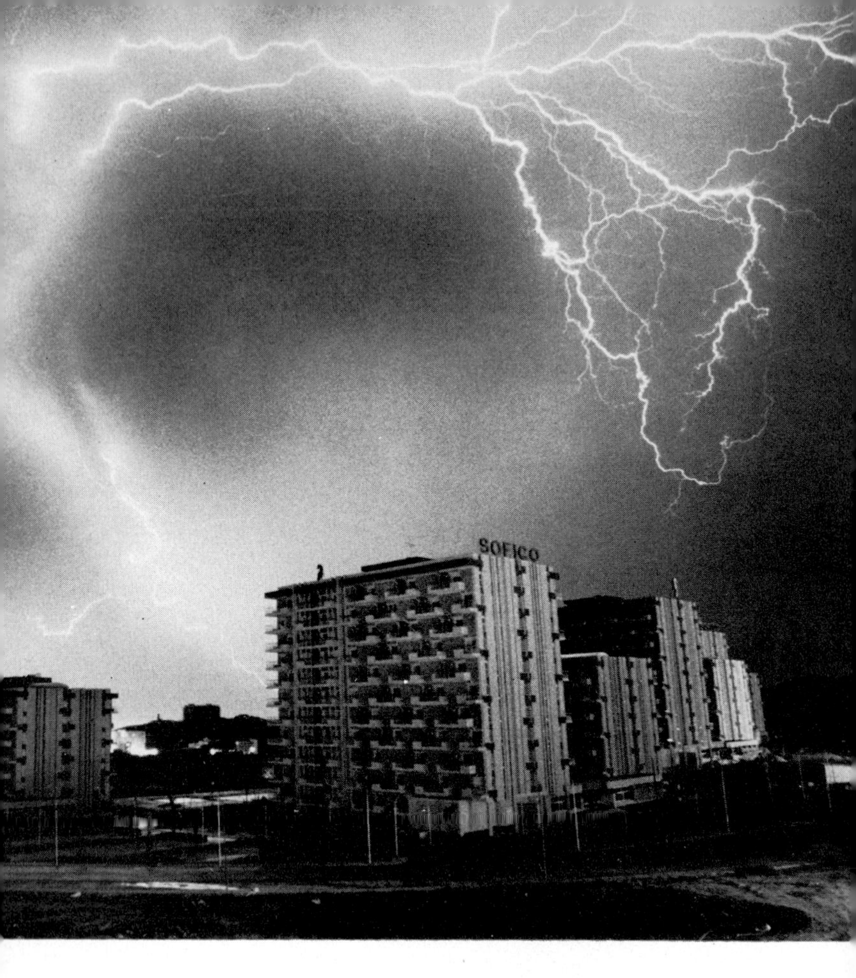

Lightning over half-built hotels. By leaving the shutter open you can build up several flashes in one picture – *P. M. J. Turner.*

Page 63: Moon through teasels. You need a long focus lens, a tripod, and an exposure of around 1/15 sec. for such an effect – *D. Doble.*

Again, you are subject to the same problems of blueness if the light is reflected directly from a clear sky. It is possible to use a reflector of gold foil to give a warmer effect, though there is a danger of overdoing it. Generally speaking, lighting the shadows with fill-in flash would risk your spoiling the effect altogether. The flash has to be very weak in order not to look artificial – certainly giving less than one quarter of the main exposure. One way to fill in with flash is to bounce it off your own body. If you hold the flash very close you might restrict the light from it sufficiently, but it is a rather hit and miss method. You are certain only that if the light comes from the camera viewpoint it will be very flat (low contrast) which is ideal for filling shadows and so reducing contrast in the subject generally. Of course, high contrast in the scene can be attractive, so you should not automatically think in terms of trying to eliminate it.

Weather and your picture taking

Bad weather suggests a variation in technique from that indicated in other, purer, low light situations. Again, much depends on what your aims are in taking the picture.

Rain is characterized by dull, heavy light of low contrast, wet surfaces visible in the scene with visibility reduced to the middle distance and no cast shadows. If you are shooting in rain you may want to emphasize the fact. You should choose viewpoints showing wet surfaces, droplets on glass, etc, places where the effects of rain are most easily discernible. Rain itself does not show up unless strongly backlit. In most cases this means that the sun must be behind the rain (ie, you are photographing the rain against the light) or it must be falling against a very dark background while being quite well lit from the sky.

If you want to preserve the heavy atmosphere or mood of a rainy scene in black and white you should increase the exposure slightly to record as much detail as possible and process for the normal length of time.

If the idea is to suppress the dull effect of the rain you should aim to increase contrast. You give the normal exposure as indicated by a meter reading and increase the development time, printing on a high contrast paper if necessary. This does not, of course, put in shadows where there were none before – it merely increases the contrast of the tone variations already in the picture. In rain, these are on a very limited scale.

Rain and mist often account for very pleasing colour rendering of nearby subjects, especially with colour transparencies. The general diffusness of the scene counteracts the tendency for excessive contrast in colour materials. So you get a smooth even colour rendering, with little loss of shadow detail and no bright, colourless highlights. The meter reading is fairly reliable, though exposures tend to be far longer than for normal outdoor work. When photographing more distant subjects there is a greater tendency for the film to respond to the predominance of blue wavelengths reflected by the mist or rain, although objects seen at great distance through mist, ie: lights, etc, tend to look reddish for much the same reason as in sunsets where the light is transmitted *through* the atmosphere, or in the case of mist and rain, water vapour and droplets.

There is no obstacle to photographing a rainbow, provided you do it in colour. The effect is hardly visible in black and white and not really worth trying. It is best to choose a view where the rainbow falls against a fairly neutral background, greyish if possible, as the colours show up more clearly. It is really more effective if you do not try to include the whole rainbow in the picture, only one end where it reaches the ground. Here the colours tend to be strongest, and there is a reasonable chance of getting good surroundings. Don't forget, in your enthusiasm for getting the picture, that the composition of the picture itself is still very important if it is going to be a good one. It is surprising how few rainbow pictures are strong on that point. The rainbow picture should not receive any more than the exposure indicated for a reading of the general scene – preferably less. Here you could bracket exposures in the direction of underexposure, but do not take your reading by pointing the meter straight up into the sky. This would indicate a far shorter exposure than you need. You have to react quite speedily to catch a rainbow at full strength, possibly with its secondary bow above, because it can fade noticeably in less than a minute, especially at the centre.

With falling snow much the same applies as in the case of rain, and in low-light snow scenes, too, there is lack of contrast. Exposure readings off snow, even in low or evening light, usually indicate far too short an exposure for the snow to be rendered as white, instead of a mid grey, and for any detail in the shadow areas. At least half as much again should be added to the meter reading, and preferably more, say, 1–2 stops increase in exposure for good results. Shadow areas in snow tend to come out bluish, but this, perhaps for psychological reasons, has come to be accepted as fairly realistic and one would not attempt to correct it.

The truth of the matter is, snow is least appealing when photographed in low light conditions, unless it be evening light with perhaps lights or some other relieving features seen in the picture also.

People, animals and other moving subjects

A low-light subject that moves to any extent is almost certain to be more difficult to photograph than one that is stationary. The very fact that the subject moves conflicts with the frequent need in existing light photography for wide apertures and slow shutter speed settings on the camera.

Any subject movement that registers on the film during the exposure will appear as a blur in the final picture. This normally happens either if the movement is violent or rapid even though a normal shutter speed is set (1/60 , 1/125 sec) or if the movement is not rapid but the shutter speed is slow, as in so many cases with existing light photography.

Another kind of blur occurs when the subject passes out of the field of sharp focus. It happens with some quick movements that do not give you time to make the necessary focus adjustments on the camera. This, too, is a common problem with shooting by existing light because the camera is so often working at the wider apertures, which do not allow much depth of field.

Despite these two main factors pulling in different directions, you can still handle moving subjects quite successfully in low light. But you must apply the aperture and shutter speed controls in the appropriate way for each case. For this, you need a camera that allows you independent control of shutter and diaphragm even if they are interlocked for the various combinations available at any exposure reading (from a built-in meter).

The method of approach for each subject depends on the direction of movement. Movements *across* the field of view (ie: parallel with the front of the camera) are more likely to be registered as a blur than those receding or approaching head-on (ie: subjects moving towards or away from the camera). In the first case the subject's image actually moves across the film surface during the period when the shutter is open. In the second it stays in the same position on the film, but grows or diminishes in size. The lateral movement, ie: across the film, may blur at even a moderately high shutter speed, whereas the head-on movement is registered as sharp. Any movements at angles between these two directions will be proportionally greater as they are nearer the lateral plane, and less as they are closer to the head-on, or axis view.

For lateral movements the critical factor is the shutter speed. The faster the shutter speed (the shorter the exposure time) the less distance the subject travels across the film. The ideal shutter setting reduces that movement to an insignificant level – to the point where no movement is visible in the final picture (unless it was desired).

Many subjects which move very rapidly nevertheless have momentary "peaks" in the action during which they are almost stationary. If you are photographing a dancer at an outdoor evening event or an athlete by stadium lighting, you might find that although the light does not allow a fast enough shutter speed to arrest most of the movements, you can still catch them at these peaks and get pictures containing little or no blur. The dancer might pause momentarily during the dance while changing direction; the athlete might reach a stationary peak at the height of a pole vault, for example. You must anticipate such moments by watching the pattern of the dancing and previous attempts at the pole vault. You then need to react just at the right moment – neither pressing the button too soon nor too late, nor jabbing at it so as to blur the whole picture with camera shake.

Both the above cases allow a focus point to be predetermined by rehearsal, whereas this is far from the case when photographing children or animals, unless the animal be restricted by some natural barrier, such as a tether or a fence, ditch or glass window. If you are working at a wide aperture, such a natural restriction is virtually essential because with the shallow depth of field there is far too great a risk of the subject moving out of sharp focus, unless it is very slow or

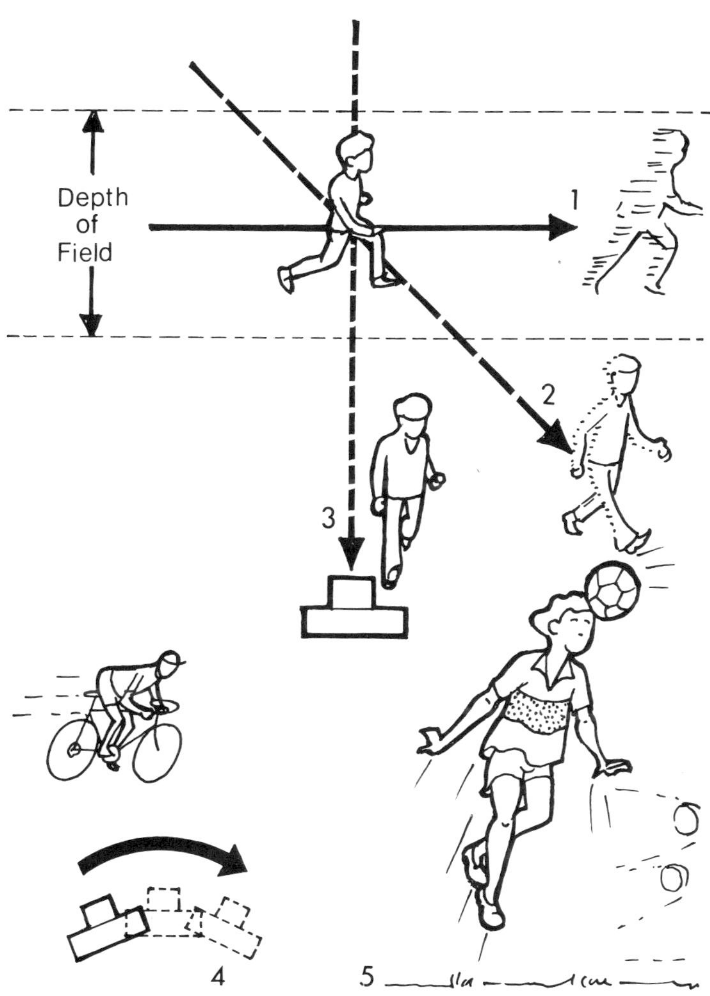

Subject movement in existing light. (1) Subjects moving across the field of view may not move out of the shallow depth of field but a fast subject may blur. (2) Oblique movement is less well covered by depth but less prone to blur. (3) Movement towards camera quickly passes out of depth unless follow-focused but gives least blur. (4) Minimise movement with a fast moving subject by panning the camera (5) or by catching movements at their peak.

you can anticipate where it will move to and so pre-focus on that point.

With subjects that move in a continuous line of action across the field of view such as speed track cyclists seen from inside the "straight" you can reduce the effect of subject movement by panning the camera with the subject. The background may blur but most of the subject should be sharp unless it contains some "internal" rapid movement such as rotating wheels. Here some movement is welcome in the picture as it can add to the impression of speed. For special effects you could let the whole subject blur in the picture. In any case a blurred background gives an increased feeling of speed compared with a picture where the background is absolutely sharp.

All these factors are common to action photography in any lighting conditions. It is more difficult to get good results in existing light, but the approaches mentioned may help. Occasionally you might be able to use flash, but this is not satisfactory for mixing with existing light sources because of the risk of obtaining one sharp image and a secondary blurred image of the same subject. Generally, this image can be disguised sufficiently only if the subject is shot against a dark or black background.

With portraiture, ordinary small movements are enough (with short exposures such as $\frac{1}{4}$ or $\frac{1}{8}$ sec) to cause a loss of critical definition in the picture. So here there is an element of luck. You can improve your chances of getting a sharp picture if you give the subject some *natural* means of support to help hold the body still. No matter how stationary your subject tries to remain, the body is naturally never completely still. In early Victorian portrait studios, where the primitive photographic materials demanded exposures of many seconds the subject could be steadied by a head or back rest, a support that was brought up from behind and placed gently against the head or body to provide the necessary steadiness, while itself remaining more or less out of sight. For outdoor portraiture you can use natural supports, having the subject rest his head on his hands or elbow which are themselves placed on a gate or wall, or leaning the body against a wall or tree. This provides enough steadiness for the longest exposures needed in modern existing light portraiture outdoors, which are certain to be less than $\frac{1}{4}$ sec.

You may have to photograph some animals in low light conditions because they do not make an appearance in full daylight. They might confine their activity to shady woodland or dark undergrowth, or may habitually emerge only in twilight or the early morning. You may have to photograph them by remote control, from a hide or other awkward conditions. The wide apertures necessary for low light work and the restricted depth of field would indicate pre-setting focus to certain points and shooting when the animal approaches. You could then make minor focus adjustments away from the basic distance. This is easier if you are waiting at the entrance to a burrow for the animal to appear, or to approach a bait.

Animals in captivity are naturally confined to some extent by the dimensions of the cage or compound they inhabit. Wild animals cannot really be photographed at speed except in full daylight.

In Town at Night

With most night photography you have to depend entirely on the lighting you find in the scene. Your subjects are in any case likely to be out of the reach of a flashgun – whose light could also be alien to the situation. Many night time pictures rely heavily on artificial lights or illiminations to provide interest in the scene owing to the absence of more "solid" visible subject matter. These lights mostly have very limited illuminating power, and pictures taken at night therefore tend to consist of extensive areas of shadow punctuated by lamps with relatively small pools of light around them.

If you want to use the lights not as subject matter themselves but as a source to illuminate another subject you normally have to confine your photography to limited areas very close to these lamps.

Generally, you should not expect to gain much detail in the background or other surrounding areas in night pictures. This absence of detail has a certain advantage in that it simplifies the picture and excludes unwanted features which might be difficult to avoid in daytime. Many people put too much in to their pictures anyway. But, with night pictures, the constant struggle to avoid "busy" backgrounds that distract the eye, or telegraph poles sticking out of people's heads is entirely avoided. In that way shooting at night should offer a head start towards better pictures.

Nearly all night scenes are of exceptionally high contrast, higher even than with indoor photography by daylight through a window. This is because in so many cases you cannot avoid, and indeed may deliberately include, lamps in the picture, immediately adjacent to completely black areas reflecting no light whatever. But you need not worry too much about contrast. It is normal enough in night-time shots and is a perfectly natural effect. In fact, greyish shadows all over such a picture tend to give the impression that in taking it something went wrong.

You may not necessarily encounter such high contrast where you are photographing a subject by the light from illuminations, floodlights or shop windows, for example. This largely depends how broad the light-giving area is. It also depends on how far the subject is from it or what the reflecting properties of the surroundings are and, con-consequently how far round the subject the light can reach. If the lighting is fairly rounded because the shadow side is "filled in" by some stray lights elsewhere, the contrast can be strong when you compare subject with background but very weak and flat-looking within the subject itself. A person photographed in black and white at night by ambient light from large areas of neon and flood light usually comes out looking rather pasty-faced although there is contrast enough in the scene. With colour film you may run in to trouble with strong colour casts from coloured lights, especially sodium discharge street lights.

By far the most interesting night shots are those that take advantage of oblique light and deep shadows, the areas of reflection, the brilliant highlights and all other features that give town scenes at night their strong atmosphere. As a rule you would be better off aiming for these if you want a distinctive flavour in the pictures.

If you are shooting in colour you should use tungsten-balanced film for preference. Daylight-balanced film tends to give night scenes a yellow-orange bias.

Where to look

The most plentiful night lighting in town is usually found in the main area of activity – the city centre or the entertainment district. Here you can capture the bustle of traffic and people out on the town. There is scope for candid photography with a less-than-normal chance of being spotted. There should be enough light about for hand held exposures with fast colour or black and white film, though as already stated the lighting may not give very exciting effects. The city centre probably offers the only chance of taking shots in various directions yet being fairly sure of having enough light on the subject.

It could be that your subject is the city centre itself. Here you have less of a problem than if you are trying to photograph people. And you can handle the subject in more ways than one. Suppose you wish to photograph the street scene with traffic, people walking about, light flooding on to the pavement from shop windows and theatres, clubs and bars with their names in lights above with neon signs high above those. With fast colour film of, say, 160 ASA you could secure all that with an exposure of 1/15 or 1/30 sec at *f*2.8. It is not normally practicable to set up a tripod in such a place but if you need support of some kind, you can often find a wall, lamp post or some other item of street furniture to lean the camera on while taking the shot. With a picture exposed to show all detail in the street, and subjects lit by all this light the colour of the illuminations themselves will probably be disappointing in your resulting pictures. If you have enough exposure to show the street you will overexpose the signs.

Lights as subjects

To get the best colour rendering of the neon signs and all other coloured lights and illuminations, you have to underexpose the rest of the scene. The signs are seen largely in darkness with perhaps only a hint of the buildings themselves visible here and there, but the colours are strong. For this effect you might try an exposure of 1/60 sec at *f*4 with the same film. Select only the most interesting illuminations and make them occupy the main part of the picture. It is sometimes difficult to visualize such a shot when, by looking through the viewfinder you can see so much more detail than you are actually going to record on the film. Seeing a picture in terms of photography rather than your own eyesight is, indeed, one of the most difficult skills to acquire and really only comes through long practice.

With longer exposures you can do one of the favourite night photography tricks – photographing the light trails made by passing traffic. You need an exposure of anything from several seconds to a minute or so depending on how many trails you want to record. The camera must be rigidly supported. If on a tripod, it should be well away from where anyone might accidentally kick it over in the dark. Most colourful effects are obtained by taking up position on traffic intersections that are not too well lit by street lamps. You can get the mixture of white front, and red rear lights. But be careful to avoid too long an exposure in case surrounding details are recorded, reducing the contrast and making the light trails less striking. Ideally perhaps, they should wind across a very dark ground. You can use the technique of covering the lens with a black card, opening the shutter and giving successive exposures by removing the card each time a car passes across the picture. On cameras not fitted with a double exposure device this avoids the need to wind on the film or risk moving the camera by opening the shutter more than once. The black card "shutter" can be used for many other night shots where you want to give several exposures on one film frame. Trick effects such as lights and signs photographed on top of one another are also possible by this means and other effects created by deliberately moving the camera during the exposure (see page 95).

Much the same technique applies to moving lights on fairground machines, display advertising and other set-piece night illuminations, and you should always take care to avoid overexposure with colour. If you are shooting against the sky it is too easy to give so long an exposure that it appears lighter than you want and so detracts from the illuminations. The deep blue of a twilight sky, on the other hand, can be a very attractive background to coloured lights, floodlit buildings, etc (see page 51).

Lights in black and white

On the whole, illuminations that contain strong contrasts are effective enough for black and white photography. Light trails are less so. Mixed coloured floodlighting loses most of its point in black and white photography and with such displays there are often too many lights trained on the subject from various directions to give the strongly defined contours that come out best with monochrome. Coloured lights on fountains also disappear and here again, there is probably an overabundance of light on the subject. Pictures which gain their main appeal from the mingling, interweaving or separating effect of different colours are almost sure to be disappointing when photographed in black and white. These are all definitely colour subjects.

Black and white photography really comes into its own where you have town scenes full of harsh contrasts, plenty of reflecting surfaces or even clear reflections, light beams caught in the atmosphere, strongly drawn forms, perhaps further defined with rim or back lighting and heavily accented highlights. This is the lighting of the back street and riverside, the city bridge and the silent wharves, the building site where floodlit work goes on through the night, or the late-night shop throwing its light across a quiet road.

Black and white night shots need the excitement of mood and pictorial effect to be really arresting. In compensation, as it were, for these demands, it avoids one of the most annoying limitations of colour film – a tendency to a sickly all-pervading yellow tinge over the picture. Indeed, it solves all colour problems at a stroke – by missing them out.

People and movement

When photographing people it is inevitable that the actual technical limitations of your photography and of your camera – shutter speed, aperture and focal length – are put to a more stringent test than with other night-time subjects.

Arresting reasonable degrees of movement, such as where people are photographed walking down the street, is not beyond the scope of the average camera if you use a fast film and you are taking your pictures in a fairly bright place. In a city centre you could expect exposures of around 1/30 sec at *f*4 to give enough shadow detail for general scenes. If your human subjects are the main feature of the picture and you are working from nearby it would be advisable to shoot at 1/60 sec. For this you may be confined to the areas immediately around shop windows, theatre entrances, etc where there is a concentration of strong light. A good technique is to find a well lit area, conceal yourself nearby just outside it and, with focus and aperture set and finger at the ready on the button, wait for subjects to appear. This is better than chasing around the streets looking for suitable victims. If you did that you would have to constantly change your exposure settings for the wide variations of light intensity you find in the average street scene. You would also have to make frequent focus changes because at night working with a wide aperture, the focus becomes really critical. The one-position technique requires only one distance setting (or, perhaps, only minor adjustment) and you just wait for your subject to walk into focus.

If you have an interchangeable-lens camera you will probably be tempted to use long focus lenses to get close ups of faces. You are really setting yourself a difficult task. The longer focus lens may have to work at full aperture the whole time (most lenses do not give of

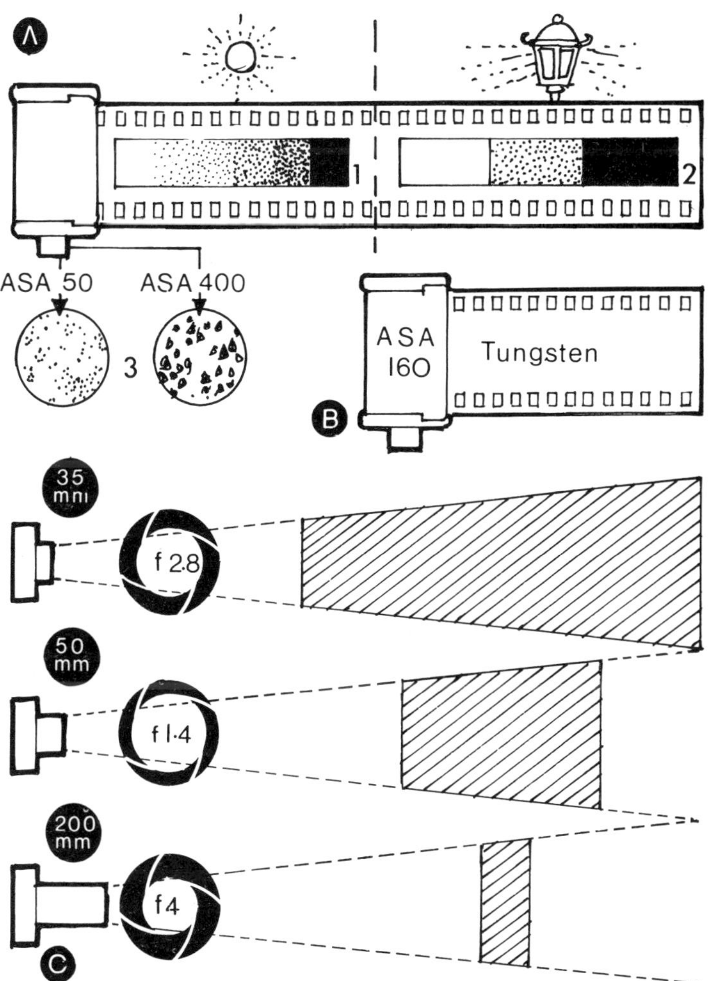

Night photography. A. Subject contrast and film speed for black and white; (1) Daylight subject contrast range is very low compared with (2) night scenes. (3) Fast films give shorter exposure but more grain. B. With colour you use a high speed film balanced for tungsten illumination. C. You may have to depend on the maximum aperture; a wide angle lens offers a reasonable maximum aperture and great depth of field, standard lenses often have an exceptionally wide maximum aperture and most long focus lenses have a smaller aperture and give little depth of field.

their best at such a setting) and as well as having little depth of field it may be difficult to hold the lens steady enough for the longer-than-normal exposure times. You would undoubtedly be better off with a standard or wide angle lens. A wide angle lens is likely to offer a reasonable working aperture, you do not have to be so careful with focus and it gives intimacy to pictures of people. You can also shoot easily from quite nearby when the pavement is rather crowded.

A long focus lens, on the other hand, tends to give a feeling of remoteness in photographing people, even though you are, in effect, magnifying the image. Somehow the distance between you and the subject is very apparent in such pictures and indeed the lens does encourage you to put a greater distance between you and your subject. The detailed view of the long focus photographer is especially noticeable in candid photography of people in the street.

Despite the certain advantages of a wide angle lens you will probably find your most versatile choice for night photography to be a lens of standard focal length. It generally offers the widest working aperture of your lenses and it allows you to take pictures of long range subjects as well as those nearby. There is therefore no disadvantage in having a non-interchangeable lens camera, and the most likely tangible advantage of the interchangeable type is that often the standard lens on such a camera has an exceptionally wide maximum aperture. In most other night photography situations the choice of lens is of little importance and, except for some special pictorial effects (such as using a wide angle lens to include huge areas of reflection in the lower foreground) there is no need to change from the standard.

Because they move, you need light when photographing people at night. So you should go where the light is. The light from shop windows is strong but one-sided. People tend to stop and look in to the windows so, for faces, you could shoot from the window side. Often you can shoot through the right angle of a shop window from the recessed entrance to the shop. You may not be seen for a long time and the people are stationary. The lighting from this angle is strong, but rather flat. You get more general lighting at entrances to hotels, theatres, etc because often there is a broad portico or canopy with rows of lights beneath it. The strong toplighting is not attractive, but it covers well for shots of people arriving from the street – such as personalities stepping out of cars, etc.

With larger groups of people, often a traffic island or crossing refuge in the middle of the street provides a good vantage point. You get clear foregrounds and so your group is not obscured by large unwanted figures. This position also offers a possibility of coloured reflections from a wet street to fill the dark and empty space in the lower part of the picture. Unfortunately, such dark areas are all too common in pictures taken at night.

Another light source suitable for photographing one stationary person or a group of two or three is a single street lamp. They can be positioned immediately underneath. The lighting is rather ghoulish, however, as it comes from immediately overhead unless you place the subjects a little beyond the lamp so that some light falls on them from the front. A well tried dodge is to arrange for a person under the lamp to be reading a newspaper, thus reflecting light up into the face. This effect, though quite dramatic, is something that you would only try once. Another, similar, treatment is to have your subject reading a map by a car headlight, again throwing light into the face. Otherwise the light from headlamps is an exceptionally unpleasant source for lighting people at night – quite as much so as using a single flash gun on the camera as the sole source.

Other small light pools are encountered at night where a working lamp or light panel illuminates the face of a person standing nearby or peering into it. This can give a strong chiaroscuro really evocative of night time conditions. These small sources do, of course, place limitations on how far the subject can be from them as well as their possible use for more than one picture. You can easily feel cramped by such a light source when trying to get a picture. So, rather than make such efforts, it would perhaps be wiser just to keep an eye open for them and take advantage of the effect if it is there.

Arranging the subject

Having found an effectual light pool at night it is possible that you may think of arranging your human subjects to take advantage of it. There are many arguments for and against producing such deliberately contrived human situations. This approach has been used to set up news pictures, often very convincingly. It seems to be acceptable practice in news photography to re-create situations that occurred a little while before by asking the persons involved to "do it again". It is said to be legitimate to do this if the objective is to piece together a picture which gives an accurate representation of a real event. The trouble with this attitude, and in manipulating people in general for the sake of a picture, is that, even if the result carries some conviction the habit tends to degenerate into mannerism. This too, is the chief danger in manufacturing situations for the sake of the light source. It is better to look for pictures that occur naturally, though this does not forbid making some minor adjustments to improve the composition. Your results should not reveal the tell-tale traits of the stage-managed "interesting" picture.

Sports and action

Sport and action pictures normally demand that your camera work in diametrically the opposite way to that required by night photography. Whereas night photography needs long exposures and wide apertures to get enough light on to the film, sport and action pictures need short exposures to arrest movement and small apertures which offer enough depth of field to contain the action without constantly refocusing. How then are these conflicting requirements reconciled?

Sports often take place under floodlighting in a city stadium. This is hardly a brilliant light source. Nevertheless, it is bright enough to allow exposures to secure reasonably sharp pictures of not too rapidly moving subjects on high speed colour film. The minimum practical shutter speed would be 1/125 sec. Even then, with many sports you will have to choose moments when there is not too much activity, or a natural pause. In football, for example, these moments occur every so often when the movement of the ball is uncertain or when, as in other sports, the players change direction or do not move laterally across the field of view (see page 68). Here the remarks made earlier concerning moving subjects apply with particular force. You can generally work at or near full aperture because unless you have a front row seat you will be so far from the action that the depth of field will probably cover most of the ground. With action nearby you have proportionally greater difficulties. With athletics you can choose moments in the action fractionally before a change in direction of movement – the high point of a jump, the handstand on parallel bars, the preparation for a long jump, the moment of landing, etc. Alternatively you may consider that a little evidence of movement in your picture is desirable. You can exaggerate this effect by setting a slower than normal shutter speed (and a correspondingly smaller aperture to compensate the extra exposure).

Problems and how to solve them

Slow speeds For night photography a camera with a range of slow shutter speeds, say, between 1/15 and 1 second is a great asset. This can take care of the typical exposures with fast film which occur outside the range of hand-held camera situations. With such shutter settings you need only steady the camera against some solid support and need not use a tripod. If you do not have such speed you have to choose a smaller aperture and set the camera on "B" for a time exposure. For this you should really use a tripod or find a very stable flat surface on which to place the camera.

Choice of film With black and white photography you have no problems with the choice of film. Only remember that, all things being equal, if you use a faster film, you tend to get more grain appearing in your pictures. Faster films tend to give lower contrast; slower films are "harder". Fast film needs care in exposure and development if you do not want a grainy result. Overexposure increases the grain, and so does development beyond the recommended time. Deliberate "forced processing" can, in effect, increase the speed of the film slightly but is more often used to increase the density of an image that only just made it. Some people habitually extend the development time to gain this advantage for night photography. But it is not a recommended practice with the fastest materials unless grain is of no account. Colour film can be similarly force-processed (see page 204).

With colour film your choice is between normal speed and fast material, and in most cases it is much more convenient to use the latter unless you are going to take pictures in bright sunlight on the same load of film. In that case you might find that you could not avoid overexposure bcause your camera might not offer a combination of fast enough shutter speed and small enough aperture. You also have to choose between daylight and artificial light film. Strictly speaking neither of these films is properly colour-balanced to match the mixture of light sources encountered in night photography. (Incidentally no film will give good colour in sodium lighting.) Daylight films tend to render such scenes in warm colours, tungsten films render them with a colder bias. So the choice is a matter of personal preference. It is possible to influence the rendering with very pale filters, but such a correction must be very slight.

Contrast The high contrast found in so many night situations can be reduced by using reflectors to fill the shadows. Or you can choose a position where the shadow side of the subject is partially filled by light reflected from the surroundings. In black and white photography contrast can be reduced by a combination of overexposure and underdevelopment, but it is doubtful if this would have a significant effect in the majority of night situations in town. It might even produce a negative which was more difficult to print satisfactorily than if it had been treated in a straightforward manner.

Exposure For most shots with such a wide contrast range, straight reflected light readings are most unreliable, and the automatic camera is sure to indicate that there is not enough light. A good method is to go up to the subject which forms the most important part of the scene and take a reading of the light reflected (bearing in mind the considerations previously discussed on page 36). Spot reading meters could be confined to areas of chief interest as viewed from a distance. Alternatively you could take a white card reading and multiply the exposure indicated by a factor of four. You could take highlight and shadow readings (if possible) in some situations and divide the difference but this would probably be the least reliable method. Whatever method you choose (see page 38) it would be safest to bracket your exposures either by taking one picture at your estimated reading and one a stop above and another a stop below, or, alternatively, you could take two only, one half a stop above and another half a stop below that calculated.

Focusing You are less likely to have trouble focusing town pictures because there are probably lights or highlights on the point you want sharp. If it *is* too dark, you can put a torch in the scene or ask someone to light a match and focus on that.

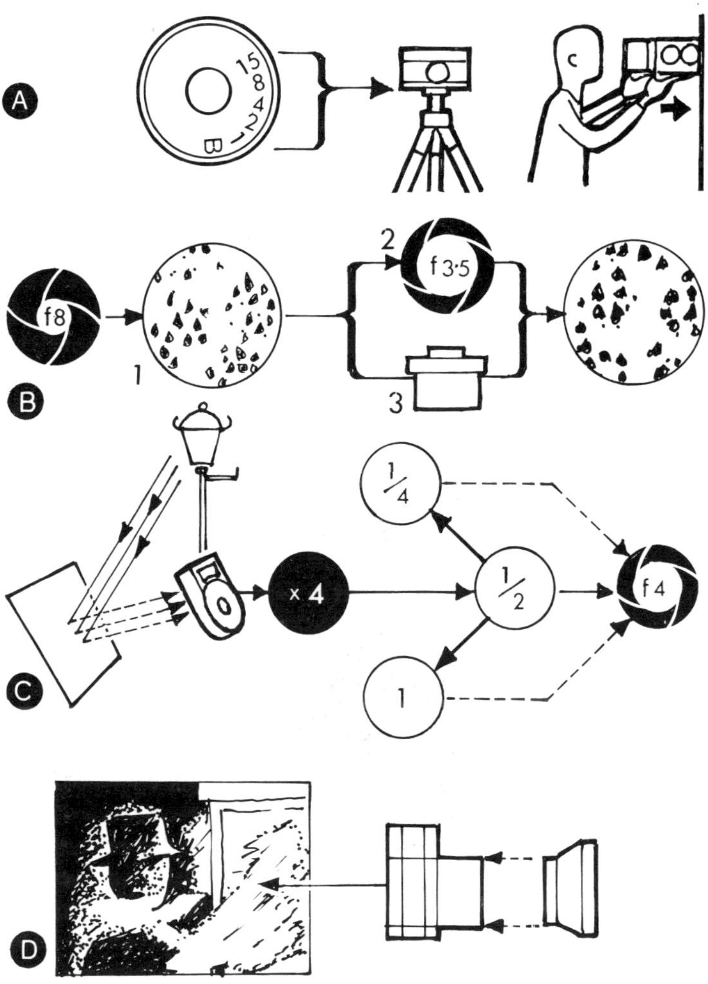

Solving night pnotography problems. A. Slow speeds help with the longer exposures needed, whether the camera is on a tripod or only steadied against the wall. B. Use fast film with care. It has (1) large grain, which becomes larger if you (2) overexpose or (3) overdevelop it. C. Direct readings are unreliable so take a reading from a white card and multiply it by 4. Bracket by giving exposures either side of that estimated. D. Protect the lens from flare with a lenshood.

If you are working at a very wide aperture the limited depth of field has to be carefully "spread" over the parts of the subject you want rendered as sharp. Remember that the closer to the subject you are the less the depth. You can assume very roughly that you have twice as much depth to spare behind the point focused on as you do in front. With very distant subjects therefore you have little need to worry. With reflections in water, glass, etc, you focus on the subject in the reflection *not* the reflecting surface itself.

Flare A strong light within, or immediately outside, the picture area can cause internal reflections within the lens and result in flare in the picture. Though modern lenses are less subject to this problem than used to be the case, it still happens. Worse, a series of reproductions of the iris diaphragm, sometimes in colour, appears across the picture. You can reduce the chance of getting unwanted flare by using a lens hood (sunshade) at all times. This is strongly advised for all night photography. You have so large an unexposed area in night pictures that any flare or halation shows up far more strongly than in pictures taken in daylight. There may, of course, be reasons for *wanting* flare in the picture. It can imbue the scene with a certain atmosphere which, though artificial, somehow has a place. Flare does occur within the human eye but the effect is quite different.

Halation is an effect in which strong highlights (usually lamps) in the picture are surrounded by a halo of light. In the days before films were provided with a special anti-halation backing, strong halation effects were easily obtained. They were caused by light bouncing off the rear surface of the film and hitting the emulsion from behind. Usually they were considered a nuisance though a few pictorialist photographers enjoyed the effect of a halo round a gas lamp or around the Christmas candle. This effect is rarely encountered by accident except in a small way if your pictures are overexposed (see page 99).

Freaks and Effects Outdoors

Many people are under the impression that trick or effect pictures are almost invariably set up for the camera under specially controlled conditions. While this is undoubtedly true in many cases, some freakish effects occur quite naturally without needing to be encouraged, and others happen with only a very little assistance from the photographer. There is great scope for shooting effect pictures by existing light. Most effects occur at one (or more) of three main stages. There are effects which are present, naturally, in the scene, others which happen in the camera, and those which owe their origin to some stage or property of the process *en route* to the finished print or transparency. Here we are concerned mainly with those in the first two categories because the process effects or tricks are common to all types of photography and are not especially applicable to pictures taken by existing light.

Effects in the scene

Existing light photography lends itself particularly to certain types of effect. The broad areas of underexposed film in many outdoor night shots are susceptible to many influences – good or bad. Light that comes from odd places, or has a strong colour is registered with full force. Lights that move can be made to track across the film leaving a clearly drawn trail behind them. Whether man-made or the product of the natural world any light gains in significance for being surrounded by darkness, dusk or just a grey day.

Lightning

Lightning is a difficult subject in that it is unpredictable. You can never be sure where it will strike or whether it is likely to reappear in the same place. You need a time exposure and a small aperture to avoid getting too much density in the sky. Sometimes you can judge the approximate time between flashes and open the shutter immediately beforehand. You can also get more than one flash in one picture. But it is advisable not to try too often, or you may overexpose the sky while waiting for the second flash. Lightning streaks alone can be combined

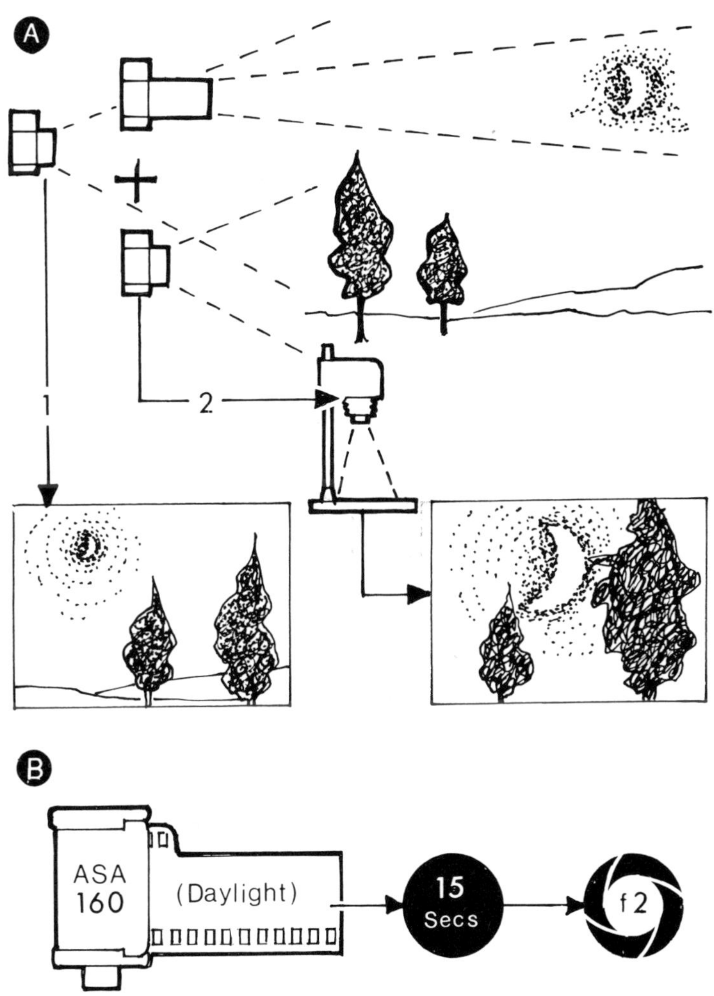

Shooting the moon. (1) With a normal camera lens the moon looks much too small. (2) A more realistic effect is obtained by shooting the moon through a telephoto lens and then combining it in the enlarger with a moonlit scene without the moon, shot with a normal lens. For a moonlit scene with fast daylight colour film give exposures of at least 15 sec at *f*2.

by sandwiching negatives at the printing stage. The most impressive lightning pictures show some outline or silhouette of landscape with the lightning flash reaching the ground. Lightning is like a giant electronic flash and repeated sheet lightning or other flashes outside the picture area can expose the whole landscape.

Shooting the moon

You can photograph the moon at night or in the early evening without any difficulty. You can also take pictures by moonlight, without including the moon itself in the picture.

To photograph the moon you set the camera on a tripod or other rigid support and expose for 1/30 sec at *f*5.6 with a fast film. But you should bracket your exposures. The moon is hardly worth photographing except through a long-focus lens, otherwise its image appears very small in the picture. If you are making prints, you can combine a negative of the moon with one of a scene photographed by moonlight (but not including the moon itself) sandwiching the two in the enlarger carrier and printing them together. If the two are properly aligned the result is very convincing.

If you are taking scenes by moonlight that are to appear natural, exposures with a fast colour film could be based on 15 seconds at *f*2 but, as with all exposures under unconventional conditions, much depends on what you want. These suggested exposures assume that the sky is clear and the moon is not veiled by mist or clouds. You should use daylight colour film, not tungsten.

If you wish to take shots by moonlight to look like daylight scenes you have to give exposures in the region of 3 minutes at full aperture with a medium speed film. You might obtain an effect resembling daylight with colour film, all colours being rendered more or less correctly. But strange things can happen when you so expose a colour film designed for short exposures. Due to the effects of what is known as reciprocity law failure, the colour balance may be seriously disturbed. With Ektachrome there is a tendency towards red, if you use daylight film. On artificial light film, moonlight scenes take on a heavy blue cast. Ektachrome used for long exposure times shows, therefore, a tendency for the red effect and the blue cast to mix, giving a purple cast across the whole picture. Such effects occur only if the picture is taken in the clear atmosphere of a rural environment and away from reflections of city lights.

It is not possible to reproduce the effect of sunlight using the moon as a substitute because with the long exposures required, rotation of the earth causes the shadows in the subject to blur instead of being sharply defined.

Fires, fireworks

The main problem with fires, fireworks and the activity that goes with them is the wide range of brightnesses that you want to accommodate in one picture.

Fires at night need a shortish exposure on account of the movement of the flames if you are photographing only the fire itself. Longer exposures give only a flat sheet of white which looks nothing like flames at all. Faces around the fire, on the other hand, need far more exposure – a fact which can be quickly ascertained by taking a reflected-light meter reading off them from nearby. You have to favour one subject or the other unless you use flash to fill-in the faces and so "cheat" the effect.

Faces can hardly be combined more successfully with fireworks, because although they both need a time exposure to gain the maximum effect, you cannot usually risk a time exposure with people who are likely to move about. With black and white you could shoot separate negatives and combine them in printing or, with colour, try a double exposure in the camera, though this is not easy. You might get one or two pictures by the rather contrived device of making someone hold a sparkler or other, safe, light-giving firework and photograph their face lit by that. But generally you have to accept and work within the limitations of the subject unless you add light.

With fireworks you should put the camera on a tripod pointing at the sky. Set a small aperture, open the shutter and give time exposures only when rockets, fountains or Roman candles go up, quickly covering the lens between times. You can use the lens cap or a piece of black card as a shutter. Catherine wheels and other low level fireworks could take a much shorter exposure time.

Camera effects

The camera itself gives you more scope for effects or tricks than you will find in any scene. As with any photography involving experiments of one kind or another, it is safest not to rely on a single "try" but to protect yourself with several attempts if possible, making any necessary variations. Some camera tricks rely on a complementary treatment at the printing or processing stage to complete the effect. Many are done quite simply and without any follow-up.

Multiple exposure

Perhaps the best known camera trick is double exposure. One image appears superimposed on another in the same picture. In the old days before cameras had a built-in device to prevent it, this "effect" sometimes used to happen quite unintentionally – much to the annoyance of the photographer. Nowadays you only have it if you choose to, because normally you can't release the camera shutter without winding on the film. Many cameras do not allow two exposures to be made on the same piece of film; others have a special override device that makes this possible. A lock is operated which allows you to tension the shutter without advancing the film to the next frame.

If you do not have a double exposure facility, on most 35 mm cameras there is a way of obtaining the same end result. First you take up any slack in the film by gently winding the rewind crank or knob as if you were rewinding the film after exposure. You then hold this knob firmly, press the rewind button (normally in the base or top plate of the camera end) and advance the transport lever in the normal way as if for one whole frame. The rewind button disengages the transport mechanism but the shutter tensioning and other functions continue as normal. So you can now take a second shot over the first on the same frame of film. You can repeat this operation again several times if you wish on the same piece of film, exposing repeatedly, but do not expect to obtain perfect register. The film generally moves slightly.

With your camera on a tripod for a shot needing a long exposure there is no need to bypass the transport mechanism. You can make the

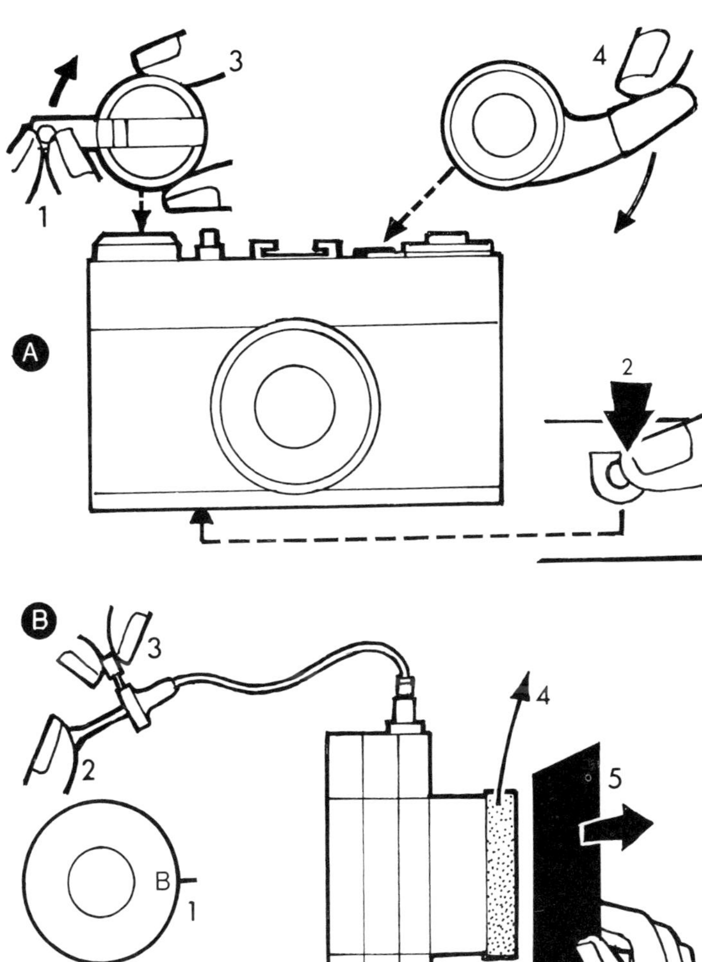

Multiple exposure in the camera. Method A: Tighten the film (1) with the rewind knob. (2) Press the rewind button and, holding the rewind knob (3) advance the film transport lever to re-tension the shutter. Then re-shoot. Method B: Longer exposures (1). Set the shutter on B and with the lens cap in place (2) press the cable release button and (3) lock it. (4) Remove the cap with a black card held in front. (5) Make each exposure by removing and replacing the black card.

exposures with the lens cap and a black card. Set the shutter on "B", press it and lock it open with a cable release. Hold a matt black card very close in front of the lens. A piece of card covered with black velvet or velour is ideal. Remove the lens cap. Allow time for any vibrations on the camera to subside, then make your first exposure with the black card. Replace the card. Second, third or any number of subsequent exposures can follow at intervals.

Between your exposures the subject in front of the camera might move, giving several separate images of the same subject within the picture. Or the subject might be replaced by another, superimposing images of different subjects. These subjects could be related in some way to represent a theme, though it is better to avoid doing that consciously because of the risk of producing pictures that make banal statements or display obvious emblematic links.

This multi-exposure method is ideal for accumulating on the film effects that are individually of only momentary duration, such as flashes of lightning or fireworks, without building up unwanted detail in other areas as with a night sky or features of the landscape. The method works well with fireworks. Not only does the whole progress of the life of a firework become traced on the film but others appearing at different intervals, when so combined, give the effect of an unusually extravagant display.

You can set up pictures deliberately for the multi-exposure technique placing different objects in the light source.

Another variation is to move the camera between exposures and take several different views of the same or different subjects alongside one another in different areas of the frame, or arranged so as to be superimposed.

Several separate exposures can be made to show different stages in the progress of a moving subject. Building up a series of images in this way normally calls for many short exposures made in quick succession. Such an effect is beyond the scope of a camera not fitted with a multiple exposure device.

Tricks and odd shots with time exposures

You can use time exposures for many night-time subjects. But if you are photographing lights, as opposed to views, you probably want to avoid the kind of long exposure that lightens the whole scene or the sky against which the subject is to appear. A dark backdrop is more effective for most such pictures. With time exposures even quite a dark sky can soon become too overexposed to give you the contrast you need. Time exposures do, however, have many other applications in trick photography.

If the subject moves, you can open the shutter and let it make a light trail across the film. You can interrupt this light trail at intervals by momentarily interrupting the exposure with the black card. Another way is to make a small wheel from black card and rotate this in front of the lens as the light-emitting object crosses the field of view. The result, for example with light trails from passing traffic, is to chop the trails into short lenghts. A series of such trials superimposed on one another can be built up in this way.

Shoot for the stars

A standard trick using a time exposure is to set the camera on a tripod pointing up at the night sky. With a long enough exposure, say, several minutes at full aperture with a fast film, you can record trails that the stars make due to the rotation of the earth. For successful results you need a very clear sky. It is impossible in urban areas.

Moving the camera

If the camera is moved during a time exposure, the image of the subject becomes a blur, while bright highlights or lamps make light trails across the picture. Tracks from coloured lights are very attractive. This deliberate camera movement can be mechanically controlled or done "freehand". If you put the camera on a tripod fitted with a pan and tilt head, you can lock off the head in one plane only and move the camera in the other during the exposure. Without a tripod, if the camera sits properly on its base you can swivel it around to get one of these effects at least.

For more adventurous effects you should hold the camera in your hand and move it. Open the shutter and move the camera according to the figure you want to make. Sometimes just waving the camera about gives a good effect, but regularity in the shapes generated is more likely to be successful. Choose a good "clean" subject to practice on. The danger is over-complication. If the effect is overdone it may just result in an uninteresting smudge of light. So keep it fairly simple both in terms of subject and the movement you give the camera. Beyond the recommended precautions success depends to a large degree on luck.

Where it is difficult to move the camera, you can get the same effect by holding a mirror at 45 degrees to the lens and moving that about instead. You are then virtually moving the subject by moving its reflected image while the camera photographs it.

Colour filters

There is enormous scope for effects with coloured light or fireworks using time exposures but if you do not have much colour in the scene you can add it by placing a suitable filter over the camera lens. Colour filters of the type used for corrective or contrast adjustment in black and white photography are ideal for playing with light in colour. You can modify your time exposure by shooting part of it through a filter of one colour and part through another. With lights in the picture, you can then get light trails of different colours with moving subjects or by moving the camera.

You can add colour filters to any low light picture to give an all-over cast of one colour, but all these filters require extra exposure from $1\frac{1}{2}$–$2\times$ upwards to compensate for the light loss due to the density of the filter. In certain low light situations this may push your exposure beyond the limits that make photography practicable, depending on the situation. It is also a strictly limited effect from a creative point of view unless you are making multiple exposures with one or more colours.

Effect filters and screens

Special filters and screens can be placed in front of the camera lens to give certain set-piece effects. The star burst filter, or cross-screen as it is sometimes known, converts all the principal highlights in a picture

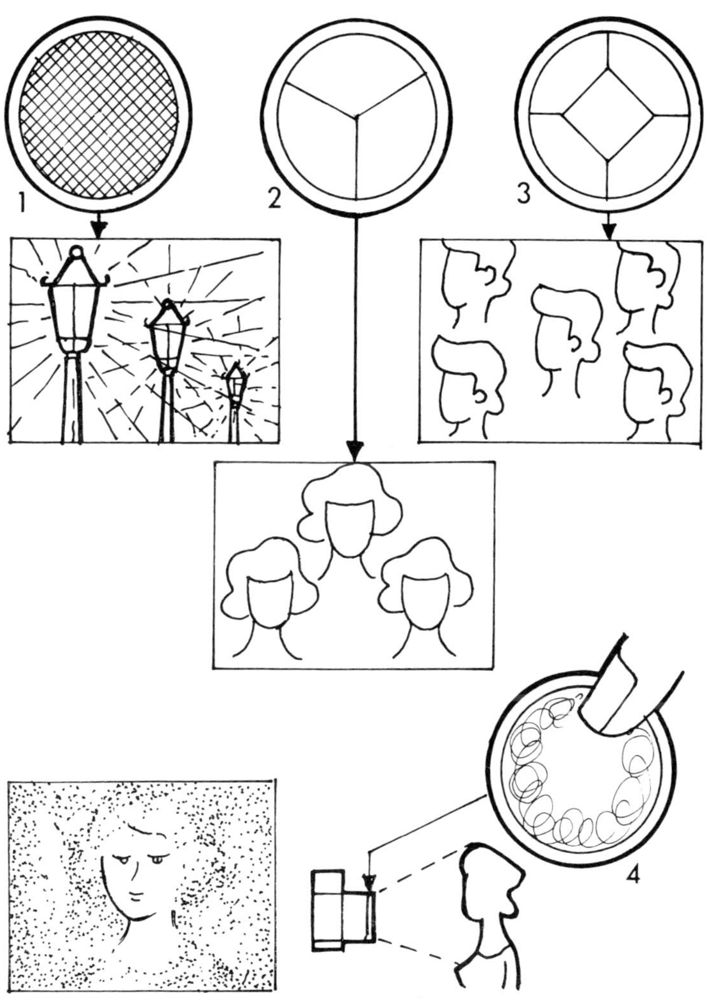

Effect filters and screens placed over the lens. (1) Star burst screen turns highlights into crosses or stars. (2) Prismatic attachment gives separate images of the subject. (3) Multi-facet attachment multiplies the images in a pattern. (4) A partial diffuser can be made by placing in front of the camera lens a piece of nylon stocking with a hole burnt in the centre with a cigarette or by smearing a sheet of glass or plastic with petroleum jelly.

into crosses varying in size (the length of emitted rays or the arms of the cross) according to the size and brightness of the particular highlight. The crosses may be rotated into the desired position by turning the screen. This screen is most effective in low light pictures which, though predominantly dark, have a few strong highlights, such as a street scene at night and an indoor situation where the lights are in the picture or are reflected off a shining subject.

A multi-faceted prismatic attachment gives multiple images of the subject in front of the lens. This might find a use in low light situations where the subject is well lit but seen against a very dark background. Some portraits where the profile, for example, is strongly picked out but everything else is in deep shade, are effective subjects for this device. Complicated subjects, or those with fussy backgrounds give a muddled result when shot through a prismatic attachment.

Diffusers and attachments, screens or filters that give flare or halation are all especially applicable to the kind of low light shot that is full of strong contrasts, provided there is sufficient flare, halation or diffusion to be picked up in the underexposed areas. In some cases where the so-called threshold of exposure is not reached (you have to give so much exposure to a film before even the minimum image density will register) there is simply not enough light spread into the darker areas to make any impression on the film. So with the typically contrasty existing light shot the flare shows up splendidly against the dark areas if you can get it at all. But do not depend on that. The film may absorb all the effect you were hoping to get and give you a reasonably straightforward picture as a result.

You can make a simple diffuser by stretching some nylon stocking across a frame and holding that in front of the lens. This slightly softens the hard edged shadows in a portrait. A much stronger effect is obtained from a glass or plastic sheet smeared with petroleum jelly. You can also buy diffusion discs. The type with concentric rings and a clear centre must be used at a wide aperture to have much effect. In all such cases the highlights in the scene are spread slightly into the shadow areas (the reverse happens if this effect is carried out in printing). Only a very slight increase in exposure over what you would normally give is called for to take account of your screen.

Flare can be induced in a picture by shooting close to the strongest light source, or more effectively by placing such a source just outside the picture area. The results in colour are sometimes very pleasing indeed, with an all-over softening effect but, again, there is a large measure of luck in it. If you are determined to get flare you would have a better chance by using an old uncoated lens.

Halation was described on page 86. Although a longer exposure should give more chance of a halo effect, in most circumstances it is not easy to obtain. With photographs which are to end up as prints, it is perhaps an effect best left to be mocked up at the enlarging stage, though it must be admitted that results are unlikely to be quite the same.

Diffusion and flare or halation effects can sometimes be found occurring naturally in the scene – wet windows, reflections off irregular surfaces or from surfaces which move during a time exposure, such as lights in water photographed at night. Diffusion, although softening the image, is not the same thing as having a subject out of focus. A diffused image is a basically sharp rendering overlaid by an unsharp one where the light rays are scattered in some way. An out of focus image has no sharp component and has little value as an effect except when placed in opposition to sharpness in some other part of the image.

Daylight Indoors

Daylight indoors is the best and most versatile light source for existing light photography. It also possesses an intrinsic beauty that has appealed to artists for centuries. You can use the daylight through a window or skylight to photograph the interior of a room, to take a portrait, or a shot of an animal, or to light an object – a still life, or a photograph you want to copy, for example. Or you can picture an effect of the light itself as it enters the building: a shaft of sunlight caught in a dusty or smoky atmosphere, or playing shapes on the wall, or projecting colours from stained glass onto the floor of a church. Window light can also be made to play tricks – you can shoot silhouettes with it or make flare effects or abstract shapes – all the time using only what is there, however low the light level.

You do not need fine weather. But the effect you get is different, according to whether it is sunny or dull. Naturally for some subjects you want as much window light as you can get. But this is affected by many factors – the number, size and position of windows in the room, any features immediately outside, and the height of the window above the ground or, indeed, any blind or curtain that may be on the window itself. Moreover, the size, colour and character of the room itself influences the lighting that a subject receives. By subtle control you can make the best of what is a very fine light source for photography. You can use it in its raw state or restrict it and govern it with curtains or blinds. By moving your subject you have almost as much control over the direction of the light as you have with a lamp. With the aid of a newspaper you can help out the window light by introducing a "filler" light to put detail in the shadows. A mirror will spotlight the daylight on any part of the subject or, if placed behind it can change the background by reflecting another part of the room or the scene outside the window. Sometimes, artificial lights inside the room are strong enough to help you model the daylight to your requirements. But full daylight is stronger than ordinary lamps, which may serve only to lighten the shadows unless they are very close to the subject. In the evening or on a very dull day, or if you bring in photoflood lamps or a flashgun, the window light may be overpowered. In that case *it* would be the secondary source serving only to light the background or fill the shadow areas. In most cases, however, the light through the window is your key light and everything is based on that premise.

In most buildings the windows are in the walls. Light from skylights is

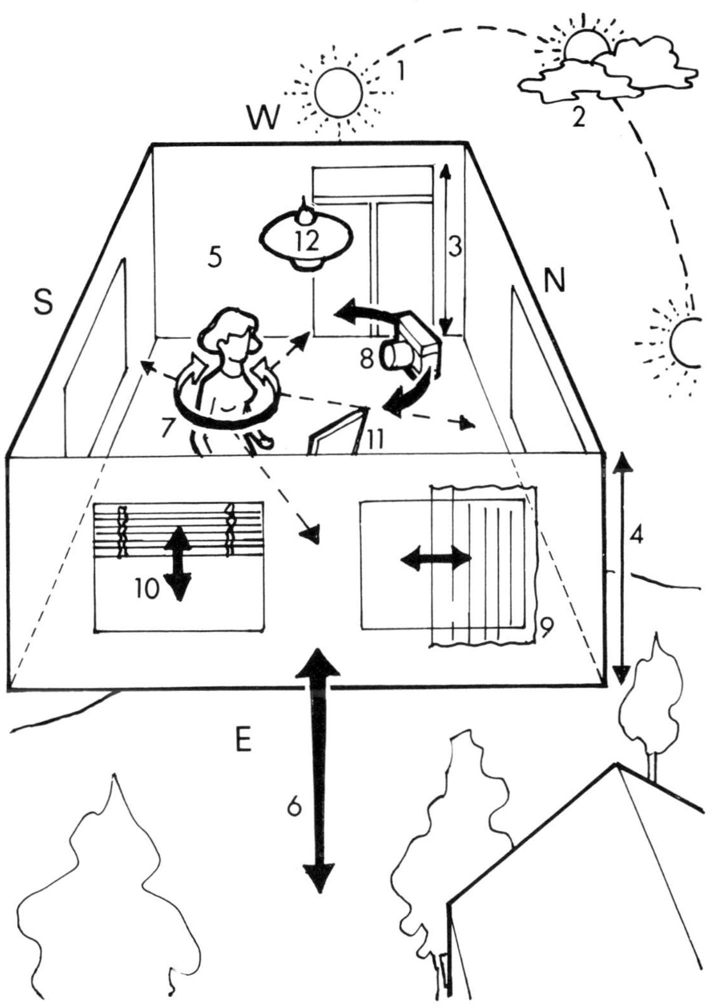

Available room light is affected by (1) Time of day (2) weather and direction which windows face, the number and (3) height of them (4) the dimensions of the room (5) colour of walls (6) height of room above ground. How the light falls on the subject is controlled by (7) placing of the subject (8) the camera (9) use of curtains or (10) blinds (11) reflectors and (12) secondary lighting.

different in character – not very controllable, if at all, often very diffuse, and unattractive if directly overhead. It may be satisfactory for illuminating spacious interiors or as a light source for flat copy work, but it is severely limited in potential for any expressive use in picture making, unless it comes from an oblique angle. Even then, pictures taken by such a source tend to lack variety of approach even though you resort to such devices as reflecting it upwards or from the side. With the light from conventional windows you have immense scope for imaginative effects that avoid any impression of repetitiveness, even if it is the only kind of lighting you ever use.

Window light is so subtle, so variable yet always so distinctive that many photographers believe there is no better light source available for photographic portraiture. It gives a rounded and firm modelling without hard edged shadows. In most cases there is at least the basis of a fill light for the shadow area to be gained from reflections inside the room. So the shaded side need not be totally devoid of interest or detail. That basic fill light can be built upon by the simple expedient of adding more reflected light into the shadows either by repositioning the subject or using a simply improvised reflector. The fill light can hardly be overdone, so the beginner's pictures are unlikely to fail in this respect. Compared with photography by lamps, window light is simple to use in the sense that it leaves you free to move the subject without also having to attend to lights. It does not diminish in power with increased subject distance in quite the way that light does from a lamp. So the light "pool" you have to work within is proportionally larger. This means that it is suitable for subjects that move around a certain amount, such as children, animals or insects. It is not ideal for those which involve rapid movement because even if it is an all-over light from above it is not as plentiful as daylight outdoors and does not allow very short exposures.

Because window light comes mainly from one or, in the case of two windows, two sources, it need not be uniform in effect from one picture to the next. There is great scope for imaginative lighting in portraiture or for other subjects and the window light can be controlled almost as much as with lamps. The results, if they do go wrong are unlikely to be too bad, or even downright ridiculous as they can be with lamps. The most adventurous experiments with window light will always be founded on something natural. This places its own

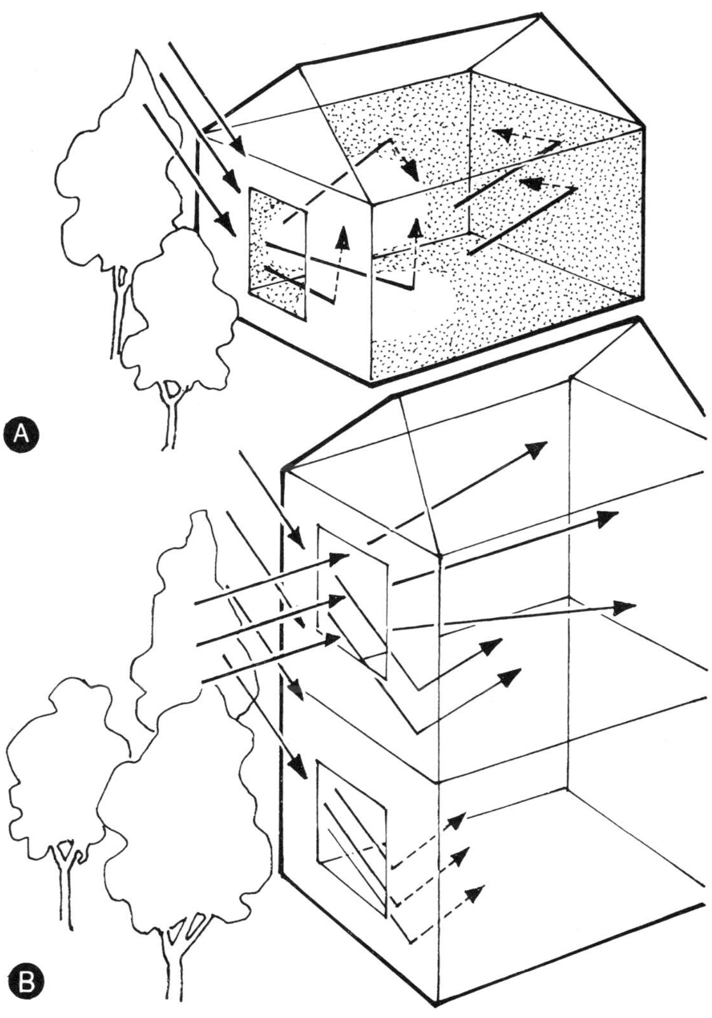

Light from the window. A. Dispersion of sky light within a room showing shady and brightly lit areas and light bounced from there. B. Upper and lower floors. Upper floor receives light from sky and lower horizon so deep room lighting is strong, whereas on the lower floor the light is strongest under the window but weak elsewhere, being largely indirect.

limits on what is done – and is certain to fall short of absurdity. So it is a very suitable source for imaginative exploits with light, shade, reflection, blur, diffusion, flare or silhouette, curious lighting, distortion and other visual excursions into the not quite real.

How window light varies

Window light differs from daylight outdoors in many ways, including its directional nature, the angle it comes from, its intensity and the kind of shadow it gives. But it is of course affected by the properties of the daylight, the part of the year, the time of day, according to the hemisphere you happen to live in, and the weather. These factors affect the strength and the colour of the daylight. Other aspects at least as important are the size of the window (particularly its height), its position in the house, any buildings or trees outside, whether you are using more than one window and, if so, how they are arranged in relation to one another. You also have to take into account the size of the room, the position of the subject within it, the reflecting efficiency of the surrounding walls and any curtains or coverings that can be placed over the windows. These all determine the character of the light reaching the subject and its effectiveness for what you want. Together, they represent a huge range of fixed and variable influences.

The right window

Skylight entering a window is from only a small segment of the sky, whereas outdoors skylight comes from all around. Obviously the larger the window the more light it admits. But the actual position and shape of the window is more significant and the larger the proportion of skylight it admits the more efficient it will be. This is why the tall windows in older houses admit so much light, even though those windows may be quite narrow. With modern houses whose ceilings are quite low, the skylight is cut off lower down. Even though the windows are often horizontally shaped in order to increase the light entering the room and placed high in the wall, the light fails to penetrate a room of any depth. The modelling from such a light is less rounded, more horizontal. The same applies to many houses built in the seventeenth century and earlier. The ideal window light – the strongest – for taking pictures anywhere in the room is found in houses built during the eighteenth and nineteenth centuries or a little later, with tall windows and high ceilings – all other things being equal. The strongest light comes from the upper part of such a window, and light striking the subject from a high angle gives good roundness with shadow underneath as well as to one side.

If the sky is partially blocked out by trees or buildings opposite, the light is reduced. The ground outside, unless covered with snow, reflects only a fraction of what comes from the sky. If the house is in open landscape or situated on a hill, ground floor windows can admit more light. But the upper windows of a house admit greater light than those on the ground floor, because they present a more open angle to the sky. In older houses, however, they are probably smaller than those on the ground floor.

The greatest concentration of light from a window is in a pool around it. The skylight enters at an angle which may cut off at, say, shoulder level only a few feet from the window whereas at floor level it may cut off more than half way across the room. There is therefore a larger area of direct skylight at floor level. This is a good situation for photographing young children or animals because they can sit on the floor and have a reasonably wide area to move within yet still be well lit and allow short exposures. At the other extreme, a person standing upright may have to be quite close to the window for the strongest light to be falling on his face. The actual positioning of the subject is important.

If there is snow on the ground or the house is flanked by a wide concrete strip, the character of the light entering the room is altered. Snow is such an efficient reflector that it may partially reverse the normal effect of window light, concentrating a very bright light on the ceiling and filling the room with diffuse illumination that seems to come from all around. The ceiling may well be a better reflector than the floor, so that the greatest amount of light comes from above, especially in ground floor rooms. In such circumstances, the far side of the room may be much better lit than usual. Subjects placed near the window might be strongly underlit, with a rounded, glowing light that is

quite pleasing – especially in the case of children. Light reflected from concrete has something of this character though in nothing like the same degree.
A whitewashed wall outside may refect direct sunlight horizontally into the room. This, too, might penetrate the room more effectively than light from the sky.

Position in the room

The colour of reflected light entering a window may be strongly enough affected by what is outside to influence the colour rendering you get on the film. It may easily account for any peculiar casts in your window light pictures that you find difficult to explain. If much of the light is reflected from a red brick wall opposite, that is enough to put a strong red cast on the subject. Grass can cause a greenish tinge if the sky is so obscured from the window that the main light comes from the ground. Light from a cloudless sky may be quite strongly tinged with blue. This blueness is retained even when the light is reflected from snow, concrete or a whitewashed wall, for example, and could account for a blue cast in the subject, particularly affecting pale colours or skin tones. Colour tinging may originate from surroundings inside the window, however. Strongly coloured curtains or the clothes the subject is wearing are common culprits.
In determining the kind of light that will reach a subject much depends on the characteristics of the individual room. With window light the strongest modelling is obtained nearest the window. Contrast is reduced the further into the room the subject moves – if the walls are pale in colour and reflect plenty of light.
In dark-walled rooms the high contrast effect is carried right across the room. At the greatest distance the window acts like a spotlight, approaching the standard half light, half shadow lighting. Full length portraits, therefore, should be taken close to the window otherwise the person may be lit less well around the head and shoulders than the rest of the body – with the strongest light concentrated on the feet! You can position someone sitting on the floor in the strongest light where, with a dark floor, the contrast is high, but that can be reduced by spreading out a newspaper (outside the picture area) to

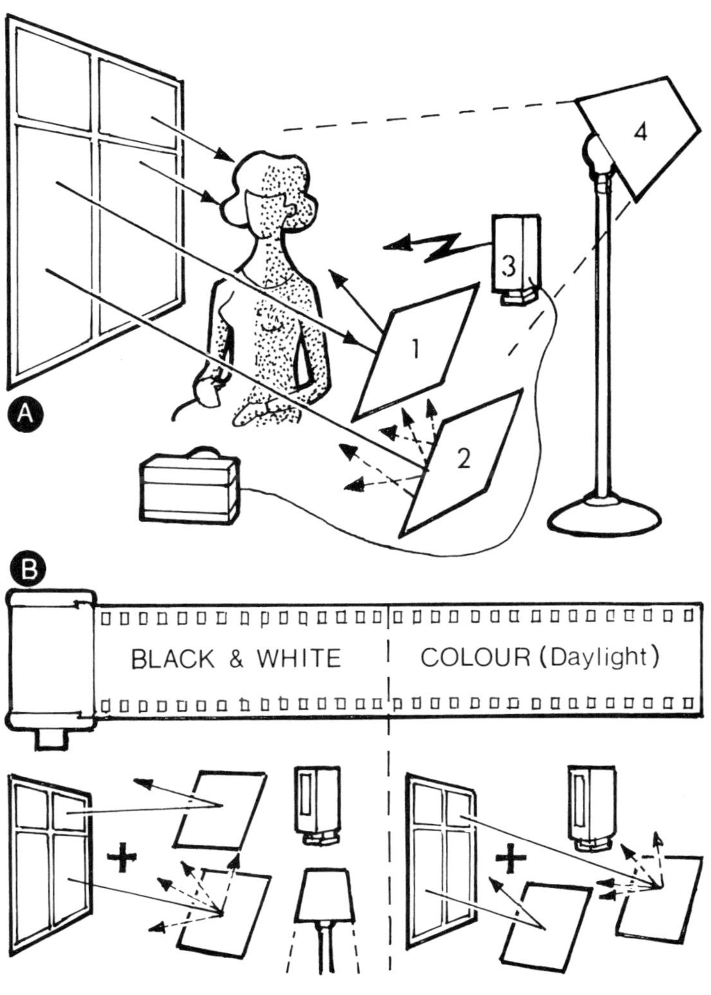

Filling shadows with window light. A. Reflect light with (1) a silvered reflector (2) white card reflector (3) lighten shadows with flash or (4) an existing lamp. B. Any of those methods can be used with black and white film but with daylight colour film lamps will cause a yellowish cast, so use reflectors or flash.

relieve the shadows by reflected light. In some rooms however, there is sufficient internal reflection from walls, etc to light a full length portrait reasonably evenly all over. All the foregoing remarks are, of course, very generalized. Shortly we shall discuss how to determine the light and place the subject in given instances.

Backgrounds

The varied lighting on walls, floor and other internal features makes it easy to choose from a wide variety of background tones for your pictures. This varies with the angle of the camera as well as its position in the room. Generally, if the camera points upwards the background will be shady. Lighter backgrounds come from choosing a higher camera angle. It is not difficult to find a pleasantly graduated background for any picture; the light fades towards the top on walls at right angles to the window. The corners of the room nearest the windows usually show a sharp fall off in brightness vertically. The subject can be positioned to allow the camera to use these background tones.

Contrast and shadows

Window light tends to be of high contrast and with direct sunlight the contrast is excessive. Typically, the subject is lit from one direction only. Shadows vary in size according to the angle of lighting in relation to camera viewpoint, but the shadows often cover quite a large portion of the subject and it is desirable to raise the light level in those areas to give some detail. This can be done in a number of ways. The subject may be repositioned near a wall from which reflected light is still insufficiently dispersed at close range to cast a significant amount into the shaded side of the subject. As the subject is moved away from the wall so the fill light is reduced. Here is scope for modification.

Another method, more convenient and versatile in practice, is to use an improvised reflector such as a white card, newspaper or white sheet. This is positioned on the shadow side of the subject reflecting light from the window into the shady areas. The efficacy of such a reflector varies greatly with small changes of distance. More highly reflecting metal foil or mirror surfaces are not really suitable in most cases as their harsh, directional reflected light is alien to the nature of a window light picture, unless the light they pick up is itself already sufficiently diffused. In any case the filling of shadows with reflected light should be very subtle, otherwise the character and charm of window light is destroyed. You should try to treat window light for what it is rather than use it as a substitute for studio lighting.

The shadows can be filled with light from lamps or flash, though care should be taken with colour in matching the light sources with each other and with the balance of the film, depending on which source, daylight or indoor light, is supposed to be the dominant.

Assuming that the subject is to be lit mainly by light through the window, the flash or lamp should be very subdued, used with multiple diffusers in front (folded handkerchiefs will serve) or bounced off a reflector of the kind just described. Alternatively, the flash can be bounced off the photographer's own body if the gun is held close enough and provided his clothes are of a neutral colour. This would, of course, only work if fill light was needed from the camera position. As a general rule, however, for the best and most realistic window light pictures it would be safer to steer clear of using flash. With black and white there is little harm in having the ordinary indoor light switched on to marginally reduce the depth of shadow. But with lamps you should always watch out for unwanted pin-point highlights. Shaded lights are best.

Sunlight through the window

Sunlight through a window falling directly onto the subject causes excessive contrast, owing to the absence of any sky surrounding that subject to "fill" the shadow areas with light. If the sun also falls on an efficient reflecting surface – light walls, a tablecloth or a reflector placed there for the purpose – the shadow side of the subject may become filled with light. It can even be lit more strongly on that side than would be the case in average outdoor conditions. In manipulating the reflector, blocking or partially masking it, positioning the subject or controlling the amount, quality or area of the sun which reaches the subject, there is an exceptionally wide choice of variations. The brighter the scene outside, the more effective are such controls because you can cut them down or redirect them yet still have enough light for exposure. For example, with the strongest light coming through the window you can narrow the curtains to a slit for angular lighting yet still have enough light to shoot by.

Unless you are actually seeking a high contrast effect it is better to keep the subject out of direct sunlight, and use it instead as a source to be reflected. If the curtains or a blind are drawn across the sunbeam, you may have a soft coloured glow or white light irradiating from the surface. Unless the blind or curtain is exceptionally thick the general light level is still likely to be high enough to permit quite short exposures. If a patterned screen, lattice blind or similar, is pulled across the window, the sun's rays are chopped up into strips or patches of light which may be made to fall across the subject. Depending on the opacity of the "clear" sections of the screen, the effect varies in contrast. If you had a wooden slat blind, for instance, with alternating solid and clear strips, the pattern would be of very high contrast for a film.

The contrast in the picture can be varied by the choice of various film/developer/exposure or printing combinations or by filling in the strips of shade and other shadows with a reflector or lamp.

Window light is naturally subject to the same effects of the time of day and season as daylight outdoors. Direct sunlight through a window is warmer in colour and lower angled towards morning and evening, reaching into a room more easily. Strong evening light effects are very beautiful where the window light is a rich golden orange, though this mood can be helped a little with a filter over the camera lens if the evening light or sunset is not as wished.

Two windows or more

Where you have more than one window you have more than one light source. This may simply serve to light a large room more effectively. But the fact that you have light coming from more places than one can be an asset in avoiding uniformity in pictures by window light and can offer scope for more lively lighting without causing problems of

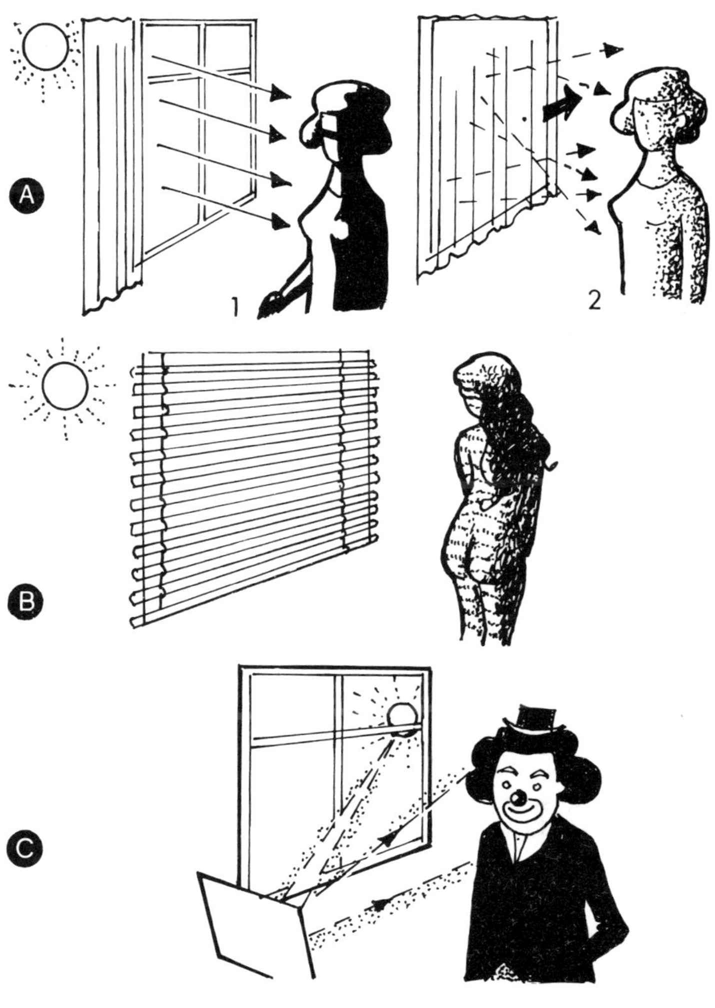

Direct sunlight through the window. A. gives (1) harsh lighting with deep shadows but (2) a curtain drawn across diffuses the light and softens the shadows and contrast. B. Blinds regulate the light and also give a shadow effect. C. A reflector in direct sunlight is very strong and allows you to alter the direction of the light at will.

matching colour balance or any of the other troubles associated with daylight work done in conjunction with an artificial light source, whether in a prime or supportive role. If the second window is in another wall at right angles to the first, the placing is useful for a number of effects in which one window assumes the role of key light and the other fills the shadows or provides effect or background illumination.

Portraits by window light

Window light is a traditional light source for portraiture of all kinds. The windows of an artist's studio are designed to admit far more sky light than those in the average home. Portraits painted in such places often either show strong modelling from the high side lighting that enters a studio, or a full, but not too directional illumination that results from a generally high level of ambient light bouncing off floor, walls, etc. It must be remembered that the north light (in the northern hemisphere) coming through an artist's studio window is consistent throughout the day and does not include direct sunshine. Such lighting nearly equalizes the brightness of subject and background and need not involve any attempt to separate them tonally. Anyway, adjustments in tone and colour can be made easily with a brush whereas with a camera you can only shoot what is there. For this reason it is dangerous to try and force too close a comparison between ideal working conditions for the artist and the photographer. Essentially, the artist seeks effects from which he can draw ideas or information – the lighting might be purely exploratory for him – whereas the photographer is aiming to build up the exact effect he wants to reproduce on film. The artist can take parts of his picture from different sources; the photographer must present it to the camera as a whole, finished and needing perhaps only minor corrective adjustment in the darkroom to compensate for deficiencies in the medium.

Light and subject position

If you place your subject close to a large window admitting a large percentage of skylight undoubtedly the greatest problem will be one

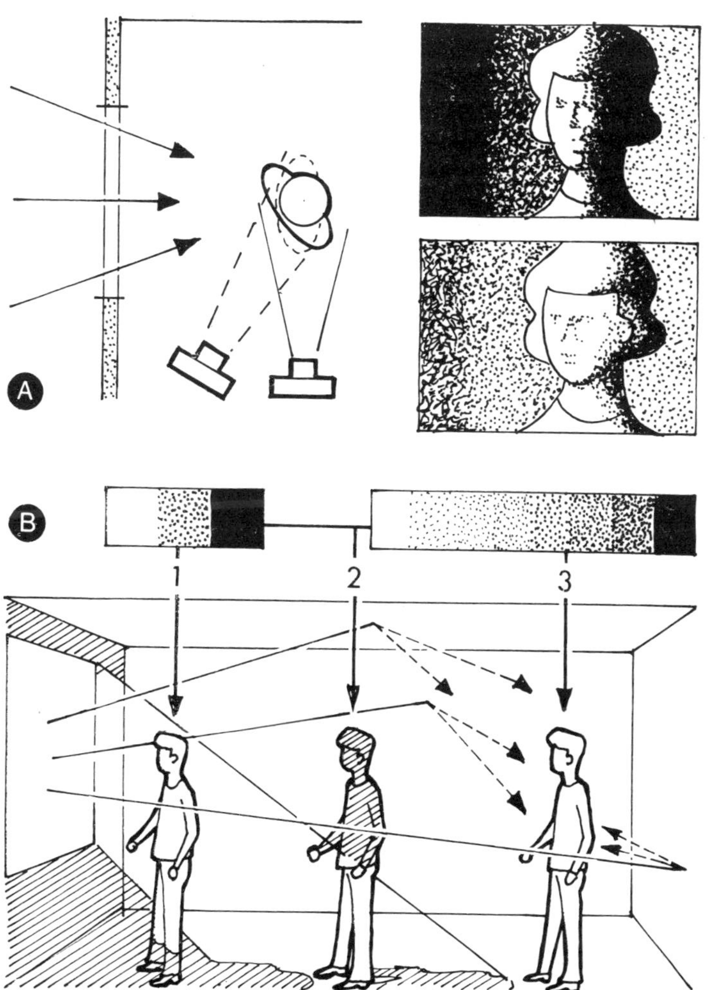

Variations in window light. You can alter the direction of window light by: A. turning the subject towards or away from the window or, B. by changing his position in the room. (1) Strong direct light on full length figure, shaded at feet (2) Strong direct light on lower part, diffused weaker light on upper part (3) Figure lit evenly all over with diffused light, even contrast generally, but depending on reflections from surroundings. Longer exposures needed.

of contrast. Remember that the photographic process tends to exaggerate the contrast you see. As we have noted, this is determined by the light. High contrast does not matter too much in clothes and surroundings but it can make a pleasant and realistic modelling of the face difficult to achieve. You lose too many of the features in darkness, the shape of the head is narrowed by the vertical edge of light and dark and, in extreme cases, the subject may be hardly recognizable. You can reduce this contrast by reflecting some light into the shadows from a large neutral coloured reflector placed on the shadow side facing the window. This is easiest with head and shoulder shots. If you are shooting in black and white you can sometimes reduce the shadow density marginally by turning on the room lights. In colour this would give a warm colour cast in these areas. You could fill the shadows with weak electronic flash though the results often look artificial unless done with great restraint. The best solution is probably to pose your subject in such a way that most of the face and body receives direct light from the window. Turn the subject more towards the window and move the camera round until you are shooting from just to one side of it. The shadow areas are now reduced to a very small proportion of the face: the lighting is flatter – the equivalent of a frontally placed key light in studio portraiture. To reduce the contrast further, with monochrome, you can use a soft gradation film, such as some of the fastest materials offer, a soft-working developer and print on a low grade of paper.

These are all variables not only in terms of contrast control but also in print quality. You should not force a reduction in contrast to the point where you lose quality in the final result. It is a matter of degree, and most people want to find general limits to work within and then make minor adjustments within those. For this reason, if you intend to photograph by window light regularly you have a great advantage if you always work in the same place. Known and familiar conditions allow you so much more control over results. If you also use the same film and processing combination you reduce the likelihood of failure even further. Take care with exposure. If you give too much you will flatten out the slight gradations of tone in the well-lit areas of the face. Too little loses all shadow detail and in the case of negatives gives insufficient density in highlights to provide enough contrast for a good quality print. To control the relative strength of the light as well as modelling and contrast, you can use the control methods previously described or move the subject around the room.

Distance from the window

The characteristic lighting from a window is basically on one side of the subject only.

If the subject is close to the window you get relatively less shadow and more "key" highlight as some of the light is coming from behind and in front as well as from the side. This gives the subject a light but well-rounded appearance but the light may cut off suddenly in the lower part of a full length figure. If the person is placed further away from the window, the "key light" gives a light nearer the half-and-half light-and-shade effect you get from small sources, because the window is now a relatively smaller area. The intensity of that light may diminish substantially, but light reflected from the ceiling, floor and surrounding walls becomes relatively more significant. This reduces the contrast in the picture generally. If these surroundings do not reflect very much then the light is, in effect, much harder and the shadows deeper. The interior of a room plays nearly as significant a role in determining your results as the kind of window light.

The light reflected from the walls and ceiling is diffused, that from the window is direct. When the subject is more than half way across the room the diffused light begins to predominate, because direct light is falling short of the subject. With a full length subject strong direct light may reach the feet and diffuse weaker light fall on the face. You may want the diffused light on the face but the lighting is unbalanced. This can be avoided by moving the subject further into the room, taking a seated pose, putting the model on the floor or moving him towards one of the side walls where the lighting may be more satisfactory. Movements of only a foot or two can often bring about a sharp change in the lighting. It helps to be familiar with individual characteristics of your particular room (and how the results appear in photographs) to make adjustments of this kind. The ideal is to experiment beforehand with pictures in various parts of the room to see what effect it has.

If the subject is out of the angle of direct daylight through the window you are working with diffused light. In upstairs rooms there may be better coverage of the room with direct skylight and therefore the lighting there is generally harder. In downstairs rooms, with light walls, placing the subject very close to the end wall can fill the shadow side so efficiently that it is of nearly equal density to an indirectly lit "key" side facing the window.

Position relative to window

The light from a window cuts off sharply at either side and light reflected from the interior of the room takes over. The lighting therefore changes very suddenly with minor adjustments in subject position relative to the window. If the subject is also turned towards or away from the light there is a remarkable degree of control available for lighting effects on the face. If you add to this the possibility of using reflectors, the range of lighting for drawing and modelling facial shapes is immense.

These controls may be used merely for their own effect with the unusual lighting drawing attention to itself. They can be made to flatter a face; to draw out the beauty that is already there, to suppress what is unattractive. They can describe efficiently the outward features, or catch a momentary expression more strongly than ordinary light would show. One stage further from this is to try to use such controls in revealing the outward evidence of character – a considerable challenge offered by portrait photography.

When the subject faces the window, viewed from the side, all prominent features in this profile view – forehead, nose, mouth and chin – are highlighted. The jaw and neck are in shadow and light draws the contours of the cheek strongly, as it falls off into shadow. If the subject turns away from the camera the side of the face becomes strongly highlighted but loses modelling. If the face is turned towards the camera position the cheeks and side of the head are more firmly modelled by oblique light cutting across the head from the extreme edges of the window, and the features are made more prominent by strengthened shadow. When the subject faces the camera you have standard half light/half shadow lighting (depending on distance) and the degree by which the light creeps round into the shadow side

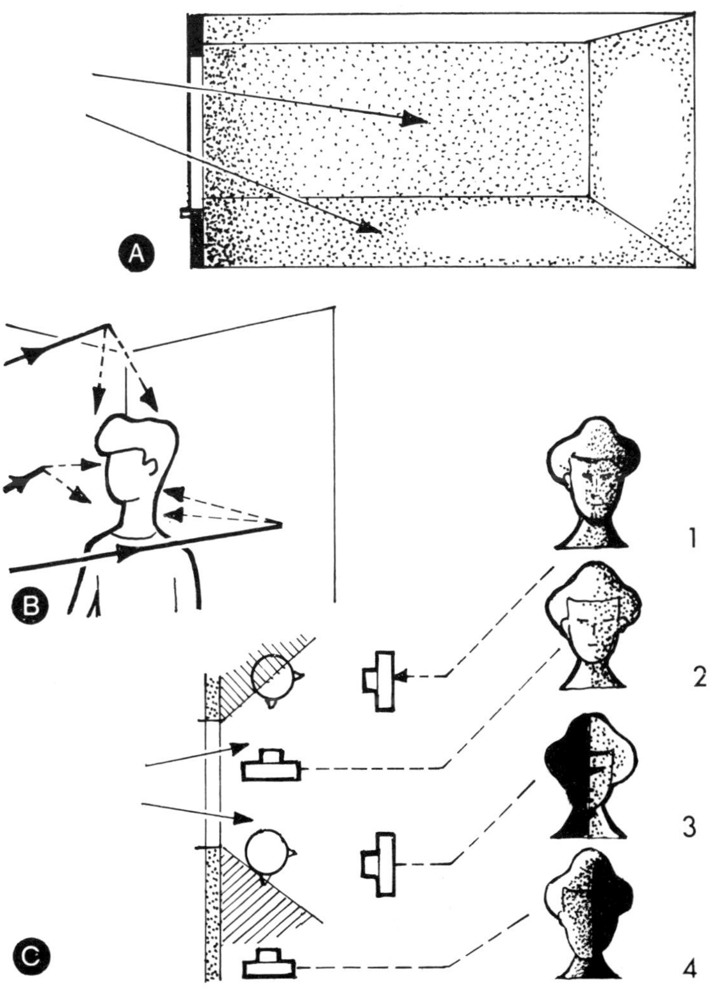

Window light for portraits. A. Light from the window falls most strongly in definite areas of the room, such as the floor and facing wall. B. Light reflected from back and side walls and the ceiling combine to form a varied source of diffused light. Light cuts off at window sides. C. Varied position relative to the window changes the lighting (1) beyond window, camera facing window (2) camera parallel: flat lighting (3) forward of window, camera facing (4) camera parallel, rim lighting only.

depends on the position of the subject relative to the window. In practice you have to move the subjct well forward of the window to get half and half lighting. Further forward still, the subject is rim lit from behind and to one side and most of the face is in shade (depending on the light level reflected from inside the room). This type of lighting is striking but hardly illustrative of the subject's features. It may catch an expression, the edge of a smile, but is not an effect for serious portraiture because the picture suffers from lack of evidence. Much the same applies to a centrally placed subject whose head is turned away from the light. The edge of the face is drawn by the light but the actual features are missing. This can be remedied with reflectors. Thus, you can combine a sharp backlit outline of the head with a softly diffused frontal lighting on the face itself. Or you can use a stronger, more directional reflector to harden this lighting. The hard-edged vertical shadow of half light/half shadow lighting tends to narrow the head. Frontal fill from a reflector makes the face look wider and fatter, as it would with fill-in flash or lamps.

Very attractive effect lighting results from near side light reflected back into the face from the opposite side, so that the strongest light *on the face* comes from the reflector, though the strongest light *in the picture* is a highlight in the hair. This is a perfectly natural looking form of lighting which, though quite exotic, could occur in the right circumstances without any artificial aids. The result is a drawing of the hair and head outline combined with a soft modelling of the face.

When the subject is placed at the far side of the window facing out, you have a flat lit profile with only the extreme back of the head in semi-shade. There is less modelling of the features generally but the head is still seen in the round. When the subject turns to face the camera you have standard three-quarter front lighting but without the fill for the shadows from the far side (which can, however, be supplied with a reflector). The edge of the lower cheek and the jawbone again become strongly modelled with oblique light because it is unlikely that light reflected within the room off walls, etc will have much effect in this position.

If the subject turns away from the window the side of the head is flatly lit and the face is so much in shadow that unless light is provided by reflection this position is well nigh useless.

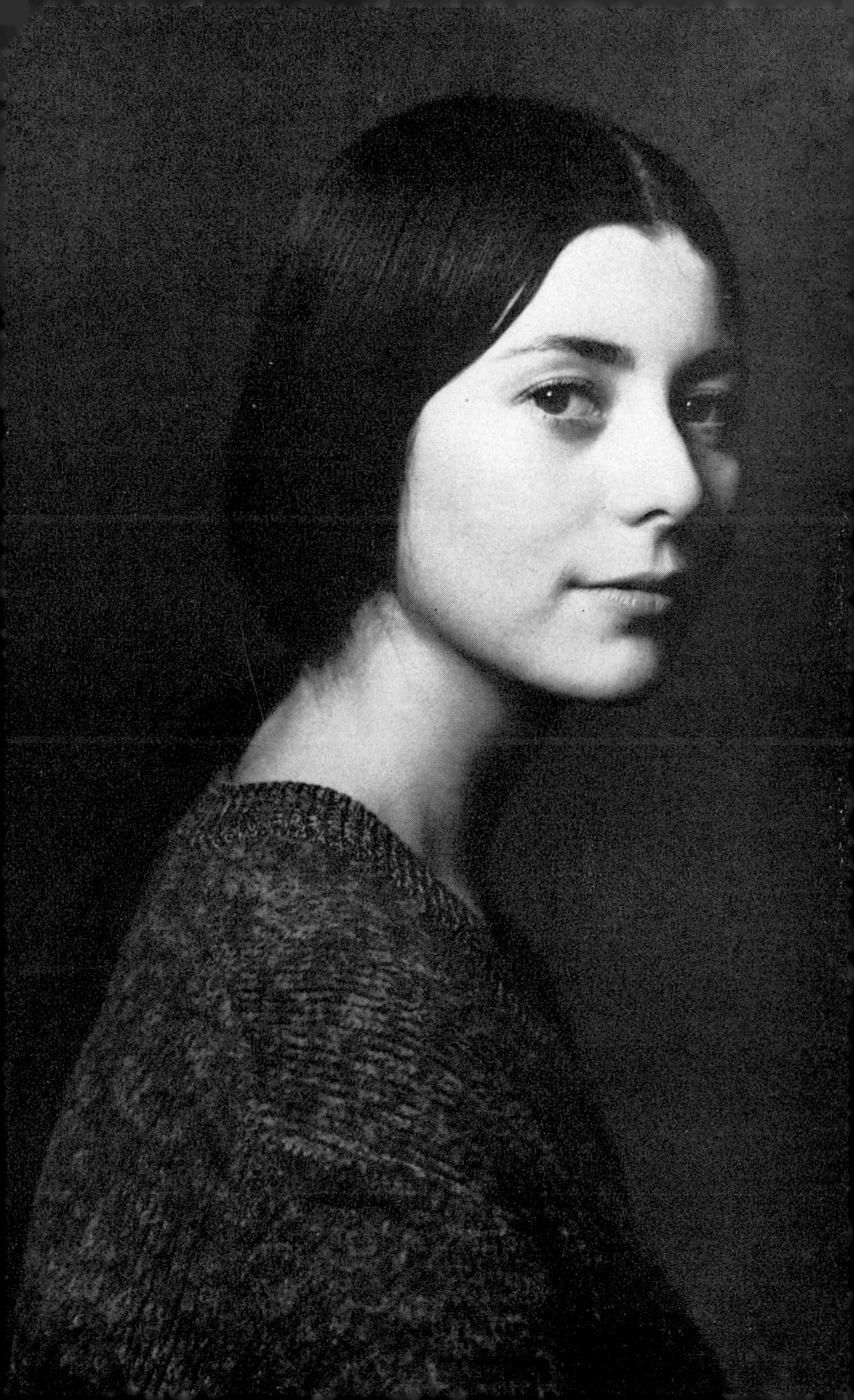

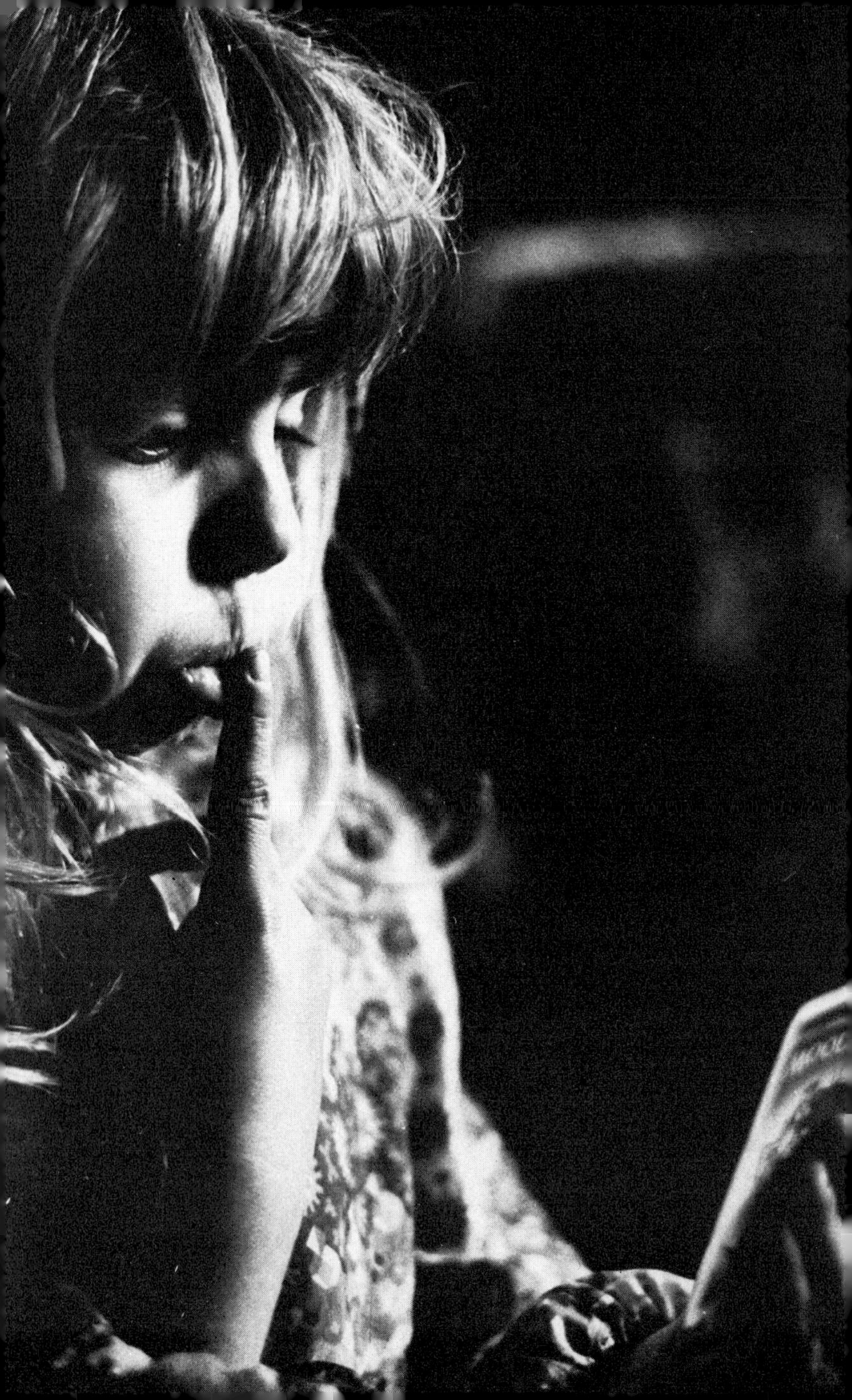

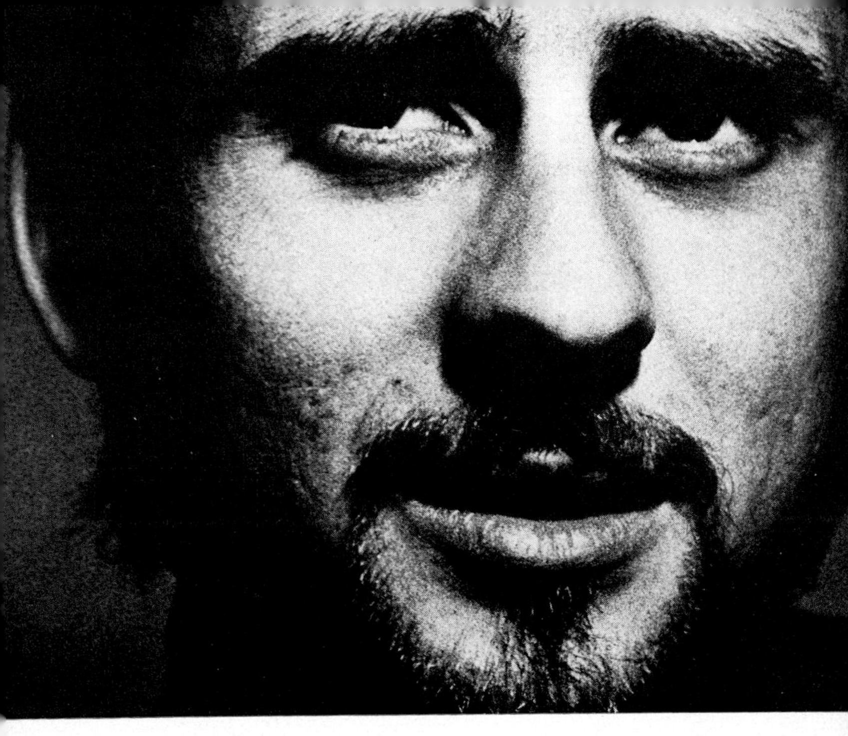

Strong overhead lighting is better for stark effects than for getting a good likeness. Oblique light draws out features which are normally suppressed or invisible. – *Harry Paland.*

Opposite: You can catch children at their natural best if you shoot by existing light. They soon lose their curiosity in the camera but a flash gun is hard to ignore – *Peter Stiles.*

Page 121: You do not need elaborate lighting for portraits. If you put your subject in the right place a single lamp can give well rounded modelling and a forceful contrast effect which is compelling to the eye – *Volkmar Herre.*

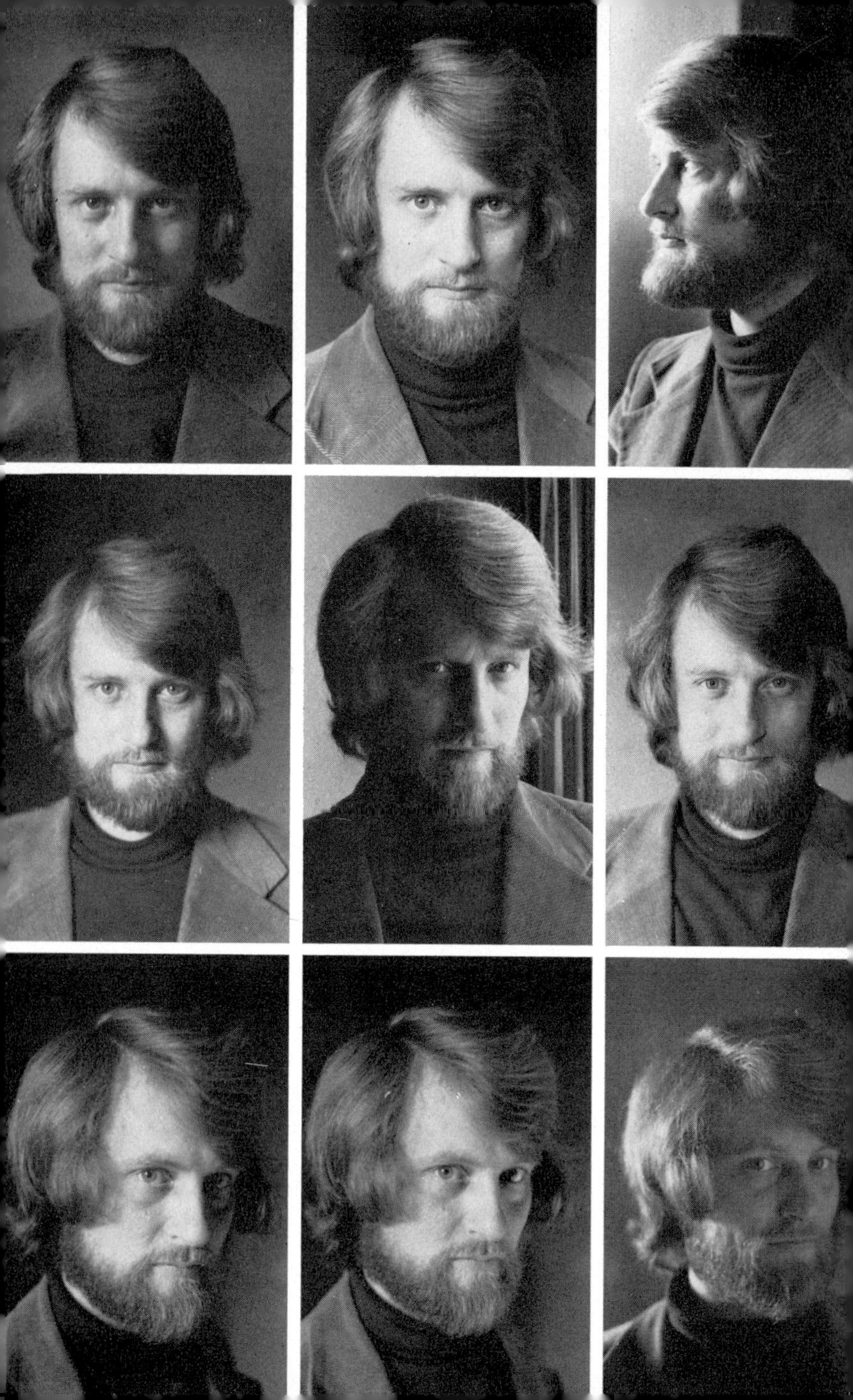

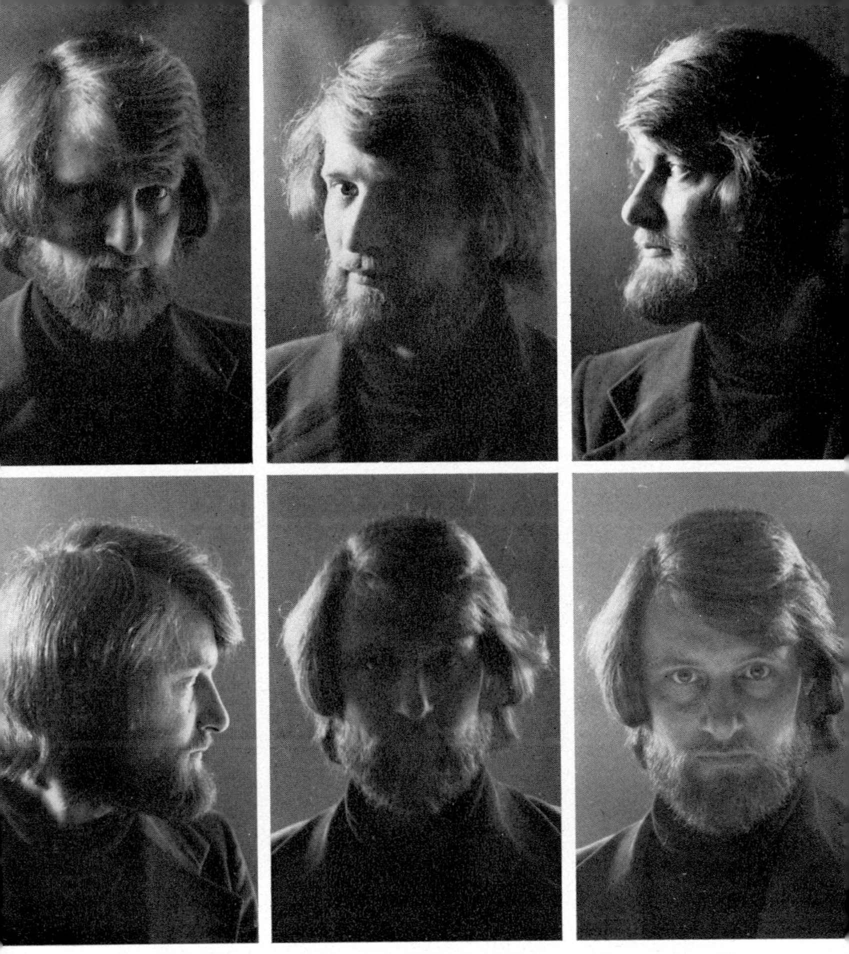

Window light. *Left:* One-window lighting ground floor. *Top row:* Side light, forward from, and alongside window, and profile. *Centre:* beyond window and contrasting background, first floor lighting in dark room, same in light room. *Bottom:* One window without, and with, newspaper reflector filling shadows, as rim light with face lit by reflector. *Right top:* Two-window lighting. Windows at right angles with one light weaker and diffused, same for three-quarter and profile views. *Bottom:* Double rim lighting for profile, same full face with, and without, reflector – *Paul Petzold.*

Pages 126 and 127: Shadows that you find on a stairway, or the slow shutter speed demanded at low light levels can produce many unexpected surprises – *Neville Newman and Dieter Korte.*

Page 128: The ballet dancer was almost motionless as the photographer caught him at the peak of his movement. The wrestler comes straight towards the camera. Neither needed a fast shutter speed – *I. Rosenberg.*

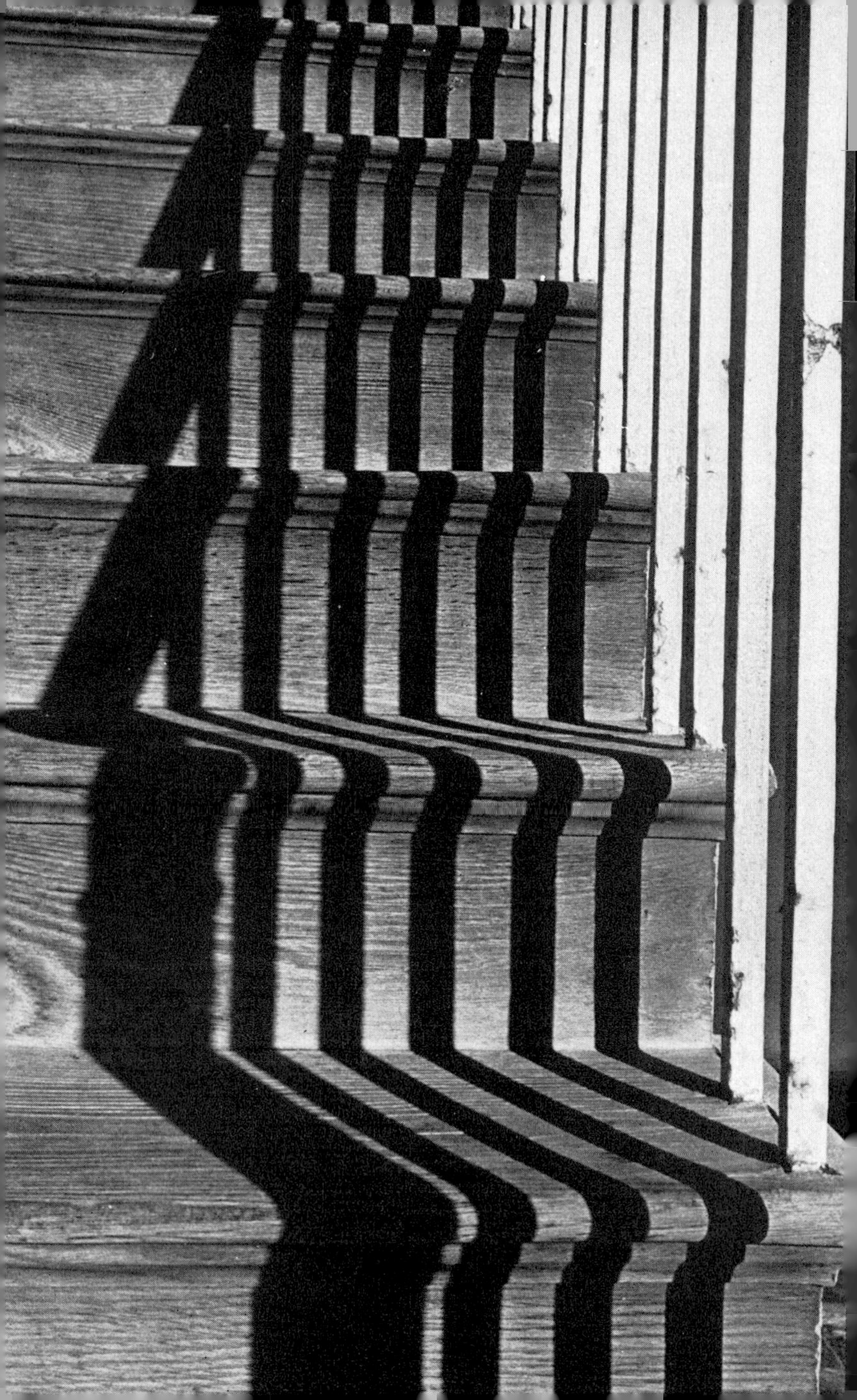

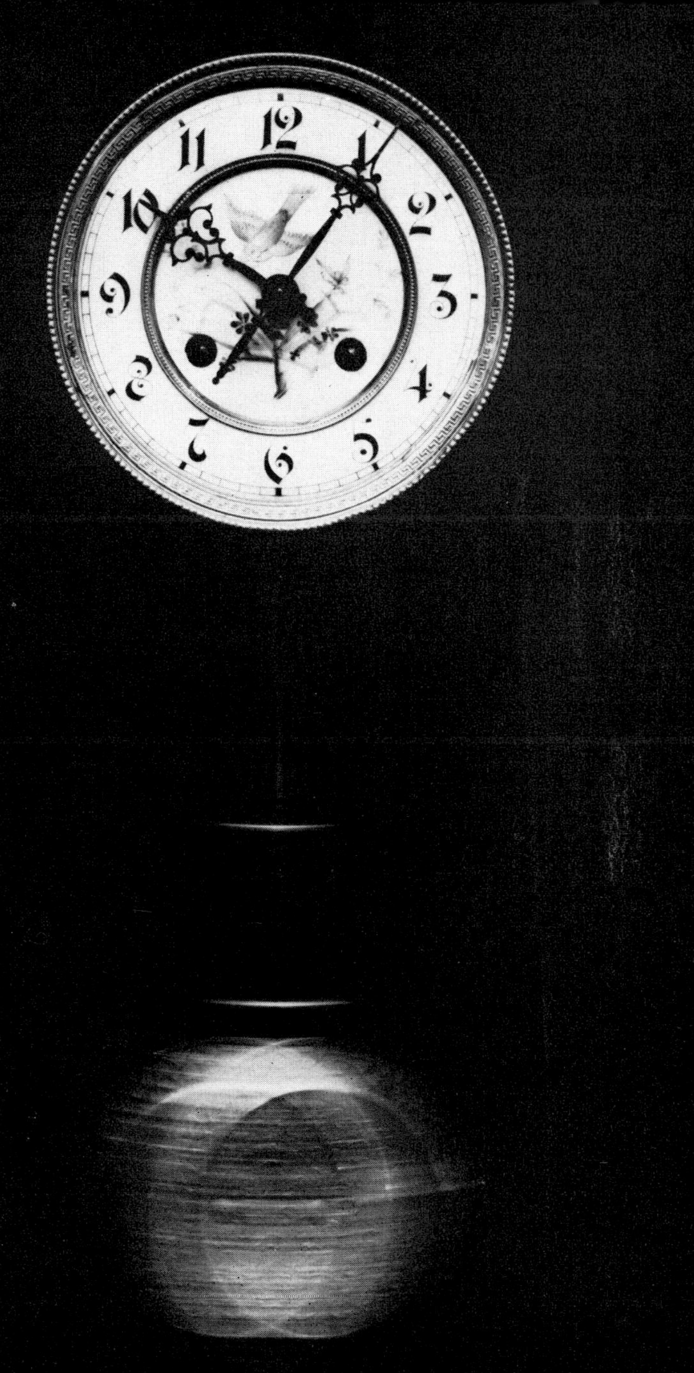

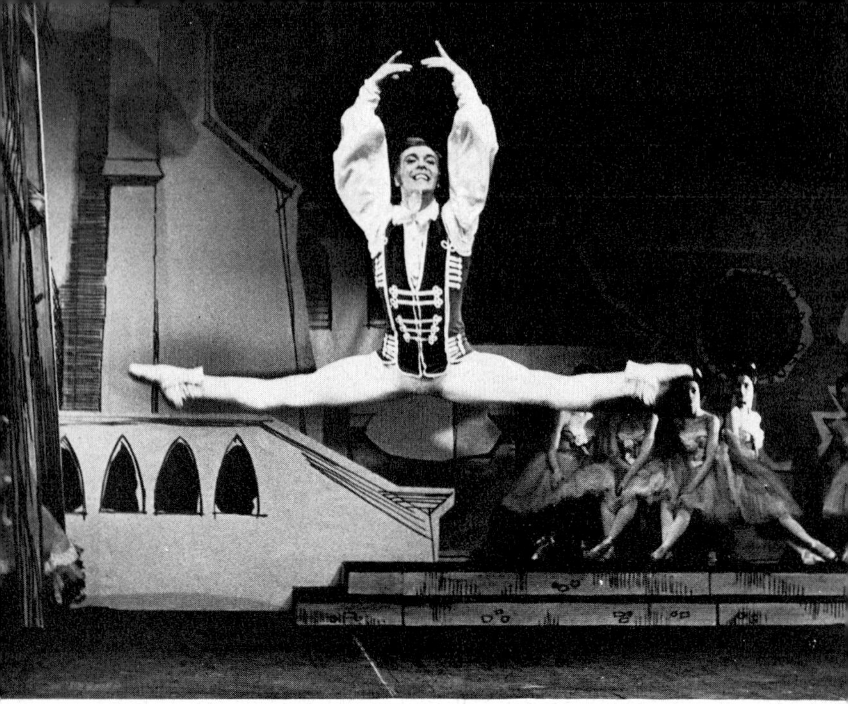

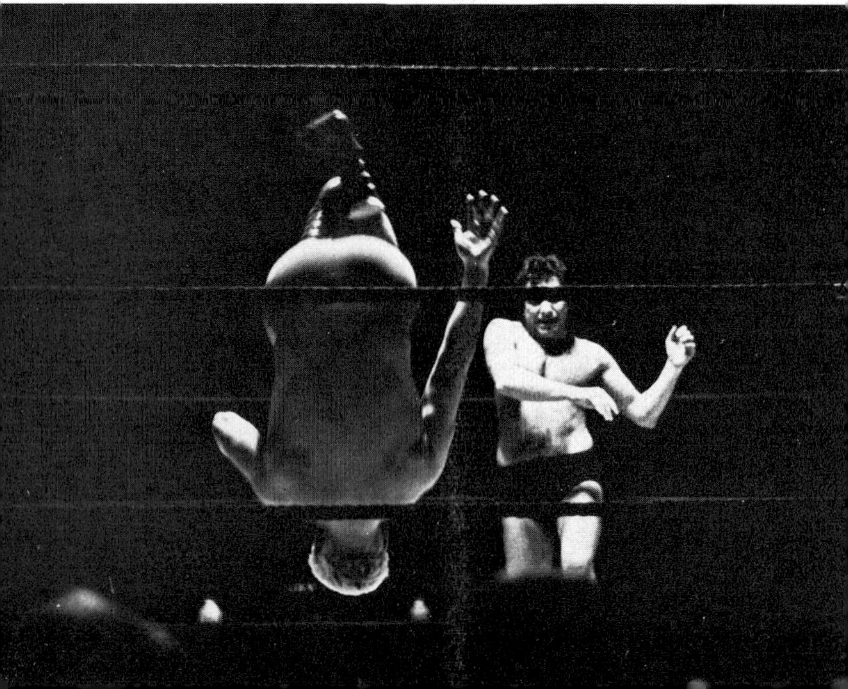

In conclusion then, subjects placed on the far side of the window tend to be more flatly lit and less strongly modelled but offer small areas of shadow. Centrally positioned subjects have the strongest modelling and increased shadow areas. Subjects placed forward of the window are top/backlit (or rim lit) putting great emphasis on the hair, which is strongly highlighted, and on the outline of the head, drawing its general shape in their outlines, but creating a huge area of shadow which can be filled with reflectors, or not, as desired. If you want an outline effect, for example for a profile, then this is the position. It would be most effectively seen against a dark ground, possibly the far wall of the room near the corner adjacent to the window where the light does not penetrate. This is also the ideal position for experiments with different reflectors, as here they have their greatest effect. Where you are photographing more than one person, you can use one of them as a reflector to throw light on to the shadow side of the other.

Two-window portrait lighting

Rooms that have windows in more than one wall can have a light source coming from more than one direction. This can be used for a variety of lighting effects in portraiture. It is especially applicable to head-and-shoulder or close-up portraits where the direction of light reaching the subject plays a more significant part in the picture as a whole. Generally, the best results are obtained where one window assumes the role of key light and the other, effect or fill. In most cases this means placing the subject closer to one than the other, so that one is stronger than the other. Cross lighting of equal power is nearly always an unattractive arrangement for portraits unless these sources are effect lights only and the main lighting or fill is provided by a reflector or lamp or by an increase in exposure.

With two windows in the same wall, the subject can be positioned at a mid-point between them facing into the room and with his back turned to the windows. An effect "rim" light surrounds the head and shoulders and the face is in complete shadow. So a reflector is arranged to fill this shadow and in that position has a very strong effect. Similar lighting can be arranged by placing the subject in the corner between windows on adjacent walls but in this case more of the face is lit (and less reflected light is needed to see the features) unless the subject is moved further into the room. You can, of course, regulate the relative strength of window light by controlling the amount coming through with curtains, blinds or physical obstructions placed between the window and the subject. But it is more satisfying in many ways to get the lighting you want by a shrewd placing of the subject – controlling the angle of lighting and its strength in one go, as it were.

Camera position

In a studio you normally light a subject relative to a particular camera viewpoint and the pose. So it is with window light. The only problem you have, especially with two windows, is to avoid getting the window itself in the picture unless you really want it. Light coming directly from the window and into the camera lens at the exposures you are likely to be giving for indoor portraiture can cause considerable flare and possibly "eat" into the profile or outline of the subject, spoiling the drawing.

The camera distance is your first consideration, for what kind of portrait is it going to be? Are the surroundings attractive enough to be worthy of inclusion in the picture or would you prefer to concentrate on the face. This is by far the best course to start with. Furnishings tend to clutter a picture or poke in awkwardly from a side or corner just when you have found the best camera angle for the subject. Sometimes they draw attention to themselves and thus away from the subject. The simpler the view the better, until you have more experience in handling large scale compositions. If you particularly want to take a picture that shows off a nice dress or suit (and with window light it helps if that is light in colour) then you have to choose a wider angle, Otherwise work from nearby. But don't go too close! If you get much nearer than four feet or so you introduce perspective distortion, causing the face to appear to bulge towards the camera.

The camera angle changes the appearance of the lighting falling on the subject, although the light itself is not moved. You cannot move

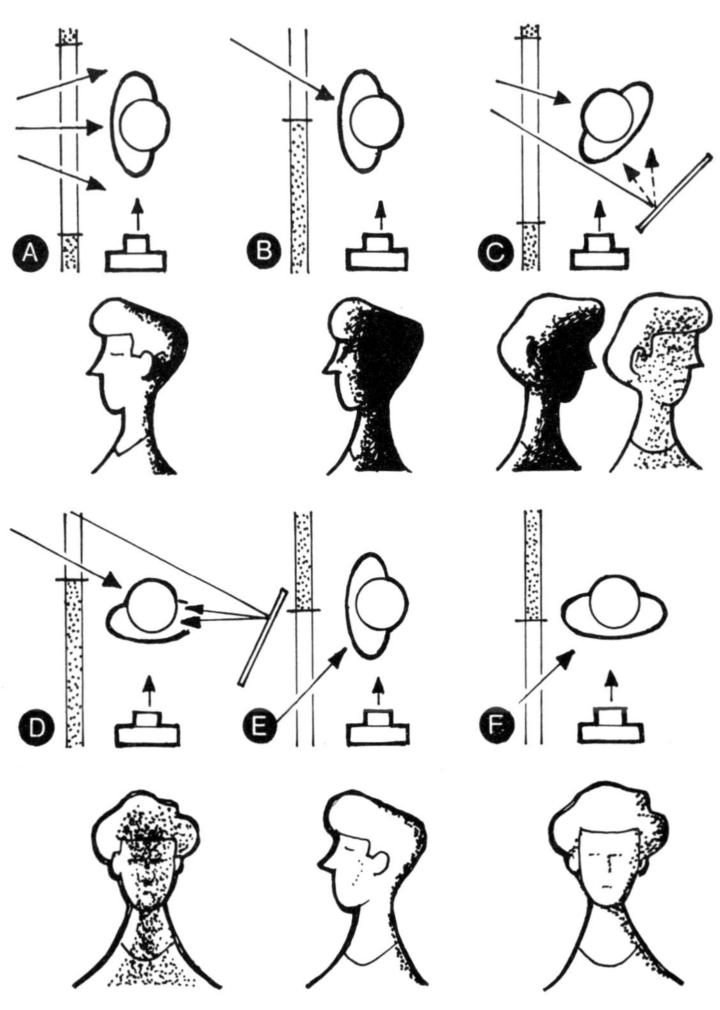

Modelling with window light. A. Profile facing window centre gives strong modelling. B. Profile forward of window rim lit. C. Profile away from window and without reflector. D. Full face well forward of window, with reflector gives rim light plus filtered shadow. E. Profile subject beyond window, almost flatly lit. F. The same in full face.

that light unless you move the subject. Hence it must be worked out in relation to a fixed camera position. If you move the camera, frontal light can turn into side light, rim light and so on. If the subject faces the window you have *side* lighting on the profile. If you move the camera round to the window position you have a full face shot with *frontal* lighting. The effect is entirely different in subject and light but all you have done is changed the camera position. A subject facing a wall at right angles to the window is side lit. If you move the camera round to a position facing the window without moving the subject, that subject is now seen in profile backlit. Increasing exposure may put more detail in the shadows; reducing it increases the silhouette effect and the likelihood of flare from window light.

Controls such as these, where possible, can contribute towards the composition of the picture whether the objective is the interpretation of character, a good representation of the person or just to gain a pleasing pictorial effect.

Choice of camera angle affects the background as well as the subject. Normally the idea is to find a background tone or colour that is distinctly separate from that of the subject. This is not difficult when shooting in colour because you are unlikely to come across a flesh-toned background although the ground may merge with the clothes in darker areas. With black and white photography you must take a little more care to avoid so close a matching of tonal values that you lose the shape of the subject's face because it merges with a ground of similar tone. This needs some careful scrutinizing because subject and background tones are difficult to judge if they are of different colours.

Ideally a background should not contain too many details; if it is a plain wall it is more pleasant to have some gradations in tone across it. This is not difficult in window light pictures – the effect occurs naturally in various parts of the room. Look for the penumbral areas between highlight and shade. The room often darkens towards the corners adjacent to the window.

It is easier to gain a dark ground if the subject is placed near the window, because he is then better lit than any part of the room. You can shoot across the window using the adjacent wall as a background for the greater contrast. Another way to secure a dark ground is to narrow the window light to a slit and place the subject in the resulting

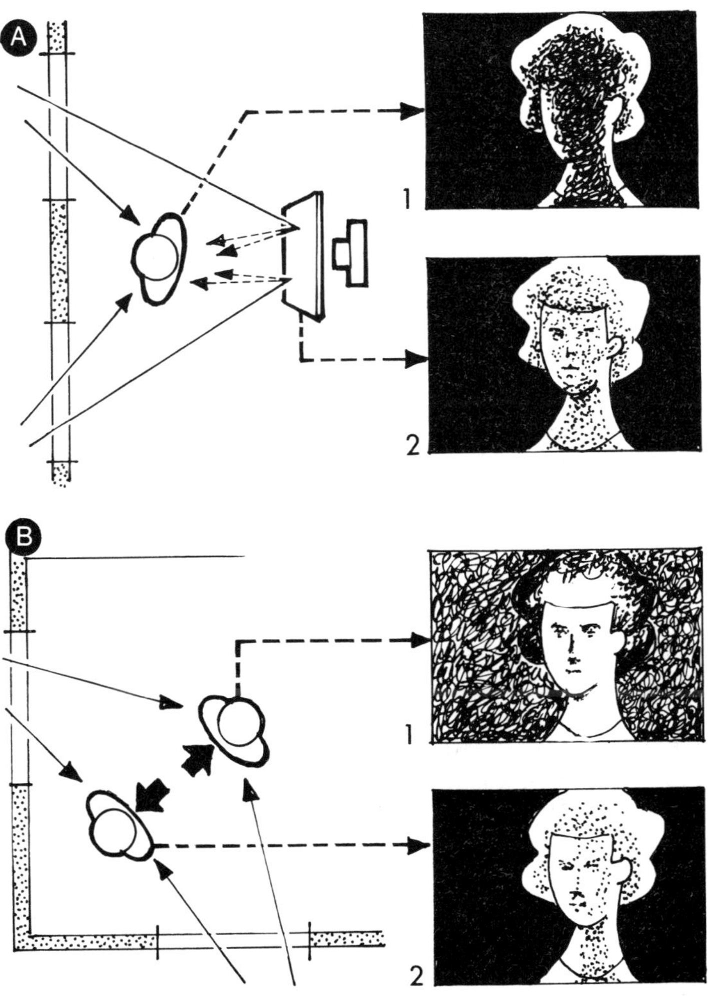

Light from two windows: A. A subject placed between two windows in one wall is (1) rim lit all round but the features are very shadowy. (2) A reflector on the other side of the subject reflects window light into the shadow areas. B. Subject between windows in adjacent walls is frontally lit as if by 'key' and 'fill' lights and (2) facing the other way is side lit from both directions.

shaft of light. The rest of the room receives very little light at all. For a light background choose the lightest walls, the bright area on the floor near the window, or the ceiling, which is usually white. The far wall and "hot spots" on the side walls, in fact any area receiving direct daylight, can provide a light background if it is basically light in tone. There may only be enough light background for close ups, but some graduation to dark towards the edges of the picture should not be unwelcome. Provided you set the right exposure for the actual subject you might even be able to use the window or sky area seen through it as a white background but this technique is fraught with the risks previously mentioned, flare, eating into the outline, etc.
The height of the camera, too, changes the effect of the lighting, the shape of the subject and the background that may be included in the picture. The majority or ordinary portraits are taken from near, or a little below, eye level if they are close up and nearer chest level if they are full length. Even slight variations away from these norms have a considerable effect on the look of the subject and the way it is lit. Extreme camera angles however, do not deceive the eye. One accepts the viewpoint as being extreme and the lighting is assumed to be correct and, in fact, the subject appears more normal this way. If the camera and subject are angled off the norm *together* and there is nothing in the picture to indicate that it is so, then you have a distinct change in the lighting angle in its own right. This would apply, for example, where the subject was looking up and the camera, level with the eyes, was looking down. The lighting would then in effect be underneath the face. In this way you can actually adjust the angle of your window light without cutting it down to a narrow slit.

Groups

Group shots are normally taken from a distance. In many cases, therefore, you have to accept one of the disadvantages of window light – its unevenness. Try and choose a position in the room where the strength of light falling on each person is as near equal as possible otherwise you will have some people very well lit and others in shade. The most even lighting for a group may be half way across the room with the subjects facing the window. Place the camera between the

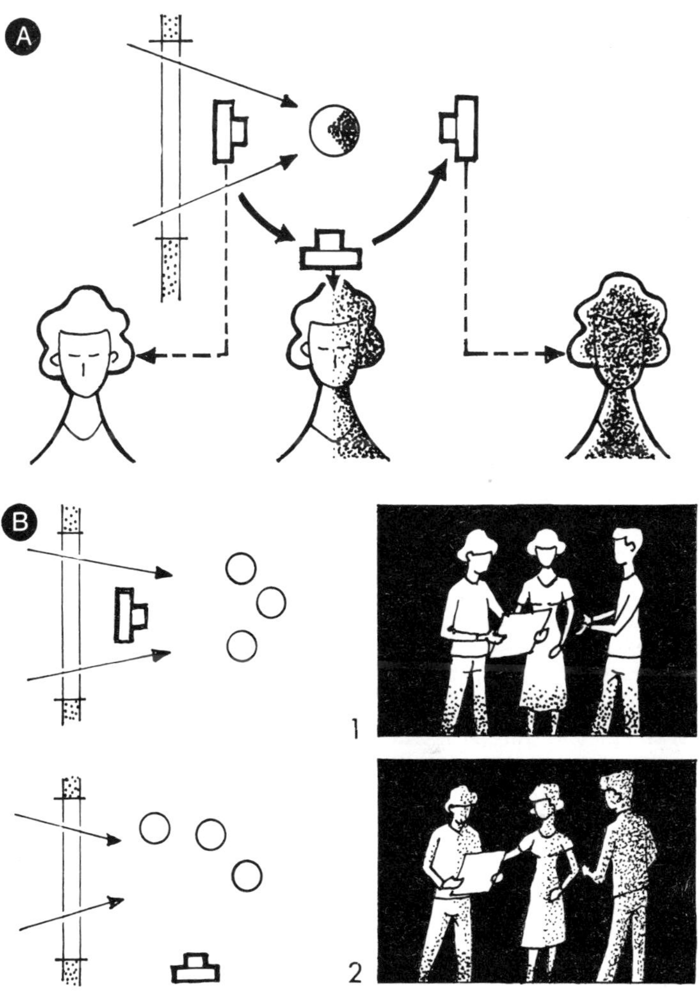

Camera position for window lighting. A. The lighting, in effect, changes according to the camera angle. B. (1) Groups positioned with each person at roughly the same distance from the window, are equally lit. (2) At different distances the lighting is uneven. Some people are more brightly lit than others and in different parts of the body, making a transparency difficult to view and a negative difficult to print satisfactorily.

window and the subjects. The lighting is flat but reasonably even, although at this point you may have the problem that the strongest light is falling on their feet. You could reduce that slightly by obstructing some of the direct sky light with your own body. Lining up the group with the window to one side is a recipe for unevenness. Although the lighting on each individual is more attractive from this point of view, there is no practical method of compensating for the heavy shadows. But, as in so many cases, much depends on the individual window and room and the arrangement of the subjects.
Another method to adopt is to work only in diffused lighting – the light reflected from the walls or ceiling. (This is quite standard practice with lamps, whose light can be bounced off these surfaces.) You do this by keeping the subjects out of reach of any direct light from the window and rely entirely on internal reflections in the room. This inevitably results in longer exposures than normal.

Children

The best place for photographing babies and very young children is in the pool of light falling on the floor below the window or in the centre of the room. The light can be diffused with a curtain or blind to give the soft effect that is so pleasing with child subjects. This is essential if direct sunlight is falling on the floor area. Reflectors can help reduce the darkness of the shadows but using a fill-in flash on the camera is more difficult because the unpredictable subject movement means that the flash to subject distance constantly changes. There is therefore a risk of overfilling the shadows. With automatic flash guns you can set two stops less than the stop recommended with the particular gun. You may have a problem with focal plane shutter cameras in that you are also hemmed in by the shutter speed you can set with electronic flash, though in window light you are unlikely to need more than 1/30 sec which is the fastest speed with X-synchronization on some cameras (see page 218). With leaf shutter cameras you can set two stops less (smaller) than that recommended for the gun and then adjust the shutter speed to a correct exposure for the key light – the daylight coming through the window.

Effects

The main effects possible with window light have already been touched on. Mostly they concern the great contrast in light levels between the light in the room and that outside, and how you expose the film. For silhouette effects you place the subject between the camera and the window, so that the scene outside forms the background. Base your exposure on a reading from the scene outside but open up by two stops to ensure over exposure of the background if you want a total silhouette. The background should not contain any large dark areas and should be thrown well out of focus. That can be ensured by selecting a large aperture to give a limited depth of field. But if that should reveal too much detail in the subject, it can be compensated by a higher shutter speed.

Flare is achieved by overexposing for the light coming through the window and is most effective if the subject is placed very close to the window, with the window forming a substantial part of the picture. This results in a soft light or haze spreading across the subject, in effect, fogging it, and reducing the contrast in the shadow areas, the more so if the lighting is dull rather than bright. This is most effective in black and white. Results in colour are less predictable as the light can take on the hue of features outside the window which may not be very pleasing. But it is worth an experiment, all the same. Another effect, window light "eating" into the subject outline comes through gross overexposure. You have to position the subject against a sky background, or in the direct sun.

Diffusion or reflection effects are possible with curtains, reflectors and mirrors, while patterned glass or acrylic sheeting with a moulded pattern can be manipulated to give effects of one kind or another (see page 96). And you can induce colour casts with coloured reflectors: even commonplace furnishings and fabrics will do this.

A lesson from others

The main appeal of window lighting is in straight portraiture. Some photographers use virtually nothing else. You will notice, if you look at the work of the best portraitists, how light has been used, often quite informally, to interpret character. One is loath, in order to prove the point, to send people scuttling back to the pioneers of photography as if no progress had been made since then. But they did work by window light and their pictures are readily accessible in books and museums. Mrs Cameron's pictures repeatedly affirm that she understood the uses of light very completely and it is remarkable how wide a variety of effects she called upon in her portraits and to what advantage they are applied to individual sitters. Remember, this was done in daylight, using only curtains or placing of the subject to control the directional effect.

Looking at work such as that is probably a much better starting point than attempting to imitate the highly wrought lighting of the "classical" artificial light studio portraits produced in the last few decades. The essence of window light is simplicity. The temptation with studio lighting is to banish shadow from the subject and fill every surface with highlights. This bad habit which so many have fallen into has long established itself as a cult.

Home Lighting

Photography by ordinary home lighting first became practicable many decades ago. It was made possible largely by the increased sensitivity of films. Coupled with the widest aperture lens then available, indoor candid photography with a hand held camera was just within reach, though the results were rather unpredictable. The best pictures were mostly obtained only where conditions were very favourable. Since the first quarter of this century not only have film speeds drastically increased, but wide aperture lenses are now commonplace. Moreover, we tend to use brighter domestic lighting in the average home than we did even twenty years ago. People are not only using lamps of greater wattage but more of them. There is also a greater variety of light fittings in use than before, giving lighting of quite widely varying character. It is by no means uncommon nowadays to find spotlights in a living room. Pencil beam lamps, multi-angle reading lamps, table lamps, standards, wall lights and a wide variety of single and multiple head central fittings are to be seen in homes these days. There is also strip lighting, which comes in several forms, colours and levels of power output, and special lamps of various kinds installed for decorative purposes rather than for any functional value.

What then, with all such light sources in mind, can home lighting do for you? In the first place it is bright enough for photographing almost any subject in colour or black and white with most cameras. It is also a more controllable light source than window light though it is rather more difficult to get pleasing results with lights. You are not confined to a single source and filling the shadows with reflected light or a lamp, though you can use a reflector if you wish. You may control the power of lamps by interchanging bulbs and often you can adjust the lighting to suit the subject by moving a lamp. With fixed lighting you can still move the subject as you did with window light. With indoor lighting you tend to be working under illumination which is all of a kind as far as colour content is concerned because most rooms are lit by the same type of light source. There need therefore be no problems of mixed light sources as there are when combining daylight and tungsten.

There are, however, a few disadvantages in working with home lighting. They are not too difficult to overcome and require only the right technique, as with other existing light sources.

The light source is not very bright compared with daylight coming through a window for example. So you must either use the fastest films or put up with the need to make slow-shutter-speed or time exposures. That means supporting the camera rigidly rather than just holding it in the hand. Inevitably you work most of the time with wide apertures. This means you nearly always have very limited depth of field available. So you have to take extra care with focusing, and in these conditions it really is critical. You may even find that the particular focusing system available on your camera is impossible to use reliably in such low-light conditions.

Colour films are not really correctly balanced for use with the kind of lamps that light the home. The tungsten illumination referred to in the accompanying leaflet or literature is either photofloods or studio lamps which, although working on the same principle as home lighting are much brighter and therefore whiter than home lighting on the same voltage. Pictures taken with home lighting therefore tend to to have a warmer image colour. Whites are yellower, reds more orange, blues less intense and flesh tones more tanned than they seem to the eye. Another problem with home lighting is the likelihood of getting excessive contrast in the picture. This, though basically more serious and less easily corrected than the other factors, is also far more subject to variation in different shooting conditions. All other things being equal, the contrast is greatest in rooms with dark walls and furnishings, and least in cases where the walls and furnishings are light. If the room is small, you are less likely to get contrast problems than if it is large. Also much depends on the tone range of your subject.

For shooting stationary objects in black and white there is absolutely no disadvantage to using home lighting. There is a slight drop in effective film sensitivity as with all general purpose materials exposed under artifical light but this is not a material problem in still life or close up work for instance, where the exposure time given can be of any length. A film rated at 64 ASA in daylight would be rated at about 40 ASA in tungsten, a 160 ASA film at 100. You need only adjust the film speed setting on the meter or give some equivalent compensation by adjustment of aperture (less than one stop extra is necessary) to give the film the same effective exposure.

With stationary subjects you normally aim for maximum sharpness because there is nothing to gain from unsharpness in most instances nor any logical reason why the image should not be completely sharp. Unsharpness tends to be far more noticeable on inanimate subjects than living ones, and one is naturally more critical of the technical quality generally. This also goes for the quality of colour rendering and lighting (shadow, modelling, highlights) and absence of unwanted reflections. (It is surprising what a wide range of tolerance applies to the rendering of skin tones, whereas a green jersey may immediately be pointed out as looking blue.). Most of these factors are normally quite easy to adjust within the scope offered by home lighting.

There is a great advantage in having scope for time exposures. You are not confined to positioning a subject in exactly the right place for the lighting as you so often are with portraiture. It is easier in many cases to move a light. With small objects you can easily use a reflector to fill shadows or concentrate light on the subject, and you can add a background of your own choice. Even a small table lamp is an adequate "key" for lighting small objects and if the exposure is still a long one it does not matter. In practice, a small lamp can be brought very close to the subject. If you want maximum depth of field you can stop down to the smallest aperture, set the camera on a solid support and give a time exposure using a cable release for preference or the delayed action (self timer) device where possible.

Time exposures also allow you to use the moving light technique. For this you need only one lamp – a small table lamp with the shade removed will do. Put the camera on a tripod and line up on the subject. Hold the table lamp and switch it on. Open the shutter and move the lamp in a complete or nearly complete circle round the camera lens and back again. Keep the light moving throughout the exposure. The result is a reasonably modelled but shadowless picture of your subject with at least some light reaching into even the most awkward crevices. You can give some slight overall direction to the light by moving the lamp rather more on one side of the lens (and subject) than the other. The moving light technique is used where it suits the subject and the result you are after and where normal lighting techniques fail.

Although home lighting can be used for colour pictures, as stated, with carefully focused static subjects one tends to be more critical of colour quality than in informal snapshots where the animation of a scene is a distraction from the questionable flesh tone rendering. On balance, you

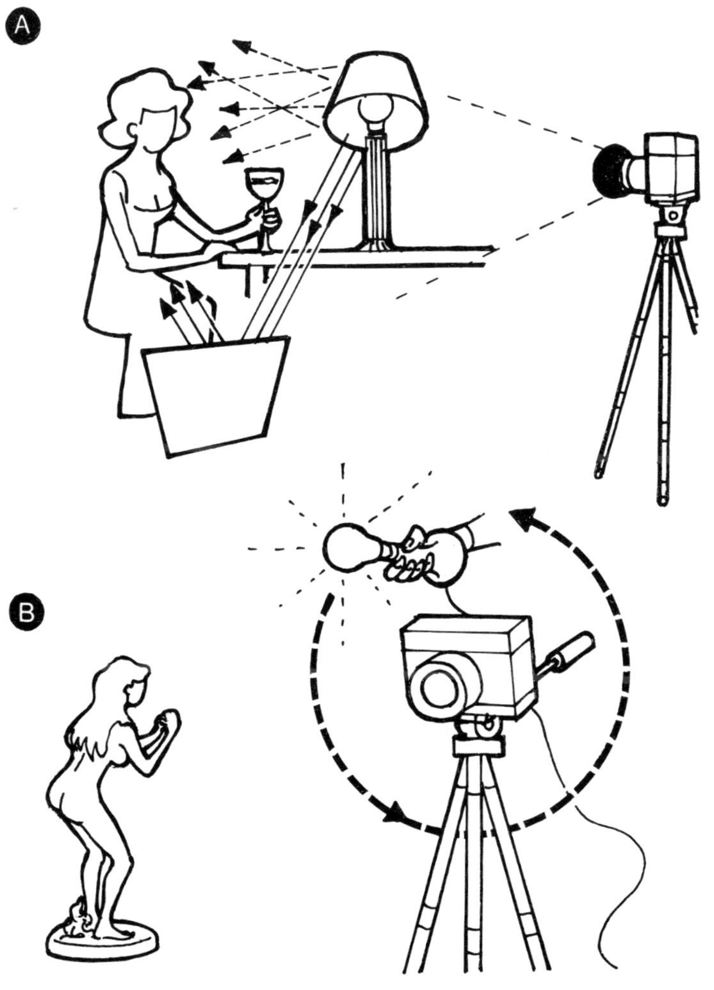

Manipulated light. A. Table lamps give two types of light direct, underneath, and diffused, through the shade. You can combine their effect on the subject by the use of a reflector. B. Moving light technique is suitable for time exposures with non-living subjects where shadowless lighting is needed.

can use home lighting for most things, but you do, of course, have the usual problems of colour casts, a drop in effective film speed and relatively high contrast.

Character of lighting from individual fittings

Light fittings are available in such a wide range of types that it would not be possible to evaluate their character and photographic value reliably by any kind of chart or listing. The following paragraphs serve only to indicate the scope and shortcomings to be expected with typical fittings. It must be remembered that the type of bulb, lampshade, wall colour, size of room and colour of furnishings all play a part in determining the ultimate appropriateness of lighting for the job. We are concerned here with aiming for best results. Most domestic lighting gives *enough* light for pictures, but the quality of those pictures, especially portraits, is not generally very pleasing unless you take care to avoid the worst pitfalls.

Central light If this is a single lamp with a shade, the "hottest" spot is immediately beneath it, which gives top lighting to subjects, and ghoulish effects to faces. The subject's face should be upturned towards the light if this is the effect you are after, otherwise he should be placed back from the lamp, perhaps with fill light picked up and directed forward in to the face from a reflector placed immediately beneath the light. In all pictures so close to the light source the background appears relatively dark (provided exposure is correct for the main subject). The central fitting with a normal shade directs a wide cone of light downwards; this cuts off at a position some way up the walls except in a large room with a low ceiling. The corners of a room are never well lit by a central fitting. An insignificant amount of light passes upwards through the shade and is reflected off the ceiling. The cut-off point of the shade on the walls makes an ugly and very noticeable join of two tones in the background of a picture and should be avoided at all costs. Clear filament lamps even project images of tassels and lamp shade seams which is worse. Remember that because of exaggerated contrast all these hallmarks of home lighting become more apparent in a photograph.

The best place for photographing with this type of shade is outside the area of direct light. Though this may call for a stop or so more exposure, the light is far less harsh and the shadows less deep. When working within the area of direct light soften it by using a diffused bulb rather than the clear type which is unsuitable for portraiture. Fill the shadow areas by matt reflectors.

If the central light is totally diffused as with a large opal globe, a Japanese lantern or similar shade, you have a source that is more flexible for photography and kinder for portraits. Light is more evenly distributed about the room and the subjects only darken with distance. This is a very adequate portrait light, though you may still find it a bit hard in dark rooms.

The shade can be removed from a lamp so that you can work with the bare bulb. This gives hard lighting which may suit your purpose, but is, again, rather cruel for portraits except in very light coloured surroundings. Reflectors such as a newspaper or large white card would bring an immediate improvement by filling shadows. The light bulb behaves more like the theoretical point light source of the inverse square law (page 33) and you have to remember to give four times the exposure (two stops) for double the subject distance from the lamp. It is safest to work with a meter the whole time.

Multi lamp central fittings are usually more suitable for portraiture if they are shaded because a number of lamps of low power give softer illumination than a single lamp equal in power to the sum of the parts. Yet because there *are* many lamps the fitting is likely to have quite a high total light output (unless that has been lost by heavy shading). An eight branch fitting with 25 watt lamps gives quite a generous output at 200 watts, for example. The problem of shade cut-off is reduced or eliminated.

Some central units are entirely indirect, almost the whole light output being reflected upwards to the ceiling and so around the room. This is very soft lighting indeed but is lacking in brightness and a feeling of direction. It does not allow the use of reflectors. Again it would be suitable for any case where you want soft light but it might not permit short enough exposures for portraits, unless you want to chance a time exposure, which indeed you can, given a co-operative subject. With this lighting arrangement the upper parts of the walls are brightest but the shading is gradual so there is no problem with the backgrounds. Areas near the floor under furniture tend to be very shadowy, and it would be advisable to allow considerably more exposure than that recommended by an exposure meter if your are seeking detail in the shadows. Otherwise, direct meter readings should be fairly reliable.

Central striplighting These tubes are either circular, or, more usually, straight in form. The illumination is unromantic but not hard, photographically. With long tubes the light is spread over a wide area and is therefore neither very directional nor prone to giving deep shadows. One tends to associate daylight tubes with even, cold illumination but this is probably because, commercially, they are used in massed rows forming a "sheet" of light overhead and are generally selected in a colour closely matched to daylight. The light from such an arrangement is flat and characterless and unsuitable for portraits as you soon see if you take a few pictures in a supermarket. Tubes are available in various colours ranging from warm pinkish tone to bluish daylight white. Domestic tubes tend to be of the warmer type which seem less hard on the eyes. But the actual quality of the light at home has as much to do with the colour of the surroundings, as the light source. Because of the colour content of these tubes, any reflections and colour casts are more likely to come from cold-coloured furnishings – blue curtains, walls, etc than from warmer coloured surfaces. At home, people tend to have only one or two strip lights in a room, and the light is rather more directional than in public buildings and shops

Wall lights These are usually tungsten lamps in dark or even opaque shades of one kind or another designed to avoid direct lighting. Most of this light may come via a neutral or coloured shade or, if opaque, the lamp is supposed to light the room by bouncing light off the wall.

In each case the colour of the shade or wall affects the colour of light reaching the subject. Tungsten lamps are less subject to influence at the colder end of the spectrum than at the warm end, because the light they emit already contains a predominance of the hotter wavelengths. Blue shades or blue wallpaper, therefore, have far less influence than red equivalents in either case. Filtering the light with blue in this way results in a very significant drop in overall light level because the blue transmitting or reflecting surface absorbs so much of the warmer wavelengths.

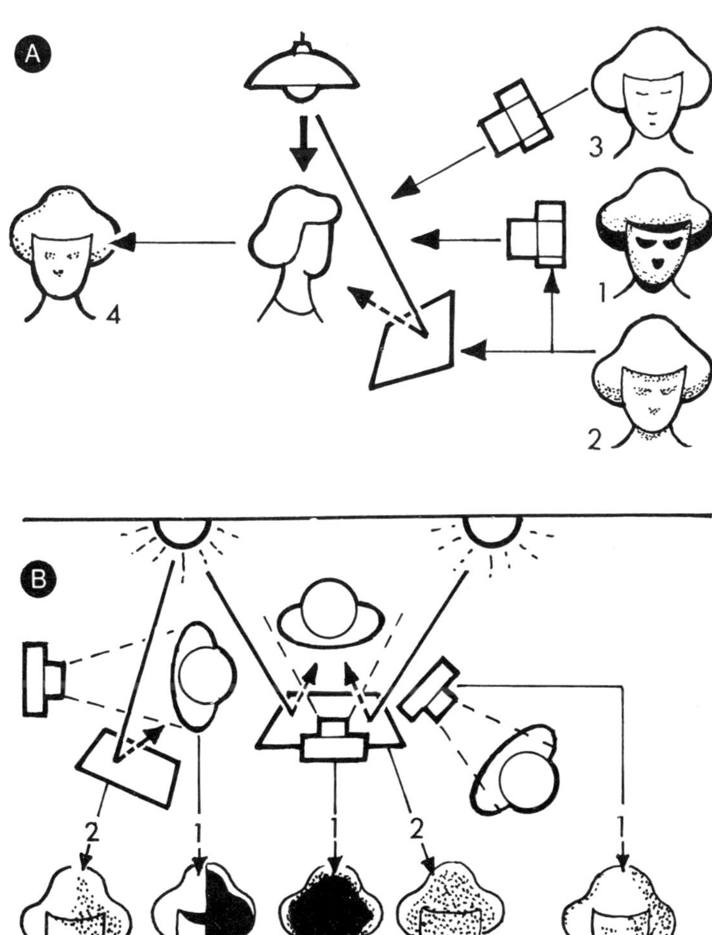

Lights in the room. A. (1) Central fitting often gives strong light with harsh shadows. (2) Soften these with a reflector. (3) Have the subject sitting on the floor looking up and the camera pointing downwards. (4) If the subject is moved from underneath into the penumbral area you have to give longer exposures. B. Lighting possibilities with wall lights: (1) Without reflectors (2) with reflectors.

Subjects placed very close to strongly coloured surfaces might pick up reflections of that colour – with tungsten lamps this could happen with red and orange. Blue and similar surfaces would have virtually no effect, but merely reflect poorly.

A room equipped solely with wall lights is very softly lit. The closer the subject is to any wall fitting the more directional is the lighting and therefore the more rounded or modelled the subject appears. In practice it may be essential to move close to one of the fittings to get enough lighting to allow a short emposure. There is no problem with this. If well positioned, lights on other walls may provide a useful fill in for the shadow side. You can also move the subject about in relation to two fittings on one wall. This can provide front-side and near-side lighting, double side lighting, frontal-side plus front fill and many other combinations (see page 172). Wall lights, if bright enough, offer far more scope for interesting and unusual lighting effects than a central fitting, particularly if there is more than one fitting on each wall. You can place the subject more or less anywhere without getting bad cut-offs of light unless almost directly underneath. Backgrounds tend to be proportionally darker unless another well-lit wall or other lamps appear there.

Standard lamps The character of standard lamps corresponds with that of the average overhead lamp except that it is at lower level. This has great advantages. The strong downward light can be use for high, side-lit facial studies, whereas light through the side of the shade is normally heavily diffused. The lamp can be drawn up to the subject, so it is not necessary to move him to vary the intensity. It is easy to insert a stronger bulb and the shade is usually large enough to allow this without risk of burning. The standard lamp is the nearest equivalent to a diffused photolamp with some of the manoeuvrability, though of course it cannot be adjusted for height. For that effect, you have to adjust the subject position. The light is not really suitable for full length shots if the subject is close by.

Table lamps can be used *in situ.* Often they are in a very good position for side lit portraiture. With people reading, for example, some of the light can be reflected up from a book. The lampshade is generally rather small and the lamp of low power. It is strictly a diffused light source suitable for use nearby. Some large table lamps can be fitted with bulbs of higher power though the fact that the lamp can be placed near to the subject makes this less important than with other lamps. A table lamp can, of course, be easily moved about the room and may be used as a handy fill light for other pictures every time the shadows need a little more detail. Or it can be used as the key light, with the general room lighting providing the fill. The shade may be removed and the light used direct or perhaps with the lamp held in the hand. A table lamp may itself be included in the picture; it is not usually bright enough to cause undue flare and fits very well in to a portrait where the face is near to the shade.

Spotlights The small type of domestic spotlight takes a lamp of relatively low power – most are limited to 75 W or 100 W maximum. Certain spot reflector fittings can take a standard bulb of any voltage below that limit so it is possible to have very low output spotlights. These can also take coloured bulbs provided they are the lacquered type. Only clear lamps will work as the reflector is in the unit and focuses the filament. It cannot focus a frosted bulb. The unit has the great advantage of low-cost replacement bulbs. With this type of spotlight all the light is reflected back into the bowl before it is directed forward in a concentrated beam. For this purpose there is an internally polished dish fitting or "back reflector" over the actual glass envelope. Another type uses a silver topped bulb instead of a built-in back reflector. The limitation here is that only the correct type of bulb can be effective. Yet another type of spotlight uses a mushroom bulb whose envelope itself forms the internal reflector. The front surface is partially frosted to soften the light slightly. The disadvantage with this is the high cost of replacement bulbs, though they are available in colours. Domestic spotlights often have a habit of leaking light out sideways and this can fall unexpectedly on the camera lens and cause flare in the picture.

Many spotlights are available as ceiling or wall fittings and free standing table models, basically using the same head. So they may be encountered in any of these positions, with the light directed into the room or bounced off a wall, furnishing or some other surface. Used indirectly, they are very subject to picking up the colour of the reflecting surface, particularly reds, and this should be noted in such cases.

The actual beam of light (except for the pencil light type of fitting which is not very common) from a domestic spotlight is not concentrated so efficiently as in a real photographic spotlight. It tends to be rather uneven and to have a hot spot in the centre which itself is not necessarily of a regular shape. Also the area covered is not in most cases adjustable and can be varied only with distance. A typical such unit gives a fully lit area of 2 ft diameter from a distance of 6 ft. A penumbral area beyond this makes the total area about 6 ft in diameter. The spot makes an excellent effect light. It also carries its (uneven) light beam over a greater distance without losing power, than any unfocused lamp does. So it can fill in dark corners or provide a useful splash of light in the background. Being a focused beam it is also very efficient at picking out the texture of rough surfaces when the light strikes them obliquely.

Using
the
Light

The lights in a room may be completely immobile because they are mounted on the wall or out of reach. The only control you have is to position the subject so that the light is both adequate and reaching the subject from the right direction. This is obviously easier if you are trying to photograph a small subject than if you are lighting a large flat surface evenly or taking a full length portrait.

Placing the subject

You can often bring a small object closer to the lamp but you may also wish to light a background for it as well. The easiest way to provide a reasonably even background for photographing small objects is to place them on a large sheet of paper which curves *gradually* up behind the object. It is not too difficult to light such a background evenly provided that it has no creases.

Ideally with such set ups you want to light the subject and background independently. But house lights do not allow sufficient control to do this. You have to find a happy medium by moving the subject and changing its angle in relation to the fixed light. If you are photographing a solid object you want to show its shape and roundness. Therefore the light should strike it from a little to one side of the camera, and further round if you want to increase the shadow area. As you move the subject round so the shadow cast by it moves away to one side of the background. If you lower the subject in relation to the light (ie, so that the light comes from a higher angle) the shadow grows shorter and may be virtually concealed by the subject. This may be done by moving the subject and background further under the fixed light source.

Any movement may change the lighting on the background as well. If you have achieved perfect background lighting but it is not quite right for the subject, sometimes a small adjustment will do the trick. You can turn the subject only; alternatively you can turn the background without adjusting the subject though this is bound to be more tricky. If your lighting is correct but the shadows are too aggressive you can fill them to some extent by using a reflector. This might reduce the shadow on the background as well. If you have a second light which cannot be moved too easily you can weaken the light by placing a diffuser in front. With two immobile lights you can sometimes position

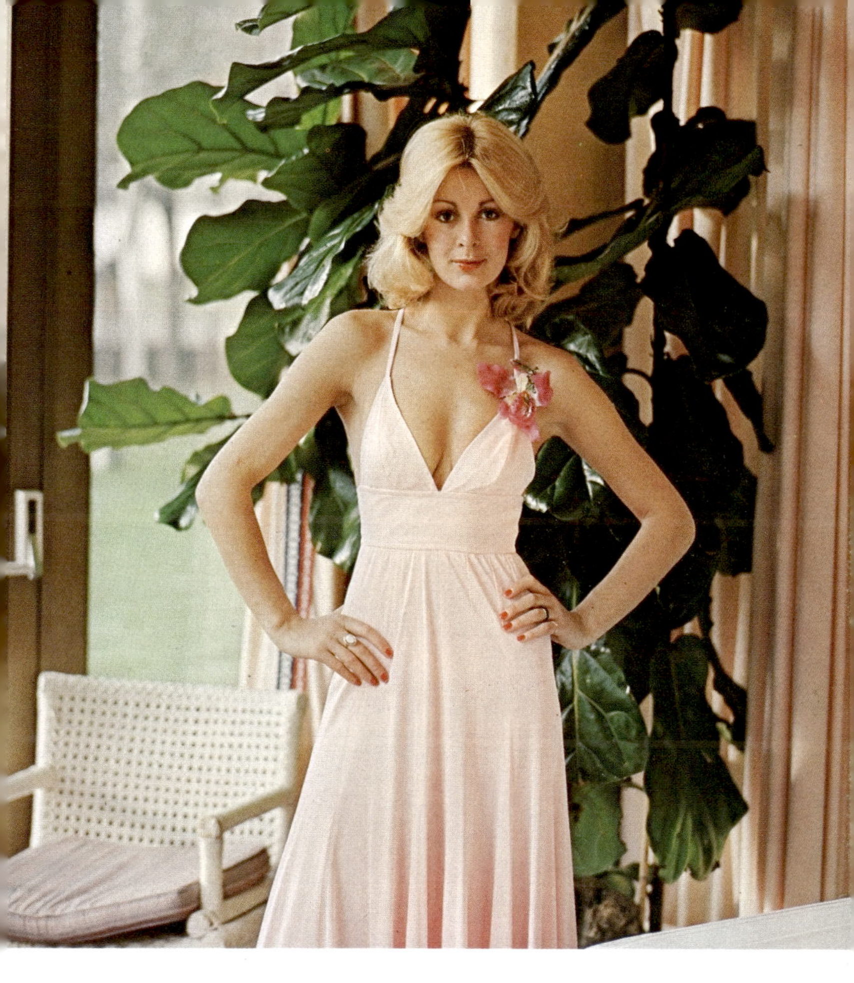

The brightest kind of 'low light' is found in a well lit modern interior with plenty of daylight through the large windows. With ordinary colour film, exposure is possible with the camera held in the hand, and there are no problems of colour balance – *Colin Ramsey.*

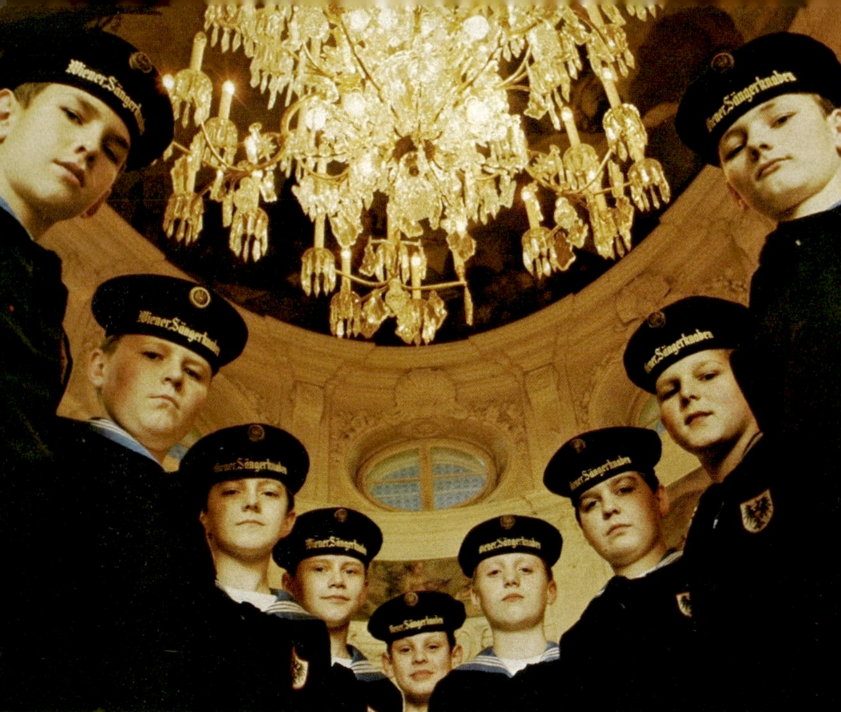

The Vienna Boys Choir by normal, though rather grand, indoor lighting. The use of daylight film gives a warm bias to the colour rendering which can still be acceptable, especially in a dramatically arranged shot such as this – *Patrick Thurston.*

Right: Stage lighting can be multi-coloured, especially for a variety show or a pop concert. True colour rendering hardly exists, but daylight film would stress the 'hotter' colours, while tungsten-balanced film would give colours nearer to what you see. Rapid movements suggest a fast film – *Peter Stiles.*

Page 156: Children in a playgroup, caught in a 'light pool'. Watch for bright areas near lamps or windows that afford sufficient brightness to show the facial expressions of your subjects. Light levels in other areas are not really important – *John Rocha.*

Page 157: Natural side/front lighting gives the most pleasing results. The subject looks well rounded and the picture is not too shadowy to suit a happy mood – *Peter Stiles.*

Page 158, top: Trafalgar Square, London. With night subjects, exposure for the main light source puts other areas in darkness – *Peter Stiles.*

Page 158, bottom: Fountains Abbey ruins by floodlight; the fading evening sky provides a happy contrast in colour – *Patrick Thurston.*

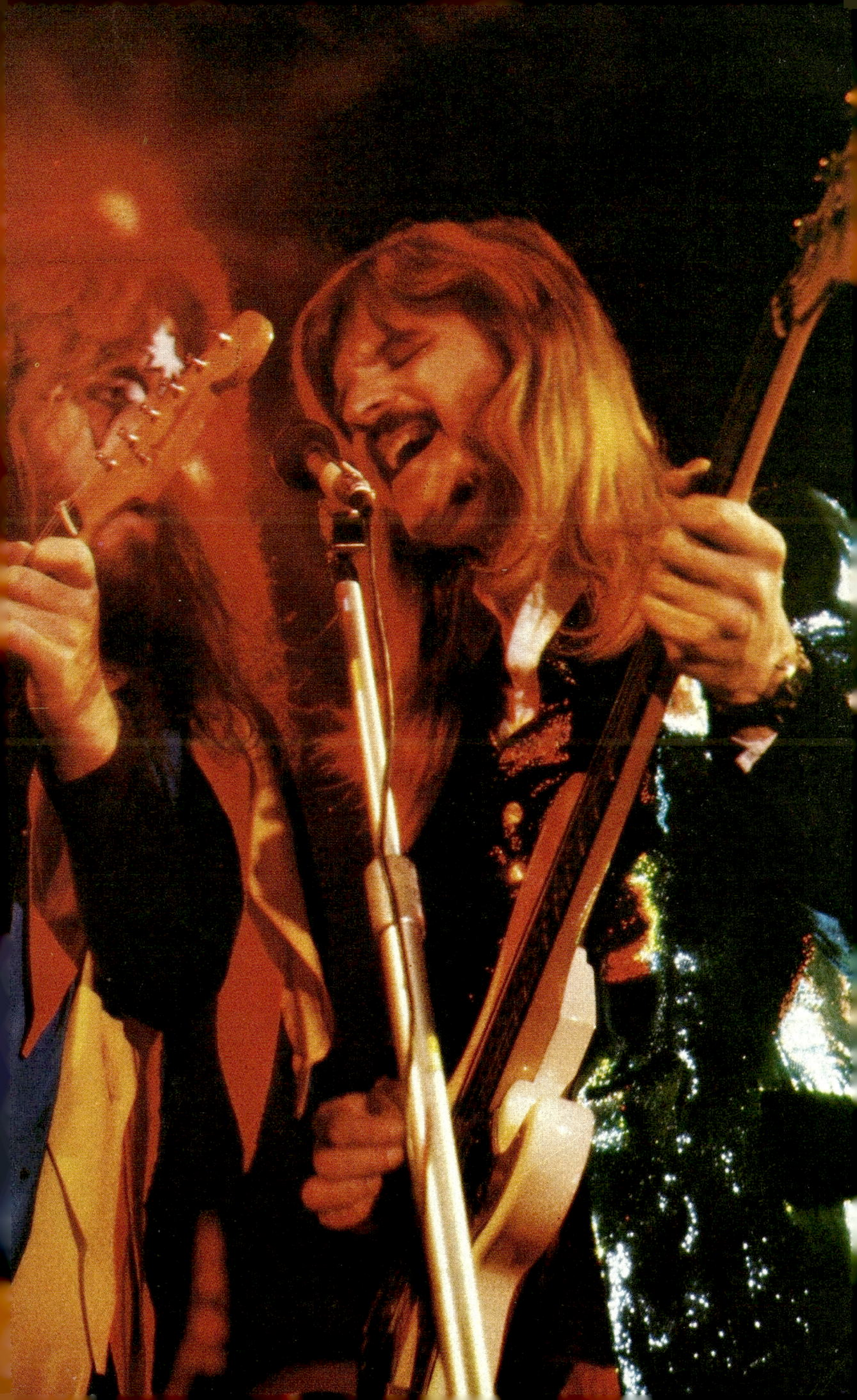

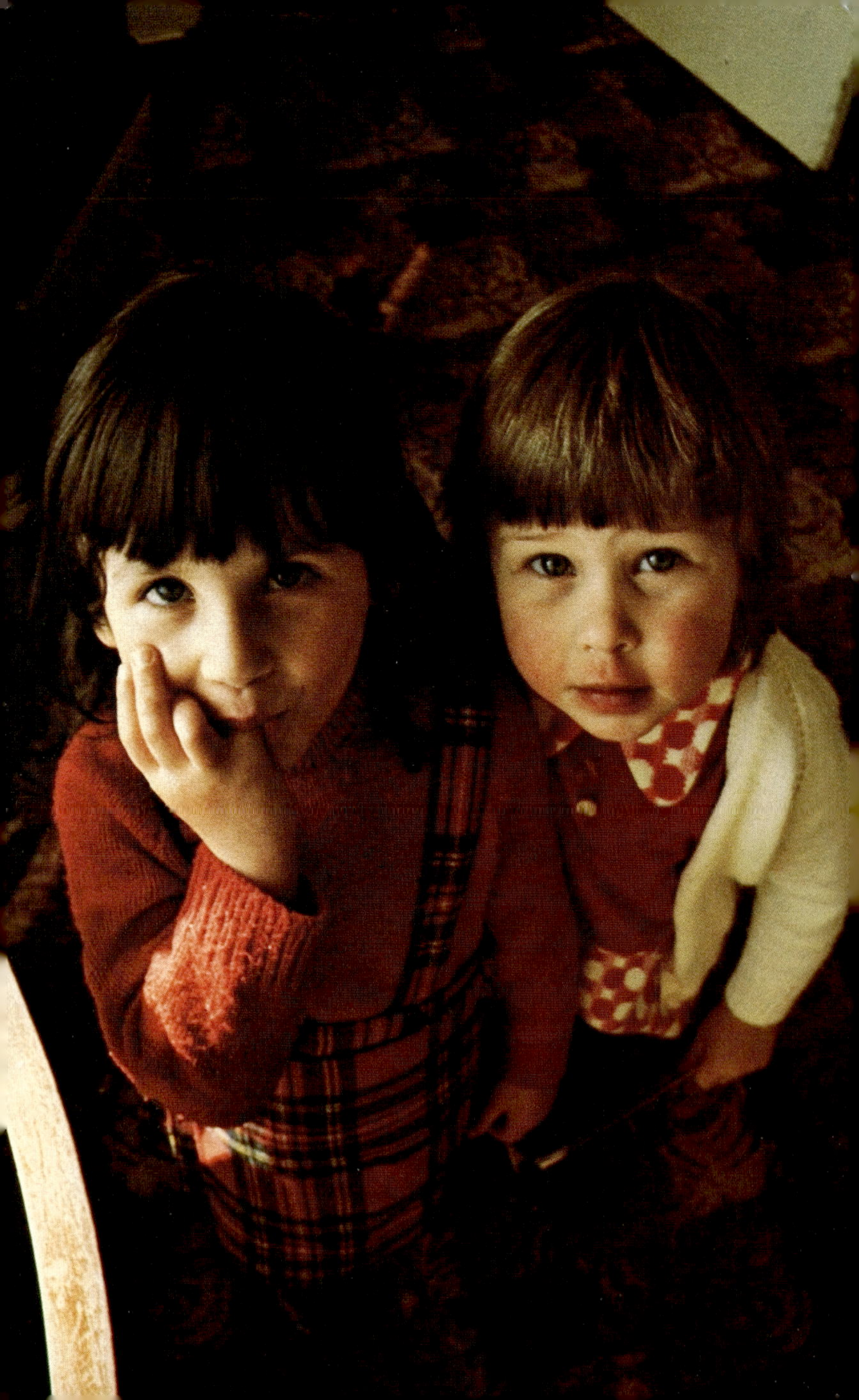

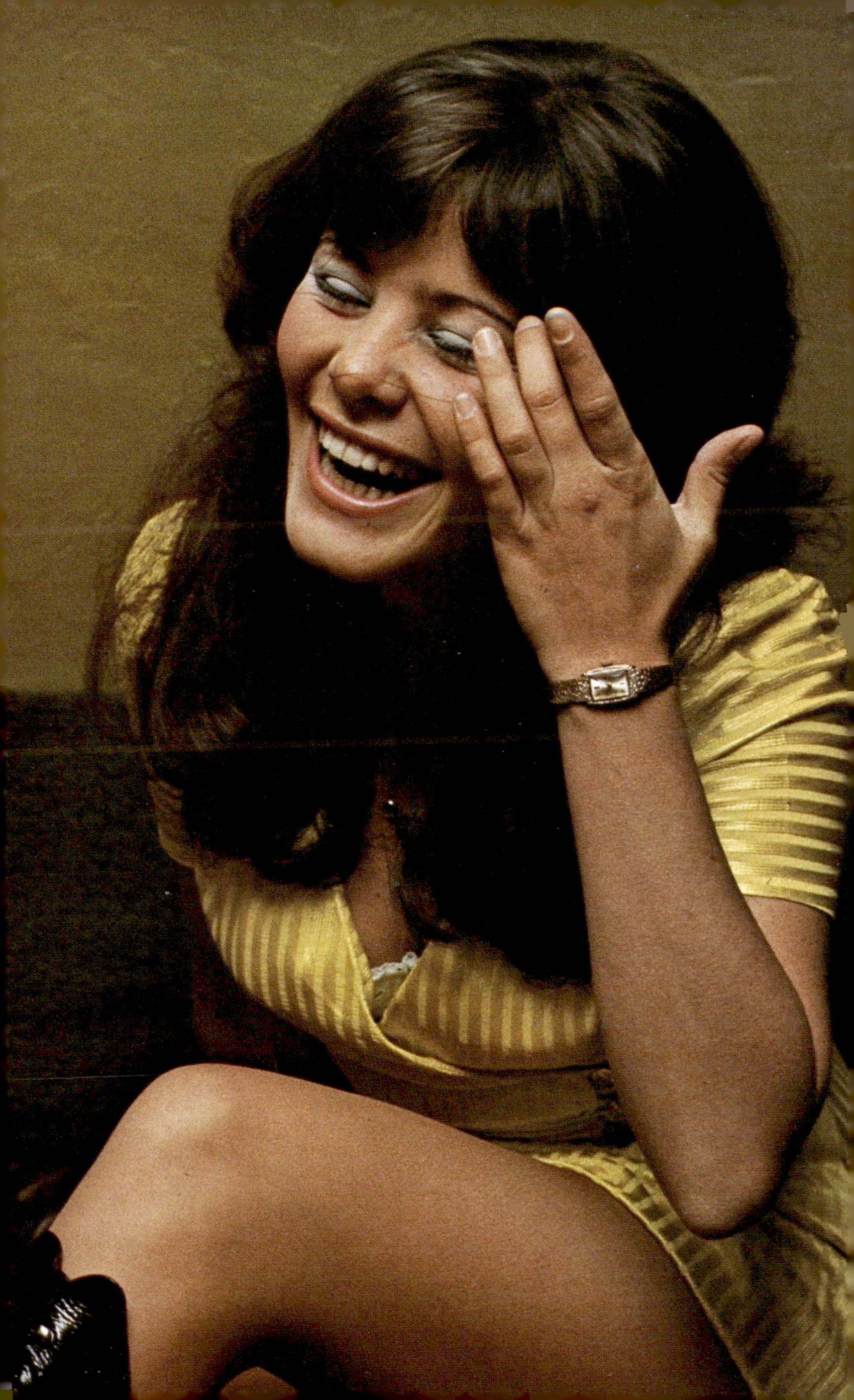

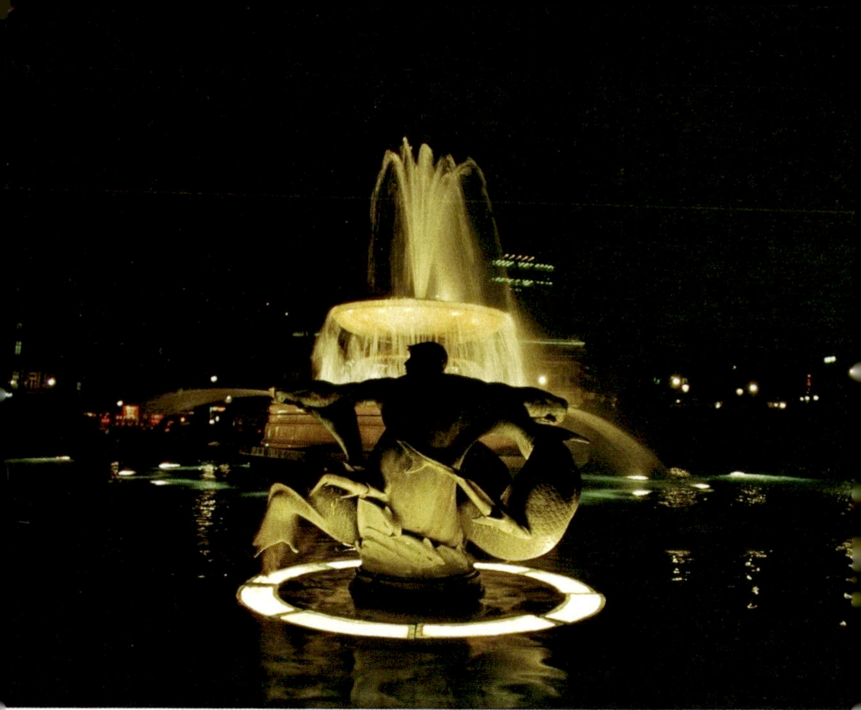

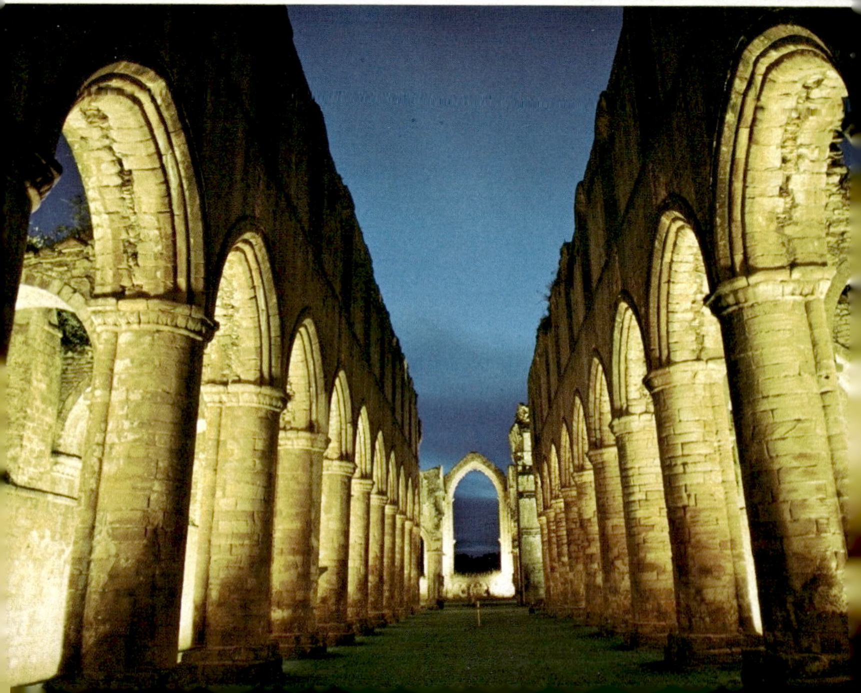

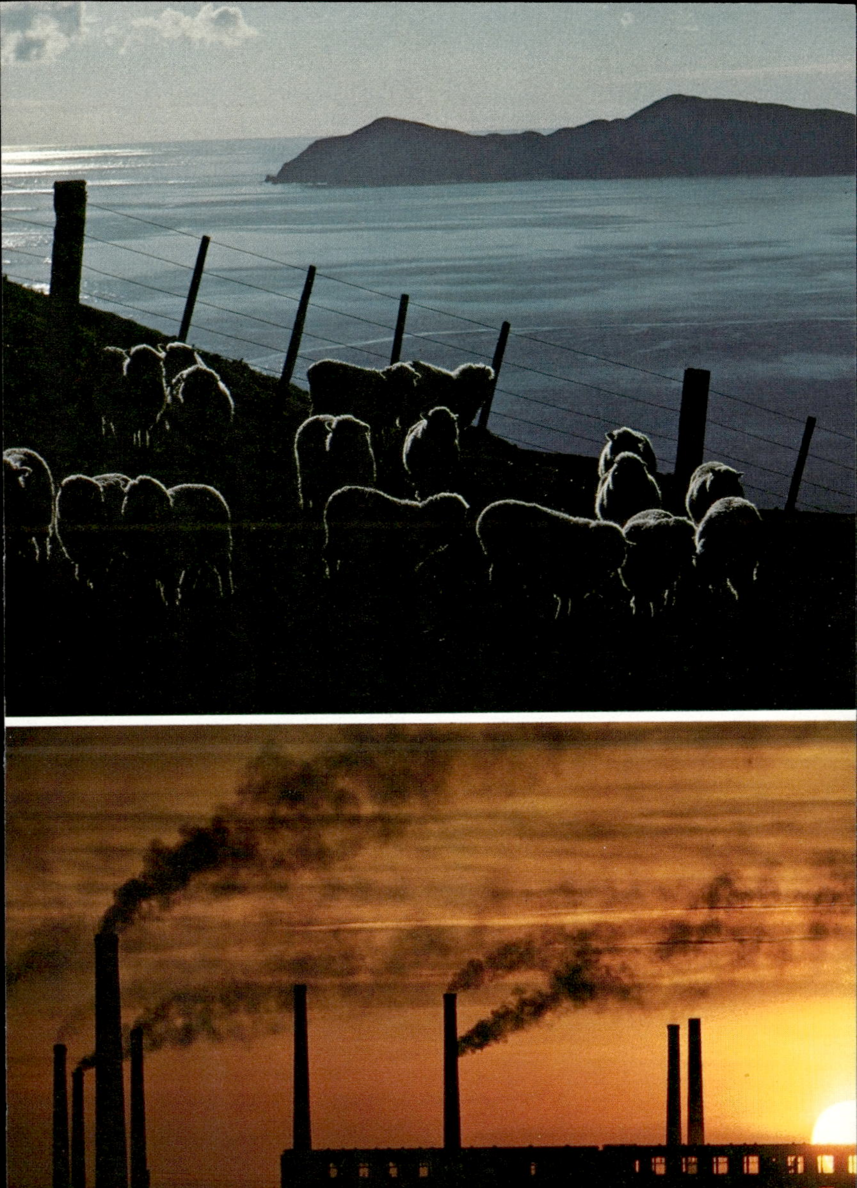

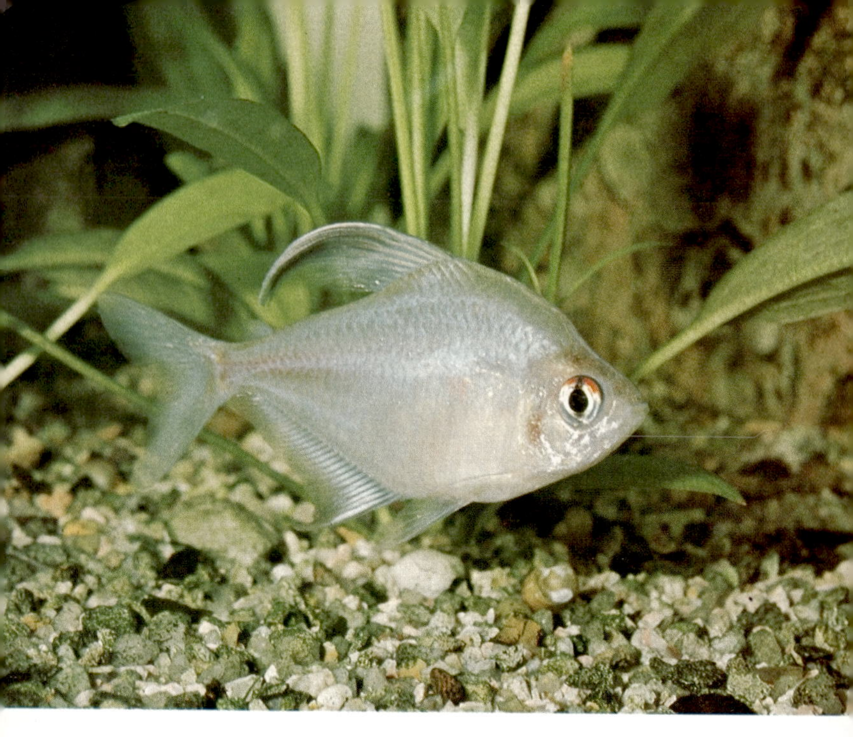

Page 159, top: Sheep. The effect of low angled evening sunlight accentuated by intentional under-exposure – *Kosmick Studios.*

Page 159, bottom: Brickworks. Exposure for the sky itself, the main colour interest, makes a silhouette of the subject – *Patrick Thurston.*

Bleeding Heart Tetra in zoo aquarium. You can avoid reflections by keeping the camera lens close to the glass front. The natural light is sufficiently bright to allow ample depth of field even at such close range – *Peter Stiles.*

the subject so that the weaker light is the key, and the stronger is adjusted to the required brightness by a diffuser. This is the reverse of the normal procedure whereby you place the subject so that the key light is the strongest.

If you are shooting a subject whose surface is in low relief you need the light to fall very obliquely to the surface to emphasize what contours there are. This is easy enough if you need only one light; you place the subject so that the light cuts across its surface. You may need some fill light to reduce the contrast or, more likely, to fill the ground, particularly with shiny objects such as coins or medallions. In a position giving good relief the ground might be too dark. A large white surface can be reflected in the flat ground bringing the embossed image to life.

Indoor home lighting is far from ideal for flat copy work, especially colour, owing to the exactness needed in placing lights and the bias in the colour of such lighting. Nevertheless it is possible to obtain reasonable results in monochrome and is certainly better than nothing. For flat copy work, for instance when photographing maps or pictures, you have to position the surface in such a way that it is illuminated as evenly as possible. Often you can nowhere near fulfil the ideal requirements of identical lights each positioned at 45 degrees to the surface – which gives very even illumination and no reflections from that surface into the camera lens. You may for instance, only have lamps of differing power. You have to place the copy surface at an angle to the lights as near to 45 degree lighting as possible but if one lamp is more powerful than the other, and neither can be moved, you have to place the copy surface nearer to the weaker light. You can check for equal power by switching off, first one light then the other, each time checking the brightness at the surface by taking a reflected light reading with an exposure meter. You can check for evenness of illumination by placing a plain white surface in front of the copy subject and inspecting it through half closed eyes. Try to make the light from each lamp as even as possible individually. Unevenness from each lamp may, however, be cancelled out when both lamps are switched on.

When there is only one lamp available it is still possible to achieve sufficiently even illumination for flat copy work – especially with small surfaces. Larger objects should be placed further away from the light source. The light should still be at an angle to the surface (even a matt surface) to avoid reflections coming straight in to the camera lens. Inevitably, therefore, part of the surface is nearer to the lamp than another part. But the further the subject is placed from the lamp the less are the relative differences in brightness at different ranges from the lamp. So the lighting on any flat surface at an angle to the light is more even at greater range. The reduction in overall illumination is not a significant factor in such copy work where the exposures can be lengthened without difficulty.

Only in the most critical colour copying job could long exposures cause any problems, where exact balance can be upset by reciprocity law failure (see also pp. 55 and 90). In simple terms the reciprocity law states that provided the sum of exposure time and quantity of light reaching the film comes to the same total the effect on the film will be the same. In fact, films are designed for use within certain limits of exposure time. When exposures are given for longer periods than the maximum intended for the film, underexposure may result, with a bias in colour rendering (see table p. 223). With domestic lamps (2600–2800 K) the light source is in effect already biased and you can anyway not expect anything but red-orange results in colour with a film balanced for photoflood lamps (3200 K). By far the best answer to lighting flat copy work in colour is to take the subject outdoors and photograph it when the sky is overcast. You should only use indoor lights as a last resort, unless the colour rendering is unimportant or you want a red-orange picture! Although fluorescent or daylight strip lighting units give very diffused illumination in the colour temperature range 3700–4800 K, they have a discontinuous spectrum. Pictures taken by their light may be lacking colour saturation at certain wavelengths. As a consequence, although the balance as a whole may be acceptable, particular colours can be poorly rendered.

Positioning for portraiture

Even though you may be taking pictures in lighting that is far from ideal you should try to follow the basic light-on-the-subject approach that you would use if you had lights of your own. In the "heat of the moment" you may be inclined to let the lighting go as it is. Of course

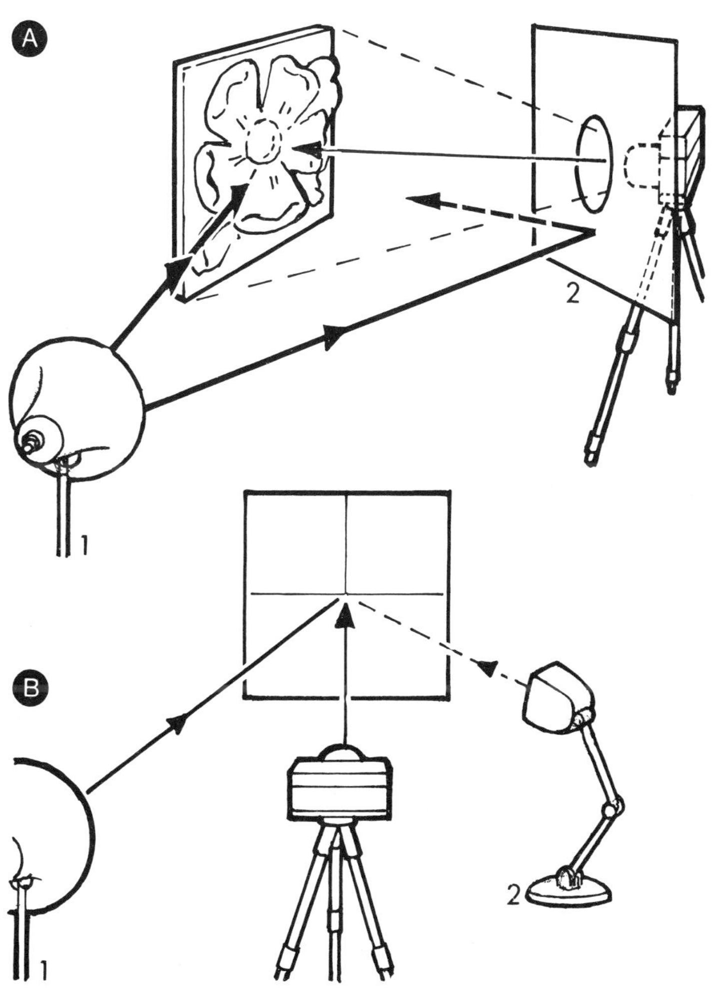

Subject in relief: A. An oblique light (1) emphasises the contours of the subject while the dark ground or shadows can be filled from the camera position with a large white reflector (2). Flat copy work: B. You have to balance up unequal lights (1, 2) to give even illumination to a flat surface.

this may do for snapshots. But whatever light you use, if you get peculiar shadows they are going to be a part of the picture and might irritate you every time you look at it. You cannot remove the effects of bad lighting even with the flexibility available to you in black and white printing. Once they are there, they are there.

One way to try and get the lighting at least about right in difficult conditions is to look at where the lights are and place your subject in such a way that at least the strongest source is coming from the right direction. This won't guarantee a good result but it will at least load the chances in your favour. It is a sensible approach in cases where the illumination is so bright that you cannot easily see its actual effect on the subject. It is easy to forget about lighting altogether this way. Some artificial light situations draw you into shooting unusual effects simply because they are there. It is a good idea to take advantage of this if it really suits the subject, and is not merely grotesque. The lighting in a scene goes a long way towards creating its atmosphere – and in the case of portraits, suggesting a mood.

In trying to find good lighting for portraits you have two slight drawbacks compared with small inanimate subjects. There is less flexibility in positioning and you need reasonably even lighting if you are to cover more than a single face in close up. Above all, you want the subject to appear naturally placed, relaxing in a chair, leaning against a table, or with an arm around another person. If you want to see the whole person, or even the larger part, it helps if they wear light coloured clothes or at least have clothes that contrast with their immediate surroundings. You can escape some of the problems of evenness or finding bright enough light by concentrating on the head – shooting either close up faces or head and shoulder portraits. This is also a sly way to get round the problems of posing the body if you are taking a reasonably formal portrait. You then have no problems of what to do with the arms and legs and how to avoid odd-looking hand positions!

Lighting the head

Considered as a physical object, the human head is a "solid" volume, rounded in form with prominent features, both protrusions and inden-

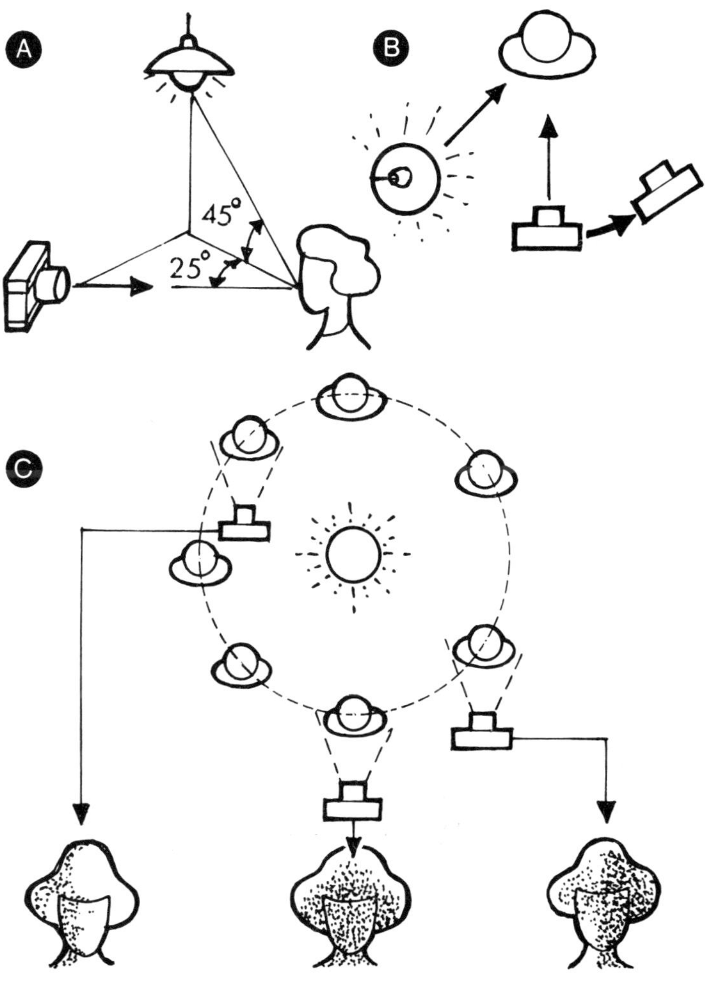

Lighting the head. A. Variables in the placing of the key light are the height in relation to the subject and the angle compared with the camera viewpoint. B. Changes in camera angle also vary the relative quantity of shadow visible in the subject. C. You can move your subject to any point in a circle around a central fitting to vary the lighting as desired.

tations on the surface, and a texture smooth in parts, not so smooth in others. The hair can be white, black or any shade between; so can the skin.

To demonstrate the volume of the head the same conditions apply as with other solid objects. The key light moulds the shape if it falls on the subject from an angle away from the viewing position. The features cast shadows. The more oblique the light to the surface of the face, the larger those shadows may be. If the light is placed too high, the forehead is brightly lit, deep shadows fill the eye sockets and obscure the eyes, the nose casts a long shadow downwards over the mouth which, too, forms a shadow. Prominent cheekbones and hollow cheeks are emphasized. The neck is largely in shade.

If the lamp is lowered, light reaches into the eye sockets bringing the eyes to life, the nose shadow is shorter, the mouth has hardly any shadow under it. The chin, however, is well rounded and some light falls on the neck. The light on the forehead is more or less equal with that on the rest of the face.

The nearer the lamp is placed to the viewing position the less modelled is the head generally, the smaller the nose shadow, and all other shadows, and the fatter the face is likely to appear. The hair which, when the lamp was to one side, cast a shadow making the face look smaller, now casts no shadow, and the unlit side of the head which made the face look more slim is now gone, so the face seems broader and more pale. Highlights that give a sparkle to the eyes move nearer the centre.

Naturally, the same factors apply if the subject is manoeuvred in relation to a fixed light source or where the light may be freely moved around the subject. If it strikes at the same angle in relation to the camera position – which, of course, moves with the subject – it does not matter how the situation was arrived at.

With existing light photography the chances are that the subject must be arranged in a position agreeable to the light that falls on it. That means, of course, that among other things you may have to accept a background that you would not have chosen originally, for the sake of getting good lighting. If you are shooting in black and white, the skin tone or the hair colour of the subject may then blend into the background so that you begin to lose the outline of the subject. This might necessitate another change – by moving the subject, switching a light on or off, drawing a curtain or changing the background in some way. If is often a matter of compromise, and you have to choose the best alternative.

Lighting the body

Largely the same principles apply when it comes to lighting the body except that you have a more complicated figure, and accurate rendering of tone or colour in the clothes is less important. It is better to sacrifice detail in the body, large though it is in the picture, rather than get unsatisfactory lighting or exposure for the face. If you are unfamiliar with with working by existing light it is a good idea to start with faces only.

You can overcome the problem of getting enough light on the body by having the subject wear light coloured clothes or hiding the body behind an object in the picture such as a table or other piece of furniture. You could reflect light into the body area without lighting the face, as such. Generally you would expect lighting on the body to be better if you are shooting by general room lighting rather than using a single small light source, such as a table lamp, near the subject's face To include the person or group full length you need to be positioned at some distance. This usually means that the lower portion of the picture area is proportionally less well lit than the upper part. It might be possible to position the person in such a way that the face were lit by one source and the remainder of the body by another. The light level may be so high generally that no special lighting technique is called for; if you expose for the face the body will come out well enough. The main problem to avoid is the tendency for unevenness and hard cut-off points in the light given from overhead fittings. There, again, it depends what standards you are applying to your photography – whether you are mainly after any reasonable shot, or you want a really first class job of work.

Clothes

Exposure can be quite a critical matter. For instance, if it is important that you show detail in a light coloured dress, then you should take care not to place the subject where the dress is so overlit that those details are lost in the final print. You have to take care with exposure in such cases. In shooting negative film, underexposure gives insufficient density on the negative to avoid printing a white dress, for example, as a medium grey. Overexposing may allow the dress to print white but obscure details both by loss of differentiation between subtle tones in the material and by the increased level of grain in the image, which could become quite marked in a print.

Single lamp: table lamp

If there is insufficient light on the subject to take a portrait you should look for the brightest area or light pool in the room which will also be convenient for portraits. This is nearly always to be found near a table or other low level lamp. The central light in a room may be too far away from a subject standing underneath. It is more than likely that the light comes from too steep an angle or, if the subject is placed far away, it is too weak to give the exposure you want. A subject can be positioned very close to a table lamp and the result will still look quite natural even with the lamp included in the picture. A single table lamp always gives enough light for a picture unless it has a very heavy shade. Even then, you can have the subject read a book or newspaper to reflect the downwardly directed light up into the face. With the average lamp, the light coming through the shade is sufficient.

You can get more than one type of lighting with a table lamp. Moreover, you can easily adjust its position rather than move the subject to make changes. The strong but diffused light coming through the shade can give a well moulded account of a person's features. It is normal to have a reading lamp beside, and slightly behind the person reading. This gives half-light, half-shade lighting to the volume of the head, with the strongest highlight down one edge. According to the camera angle this can become anything from a well lit side view through side lighting to a full silhouette or, with sufficient exposure, a flat lighting with a strong highlight running round the shape of the head and hair. With the lamp visible in the picture flare effects could result – pleasant or otherwise.

Assuming that your subject is sitting down facing the camera with the table lamp placed on one side you may find that the light is far too uneven for a straightforward type of portrait. Move the lamp forward, towards the camera, or the subject back, so that the light comes from a more frontal direction, 45 degrees to the camera would do. Most of the face should now be lit adequately, the shadows will be small except that a dark shadow of the head may appear immediately behind it. (This naturally depends how far away the background is.) With the lamp in this position the lighting should radiate quite naturally from that source and shadows in the face need not be weakened by a reflector. A variation of this is to place the subject higher or lower than the single lamp. In the first case they can look down into it – a very attractive effect. If the light is above the subject the face is made to appear wider, and the features more rounded.

A very good profile is obtained, particularly if the subject has good bone structure, by having him look straight at the light, placing the camera at right angles. The slightest adjustment of lamp or subject towards the camera modifies this lighting to a marked degree. Moving the subject a few inches forward makes the light more oblique, hardens the modelling and deepens shadows. A movement in the other direction reduces this modelling effect and brings shadows nearer to the general brightness of the face.

One problem with close ups using a table lamp is the risk of getting light in the lens causing the whole picture to flare, or flare spots or repeated shapes to appear across the picture. If, however, flare takes the form of an even cast across the picture the result can be quite attractive. Shadows and mid tones are overlaid by a whitish haze. In colour the result is a yellow-orange haze something like the effect gained by the pre-exposure fogging technique (where, before exposure, the film is first evenly fogged with a white light giving just enough exposure to establish a neutral haze across the film). All colours are rendered as a series of pastel shades; in the case of film not balanced for the light source this haze takes on the general colour bias.

If the table lamp bulb is replaced by a photoflood, the haze is neutral and not coloured.

If you take portraits in colour, avoid strongly coloured lampshades. They can give a heavy colour cast over the whole subject. How unfortunate if it happens to be green! If in doubt, take the shade off and shoot with the bare bulb, leaving the lamp itself out of the picture. If the light is too strong you can diffuse it with a net curtain, muslin, or a white sheet, though this last might be too thick and cut out too much light.

With multi branch table lamps there are two additional problems. First, unless heavily diffused by shades, and sometimes despite that, there is a danger of lighting the subject with multiple shadows. Multiple shadows are ugly in themselves and also give the impression that the picture is unsharp. Worse, the multiple lamps may be reflected in the eyes. This gives them a watery effect, which is unpleasant and destroys the clarity and concentration in the person's expression. The effect is even worse if the subject wears spectacles.

Do not place the table lamp so close that heat or brilliance worries the subject. You cannot hope for a good picture if they are uncomfortable and they want to screw up their eyes to avoid the glare. Be prepared to use a weaker light and a wider aperture.

Other effects can be produced with the single table lamp. Placing it directly in front of the camera gives flat frontal illumination with no shadows. Placing it frontally but well below the subject gives a rather grotesque effect if the light is very oblique to the face. If the lamp is not directly underneath but placed somewhat forward and the subject looks down into it, you can simulate the effect of firelight. With the camera facing the subject and the light positioned behind and to one side of the subject you can get a strong edge lighting with a full soft fill in from the front provided that the surroundings reflect sufficient light back on to the subject from in front. If not you can use a reflector.

A reflector can be used in any of the lightings outlined above, but the best results are gained when the light falls directly on the reflector, rather than by relying on the reflector to pick up ambient light. Do not overdo a reflector effect. If it balances too favourably with the main source, the picture is apt to look contrived.

One objective of existing light photography is to avoid the concocted appearance of the worst type of studio portraiture. You are relying on the naturalness of all the component parts of the picture to give the final appearance of genuineness – a relaxed home atmosphere, an outdoor situation in the late evening, or a person in their normal working surroundings, for instance.

Single lamp: overhead

The overhead lighting in a room does not allow you the scope for imaginative lighting effects that you can obtain with the relatively manoeuvrable table lamp. It may simply give a generous overall light level lacking in any individual interest or character. You may feel this is ideal for colour. In black and white work, where there is more need to show the shapes and depth of things, such even lighting is not so much of a virtue.

The single lamp in the centre of a room corresponds, in a way, to the position and elevation of the sun. If you choose the right spot for your subject and the lampshade does not interfere with things too much, you can get quite an acceptable result.

If your fitting emits reasonably even light all round, for a start try placing your subject a few feet away so that the light is 45 degrees up and 45 degrees forward – ie, the approximate angle between the camera and the subject. You can reduce the angle at which the light strikes the subject from above by moving him further away from the lamp. You open or close the angle of lighting by turning the subject and repositioning the camera.

Very satisfactory lighting for portraits can be obtained by taking the sitter some distance away and, using only the light from the central fitting, arrange him so that the light, while coming from quite a high angle, is somewhere about 25 degrees off the camera axis. The shadows arising from this are small but the head is well modelled, while the subject is at sufficient distance for the light reaching the head and body to be more or less equalized. The background, too, will be full of detail because the exposure for the subject at a great distance is not far off the correct exposure for the background. The relative brightness of subject and background can be adjusted by moving the subject towards or away from that light. Bringing the subject closer to the light gives far more severe lighting effects.

If your light fitting has a heavy shade avoid the "hot" cone of light emerging from beneath and keep your subject within the diffused area lit through the shade. Flat lighting from such a lamp serves well enough for colour. If the walls of the room reflect well enough for sufficient light level in the subject you can move it all round the central fitting and vary the lighting accordingly. This effectually gives you part-key, part-fill (reflected) lighting. Either can predominate, according to the position chosen in relation to the light and the amount of subject visible from the camera angle selected. Shadows can be reinforced with reflectors, or the main lighting provided by them.

Multi-lamp portraits

The more lamps there are in the room, the more light you have to take pictures by. If the lights are suitably positioned you can get very good results. People who use many lamps to light a room are usually aiming for an even, soft effect. You can, by the same token, expect to achieve soft, even lighting in your pictures. Where you encounter bare bulbs, open lights, or hard lights, the lighting can be very troublesome, with cross shadows, multiple shadows and many highlights in the eyes. In this type of situation it is often a good idea to turn off one or two lamps to keep the effect simple.

A good combination for a portrait is the centre light and a table lamp. Either can serve as the key light, but the table lamp can be closer without shedding light from an undesirable angle. So, before deciding where your subject should be, consider the key light and fill in principle and the many variations in placing that can give you good lighting. An additional light, say a wall light or existing standard lamp, can serve as an effect light. It can illuminate the background or shed light on the back of the subject, adding a catch light in the hair or some edge light to the side of the face. This may help in differentiating between subject and background where they blend into one another and you lose the outline of the head. But avoid a deliberate imitation of glossy studio lighting when moving these lights about. A simple arrangement is by far the most effective.

Background light

If you *have* to use a background that you do not really want, simply because of the positioning problem for subject and lights, you can move the subject closer to the light, use a small aperture and so darken the background. Occasionally you can switch off a light or shield it so that its light no longer falls on the background. Plain backgrounds can be broken up by the shadows of objects placed in front of the lamp. Such shading can lend some variation to the tone of a plain background without introducing a noticeable pattern.

Do not automatically remove all objects from an irritating background. Take only those that spoil the picture, such as a reflecting mirror or a circular shape that echoes the shape of the head, or a straight object that juts out of it. You can sometimes focus forward a little to keep a background out of focus but this is a little risky as you may miss the subject too! If you avoid strongly patterned wallpaper in portraits and aim wherever possible for clean and undistracting surroundings you will get an effect nearer to that of the standard studio portrait.

But ancilliaries can add charm to the informal portrait and, if they are attractive and appropriate, can be made a part of the composition.

Focus and sharpness

There is no reason why you should not take portraits with a wide aperture provided that your focusing is accurate. If you move the lamp further off, the narrow plane of focus that results from the wider aperture should generally fall across the eyes. This is the *general* rule. It gives you best sharpness where the centre of interest lies.

The famous Victorian portrait photographer, Julia Margaret Cameron, produced many pictures in which the focus was decidedly soft, though not taken with the special soft focus lenses then available. Whether intended or not, her pictures often seem to gain from the more generalised view afforded by this lack of precision.

But what you must avoid is having the face out of focus and the shoulder, for example, which is unimportant, aggressively sharp in the foreground. Even if you are going to aim for slight unsharpness deliberately to soften the effect of a certain lens, the head and particularly the eyes should still be the sharpest part of the picture.

If you focus correctly on the eyes, the remainder of the head can be at least partially well out of focus with little loss. Many people feel that the biting sharpness of modern high quality lenses gives a degree of hardness that is unsuited to portraiture. This is based on the notion that at a normal viewing or speaking distance one is not conscious of every pore and tiny hair on a face. It may be felt that the more general impression afforded by a slightly softened image is nearer to the real effect of looking at a living person.

Camera and film

In an earlier chapter we discussed features which make a camera particularly suitable for existing light photography of a more general kind. These factors still hold good when it comes to using the camera for taking pictures by artificial light in the home. A camera with a wide aperture lens, *f*2.8 or larger, low shutter speeds and the ability to give time exposures, makes it easier to take indoor pictures – but at the same time they became less essential. Why?

The vast majority of indoor pictures are of stationary or near-stationary subjects. It is much easier to ask people at home to stop jumping about than it is to persuade all the traffic in a street at night to stop moving. It is also easier to put up a tripod in a living room than on a busy pavement, and there are probably plenty of solid objects around the room on which to support the camera. So you can risk much longer exposures than in many other places.

Look at it this way. The difference in cost betwen an *f*2 lens and one of *f*2.8 is often very great. Yet the difference in exposure is only the equivalent of one shutter speed. So if you can take a picture at 1/30 sec at *f*2 you can take it at 1/15 at *f*2.8 – all other things being equal. If you are supporting the camera adequately either shutter speed will do for most cases except perhaps when photographing small children and animals constantly on the move.

For ordinary portraiture you will probably elect to use a smaller aperture anyway to get enough depth of field. The depth available on an *f*1.4 lens, for example, when used wide open is very small, and requires great accuracy in focusing. Again, to do this, and to be able to rely on it, you need a camera with a very clear viewfinder system for use at low light levels and a method of focusing that really suits you.

The question of suitability is an individual one. Some people have great difficulty with one type that others find very easy to use. For low light work it must be very positive. On rangefinder cameras you almost invariably have the coincident image finder. As you turn the focusing ring two images of the subject coincide when they are within the plane of sharpest focus. This seemingly infallible method nevertheless causes problems for some people. They simply cannot see the two images. In taking pictures by indoor light the problem is exacerbated; one of the images is often tinged with yellow and this makes it doubly hard to see by the warm colour of ordinary room lighting.

Reflex cameras with split image rangefinder or microprism focusing do not present any special difficulties. They are tricky to use at the smallest maximum apertures available on some long focus lenses but you are unlikely to need such lenses indoors unless you are taking a close up portrait, and for this a 90 mm lens on a 35 mm camera would be adequate. This lens may have quite a wide maximum aperture, say, *f*2.8.

Some people prefer to focus on a ground glass image and this is certainly a very positive method if that image is sufficiently magnified. Failing all these methods, the best bet is to take a leaf out of the book of the professional cinematographer: measure the distance with a tape and set the figure manually on the focusing ring.

As for seeing the general view, undoubtedly a modern rangefinder camera gives you the brightest image. The brightness in a reflex varies from model to model, and also from one lens to another or according to what aperture has been set. But you should never use the camera as a substitute for the eye by scanning around to find a picture. Look at the subject direct, only use the camera to get the framing. That way, seeing a bright image becomes less important. You won't see very well through the viewfinder at low light levels whatever the camera.

Shutter speeds are more important. If your camera has a full range of low speeds (1/15 –1 sec) you have an advantage. Some cameras do not provide speeds lower than 1/30 sec or even 1/60 which is too short for many situations even with fast film. Ideally you should have intermediate speeds down to one second. Otherwise you have to support the camera firmly and take time exposures. The shortest you can achieve with a cable release is about $\frac{1}{4}$ sec – but not reliably. Most people could not manage less than one second with any degree of accuracy. So the lack of low shutter speeds is inconvenient but not fatal. You may be able to secure a few well lit shots at 1/60 sec, especially

with the aid of special processing to increase film speed (page 206). Some cameras with electronically timed shutters allow longer exposures than the one second maximum on more orthodox models. The maximum on such cameras may be for 8 to 60 sec according to model. This timing device can be linked to a metering system in the camera which establishes the "correct" exposure for the scene being photographed. The problem here, as indeed with so many types of automation, is that with your indoor lighting pictures you may be working in one of the situations where an exposure meter cannot function properly – at least it does not give you the exposure you want.
Assessing the correct exposure is the greatest single difficulty with indoor pictures. The majority of cameras these days have a built in light measuring device of some kind. Most cameras have a CdS (cadmium sulphide) exposure meter. Older models have the less sensitive selenium photo cell. The most recent introduction is the silicon blue type of meter. Briefly the advantages of the CdS meter over the selenium type which apply in the present context, are that it has a narrower "angle of view" and is therefore less susceptible to influences outside the picture area as well as being capable of responding to a small area of the subject. It is small enough to be built inside a camera behind the lens to provide effective spot metering of selected local areas of the subject. Size for size, it is more sensitive to low light levels. The silicon blue exposure meter has the advantages of the CdS type but is said to be less susceptible to bias in colour response. It can also react more quickly to low light levels and give a reliable reading in a shorter time. A CdS meter can take minutes to arrive at an accurate reading in very low light. CdS also has a "memorizing" effect, whereby a high level reading influences readings taken shortly afterwards to give a misleadingly optimistic reckoning of a low light level.

Taking exposure readings

Cameras with built in meters can give you some trouble in finding the correct exposure. You are often seeking a reading for an area which forms a very small part of the general view in front of the camera. A

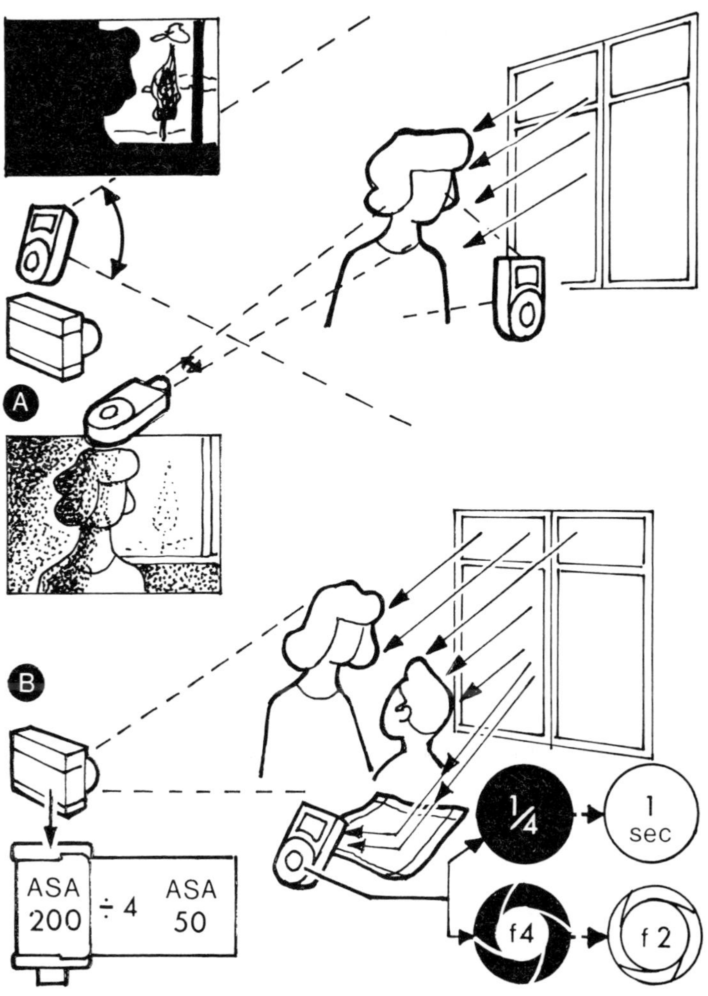

Meter readings for window light: A. Selenium meters with a wide acceptance angle can give wrong readings when taken from the camera viewpoint. The narrower angle of a TTL or separate CdS meter makes it less prone to this effect but the most reliable readings are taken from close up, excluding the window itself. B. Where the light is too low to obtain reliable direct readings take a reading from a white surface at the subject position and then either multiply the exposure by four or divide the film speed by the same factor.

selenium meter takes a relatively wide-angle reading and is subject to misleading influences such as a lamp shining obliquely on the front of the camera but just out of picture. Separate (non TTL) CdS meters take a narrower angle of view that is not so subject to the hazard of strong oblique light. But the angle of view of both types of meter is far too wide to give accurate pin point readings of small areas from a distance. If, for example, you want to expose correctly for a small well lit area in the picture you have to go up to the subject and take a reading from close range, excluding the less well lit surroundings from that reading. If, on the other hand, your scene is lit reasonably evenly all over, this type of meter is fine for taking readings from the shooting position.

Cameras with an exposure meter reading through the taking lens (TTL meter) limit the area metered to that covered by the lens or, in some cases, to a small part of it. These meters are not really susceptible to influences outside the picture area.

The meters that measure only a part of the picture area are sometimes called spot meters. They allow you to take readings of the important area from the camera position, or several readings of selected areas of the subject without moving in close. Indeed, in conditions where you cannot get close to the subject, reading by this method has distinct advantages. That is not, however, generally the situation with indoor photography.

If a long focus lens is fitted to a TTL metering camera which reads from the whole picture area you do, in effect, have a form of spot metering. Some cameras combine spot metering with a percentage of acceptance from the whole picture area. This does not give reliable results in the conditions described earlier where you want a reading from a selected area although taken from the camera position.

If your camera meter or separate exposure meter does not respond to the light either because it is insufficiently sensitive or you are working at an exceptionally low light level, you can often still obtain a reading. Point the meter at a white sheet of paper or a handkerchief spread out to fill its field of view. This should be in a position where the strength of light falling on it is similar to that reaching your subject. Now multiply the resulting reading by a factor of four. This is two shutter speeds or two *f* stops. So, for example, if the meter reading indicates *f*4 at $\frac{1}{4}$ sec, set either *f*2 at $\frac{1}{4}$ sec or *f*4 at 1 sec. Alternatively, you can re-set the meter ASA dial to one quarter the correct speed, ie, 200 ASA becomes 50 ASA. If you are making exposures of several seconds you should give slightly longer exposures that those indicated by the meter.

If your areas of main interest are of different light levels you can take a close up reading of each and set your exposure at a point midway between the two indicated exposures. If you suspect that your meter is being influenced by lamps external to the shot, shield it from those lights with your hand while taking a reading.

If a light source is to appear in the picture, *do not* include it in the area read by the meter. Base your exposure on the subject only and let the light source take care of itself.

There is an alternative method to measuring the light reflected by the subject. You can use an "incident" light meter, which measures the light falling on the subject. You take a reading from the subject position, pointing the meter back towards the camera. The meter adds together all the light falling on the subject and indicates a reading for correct exposure with a mid-toned subject. You can make compensatory adjustments to take account of subjects which are especially light or dark in tone. Incident light meters are normally separate reflected light reading instruments which have an incident light attachment such as a translucent white plastic dome which fits over the meter window or a switch which has the same effect. They may thus be used for either type of meter reading. The meters built in to cameras are almost invariably the reflected reading type.

If your camera has no meter or it is inconvenient to use, work out the exposure using the table on page 223 or set exposures recommended in the leaflet supplied with the film. In such cases it would be wise to bracket your exposures by at least a stop either way of that recommended or assessed. If you suspect that you may be very wide of the mark, bracket at two stops either side of the basic exposure.

In a situation where you are often confined to placing the camera on a tripod because of the length of exposure times there is something to be said for using a large format camera such as a quarter plate, 5 × 4 in, or half plate. It makes a very satisfactory portrait camera and the more leisurely working rate which it imposes, tends to aid concentration on the exact arrangement of the subject within the picture area, the lighting and the appropriateness of the setting. You can, in fact, "plan" your pictures to some extent by adopting this approach, even though they may be portraits. Such equipment and the care that goes in to taking the picture gives the subject more sense of occasion, perhaps making him or her feel more important. The film is more expensive but the failure rate is probably much lower than with 35 mm or roll film cameras. The exposures may be quite lengthy but you can use fast film because of the small degree of enlargement required to make a print. You can even contact print from the larger sizes.

There is much pleasure to be gained from working with such equipment. Large format negatives secure very smooth skin tones and also lend themselves to retouching (if you agree with it).

For indoor portraiture the author sometimes uses a fairly large Victorian portrait camera with a variety of old lenses of differing construction. Primitive lenses can have very individual characteristics. They give a firm drawing to the image without the cruelly hard definition of the modern lens. At the same time they avoid the contrived "soft focus" effect of the special portrait lens or diffusing screen.

It must be remembered that a film has to receive a certain minimum of exposure to light before an image can be made to register at all. Whereas the modern lens is designed to give maximum image contrast by reducing internal reflection with special multilayer fluoride lens coatings, the old lenses produce a certain level of internal flare which may provide that minimum exposure required to overcome the "inertia" effect. For working indoors by artificial light or by daylight through a window such a lens has advantages because these are situations where the subject is inherently of high contrast. The general level of flare reaching the film raises the exposure level to the threshold point at which a developable image beings to register and lowers the contrast of the final image.

Film characteristics

The films you may use for indoor photography by artificial light are of four main speed groups, or categories of sensitivity.

Slow films These include all fine grain emulsions with speed ratings in daylight of 25–50 ASA. They are usually of high contrast and unsuited to photography in home lighting for that reason and also because they require very lengthy exposure times. You would generally only use such a film for copying or similar work on static subjects or because you happen to have the film already loaded in the camera from another occasion.

Medium speed 64 ASA–125 ASA (daylight). This speed is adequate for some subjects indoors though you still need fairly lengthy exposure times and portraits may be difficult. The camera has to be rigidly supported to take pictures in the majority of interiors. These films deliver a superb quality image, possibly the best of any films, especially the black and white materials. They are of lower contrast than the slow speed films. Colour films are available in tungsten and daylight versions.

High speed 160 ASA–400 ASA (daylight), 125–320 (tungsten). This is the film normally recommended for shooting indoors in home lighting. High speed films can have their sensitivity more than doubled by special processing (see page 206).

With normal processing they allow pictures to be taken with the camera held in the hand in most averagely well lit interiors. You are likely to have to use fairly wide aperture settings and low shutter speeds, however. The image quality in terms of grain and resolution is not quite up to the standard of medium speed films with equivalent processing. You should only discount their use if you insist on the very highest possible image quality. But they are satisfactory for all general work even where the printing demands a considerable degree of enlargement.

Ultra high speed 800–1200 ASA. Ultra high speed films are available for black and white photography only. They are of low contrast and have a very coarse grain structure. Therefore they are not suited to photography involving very considerable degrees of enlargement unless the presence of grain is unimportant. They are, of course, convenient for taking pictures at the very lowest light levels, and for all ordinary indoor work it is not necessary to put the camera on a tripod.

The right film

Colour films balanced for 3200 K photo lamps give a slightly warm-toned image when used in normal domestic lighting with its slightly lower colour temperature (2600–2800 K). This bias in rendering is normally quite acceptable if you are not actually making direct comparisons with known colour references. Such warm renderings are usually fairly pleasant in skin tones and slightly evocative of the warm atmosphere of home lighting generally. Daylight colour film is not suitable for home lighting because resulting pictures have a heavy yellow-orange cast.

The main difficulty with colour rendering when using colour film indoors is encountered in shooting under fluorescent illumination. The colour output of these lights is so variable that you can only "correct" it with the aid of a filter. A table of recommended filterings is given on page 224. This covers the use of daylight and tungsten balanced film under fluorescent lighting.

It is possible to use filters placed over the camera lens to adjust the colour balance of the light if you want to take pictures indoors and outdoors on the same roll of film. You can use tungsten film in daylight by fitting a Wratten 85B filter over the lens. Filtering inevitably brings some loss of effective film speed. It is not recommended to filter daylight film for use in artificial light because the filter required demands such a massive increase in exposure as to make the adjustment impracticable. Colour negative film, designed for making prints, can be exposed in any light source although the film is basically designed for use in daylight. Adjustments in colour balance can be made in printing, but there are limits. If you are working at the extremes, as indeed you are when exposing this film under home lighting, you could help out the printer by very *slight* filtering. A very pale blue filter over the camera lens would do, though even that causes significant loss of effective film speed. Such filtering is only called for if you are aiming for perfection. Normally, when shooting in low light it is best to avoid the use of filters altogether. You need all the light you can get on to the film.

Another approach, if you want colour prints of existing light scenes indoors, is to shoot on high speed (tungsten) transparency film and have prints made from the slides. This process is, however, rather expensive compared with the more orthodox method.

The colour response (rendering in terms of greys) with all modern black and white panchromatic films is excellent for portraiture. But some super speed films still have a slight extra red sensitivity making

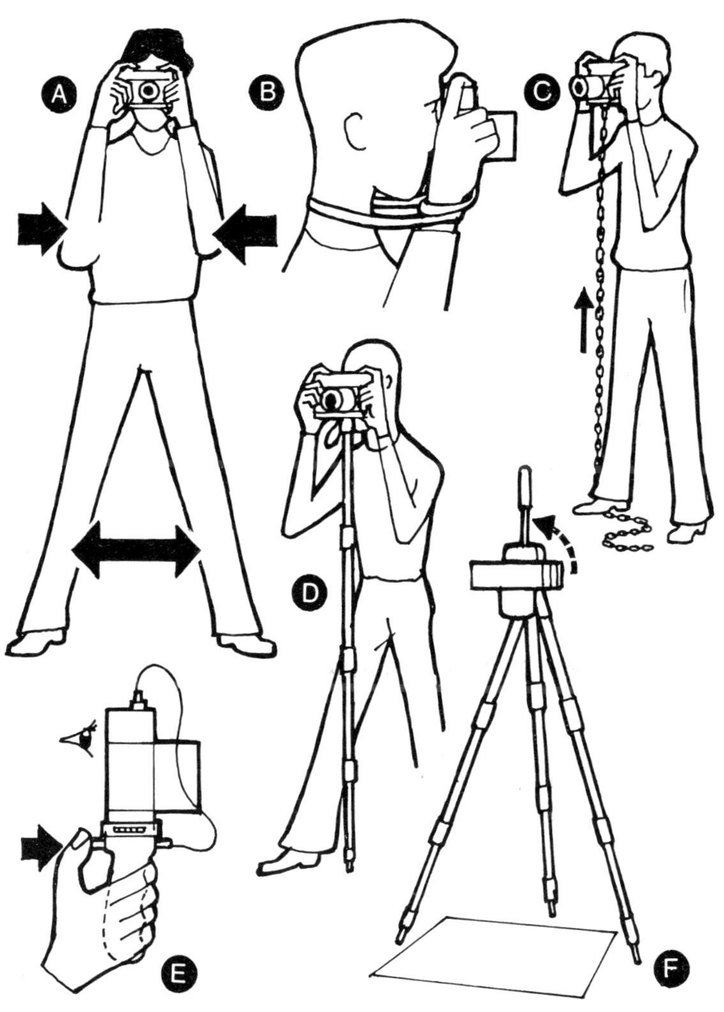

Handling the camera for long exposures. A. Hand holding works for medium-slow shutter speeds. Tuck the elbows in to the body and place the feet well apart. B. Steady the camera against the face by tensioning the camera strap round wrist and neck. C. Use a chain-pod, treading on the lower end. D. A monopod gives vertical stability also. E. Handgrips allow single-handed operation. F. A tripod is ideal for long exposures.

lips and other red areas in the subject appear rather pale. The warm tones of tungsten home lighting have a similar effect and so some people like to use a pale blue filter to slightly darken the lips and lighten blue eyes. This filter requires an increase in explosure of $\frac{1}{2}$–1 stop.

If you use a special film such as orthochromatic (non red-sensitive, available only as sheet film), all red parts of the subject are registered very emphatically as dark areas. Not only lips, but spots, pimples, veins and red cheeks come out strongly in the picture. Take care that you use it only on the right subject, usually male, and avoid photographing people with red noses!

Handling the camera

In some indoor situations the exposures required are so lengthy that you have no alternative but to support the camera rigidly in one way or another in order to get a sharp picture. In other lighting conditions exposure times are short enough for you to hand hold the camera quite easily, and a camera support becomes unnecessary. Between these two extremes lies a neutral area where the exposures could be done either way and you have to make a decision as to which is better.

The question of hand holding or using a tripod or other support is largely a matter of convenience. Hand held exposure times of $^1/_{15}$ to $\frac{1}{4}$ sec can be successful if the camera is kept very steady or you are just lucky. Longer exposure times than this call for some support though not necessarily total support. It is possible to get acceptably sharp pictures by holding the camera against the wall, resting your elbows against a piece of furniture or using some other solid object to help steady the camera. If you are anticipating great degrees of enlargement you must fully support the camera for slow shutter speeds or time exposures.

Tripods and other supports

The tripod is said to be restrictive in terms of finding shots, good angles, etc. It certainly is if you have to follow a moving subject indoors. For portraiture, on the other hand, it can be very convenient. You frame up and, while making adjustments within the picture, getting the subject to move a little or moving unwanted objects out of the way, the camera holds the exact position you chose and the focus you set. There is something to be said for that. For copying or close up work in low light a tripod or solid support is essential especially where the use of extension tubes or bellows means longer exposures and the slightest camera movement is greatly magnified.

When you set your camera on a tripod you should position it with the lens (especially a long lens) directly over one leg for greatest stability. It is most convenient to use a tripod fitted with movie pan and tilt head as this allows you to lock off camera movement in one plane and make adjustments in the other with a greater degree of control. Make sure that the tripod feet are firmly placed on the floor and will not "do the splits" when you put the camera on it. If the tripod has a centre pillar use it for greater height only if there is insufficient extension in the legs. Never use a short leg extension and a raised centre column. This makes the tripod particularly unstable. Fire the shutter with a cable release so that you do not have to touch the camera during the exposure. An air release offers a great extension so that you can shoot without necessarily standing next to the camera.

Various other forms of steadying device are suitable for indoor low light work. A monopod (a one-legged tripod) steadies the camera in one plane and allows greater freedom of movement about the room. A chainpod is a chain screwed into the camera base and hanging down to the floor. To use it you tread on the end of the chain and steady the camera by pulling upwards, keeping the chain taut all the time.

Hand holding

To keep the camera steady in the hands, you should use a good stance for the whole of the body. Stand with your feet slightly apart and elbows tucked into your ribs. Hold the camera firmly against the face with the hands round it in such a way that you can squeeze the release slowly and firmly with no other hand movement. It is much easier to release the shutter smoothly with a camera you know, as you are familiar with the response of the shutter button. If the camera is in a case you can steady it with the strap. Put the carrying strap around your neck or over one shoulder across the chest and take up the slack around your right wrist until it is an effort to bring the eypiece to the eye. The left hand should be free to adjust focus and aperture but should grip the camera firmly during the exposure.

You can gain extra support for hand holding from solid objects, as described earlier, but if you depend on those too much you are likely to be restricted by the position of the nearest usable support. Having lost that freedom it is worth reconsidering using a tripod.

Various camera clamps and grips are available to attach to the camera for convenient hand holding. Sometimes they have a built in trigger connecting via a cable release to the camera. The value of these grips is largely a matter of personal opinion.

Around and About in Existing Light

There are numerous opportunities for taking pictures by existing light in public places. You can shoot in galleries, museums and churches, pubs, clubs, theatres, shows, sports grounds or other places which are lit by window light, artificial illumination or a combination of the two. You may be interested in the building itself, or an exhibit. Or your subject may be the people you find there. Photography is well within your reach in almost any of these situations, each of which requires a different technique.

Dealing with reflections

Galleries and museums are usually well lit by either daylight or artificial light. The daylight may come from a glazed roof or skylight. This gives interesting top lighting to the exhibits, and is usually widespread enough over the area of each room to avoid very sharp contrasts of light and shade. Such lighting makes it easier to take pictures of paintings than a room with windows, such as the average country house interior or some minor galleries where light from the windows is strongly reflected in the picture glass. Even a polarizing screen is of little help because it requires you to shoot from a fairly acute angle and so reproduce the painting as a shape which is not strictly rectangular. It is better to concentrate your attention on pictures which are well lit initially. Even with skylights, or indeed with any specially arranged lighting it is difficult to avoid picking up reflections of highlights from other parts of the room, particularly from the gilt frames of paintings on facing walls. You can use a polarizing screen if you are shooting from a suitable angle but even then there is no guarantee that it will work effectively because it can only remove light reflections which happen to be polarized: random light reflections will stubbornly persist. Reflections in glass are fully polarized only when they strike the reflecting surface at about 57° to the normal. At other angles they are progressively less polarized and can be only partially eliminated. Thus, any reflections picked up when the camera is square on to the subject are likely to be largely depolarized and a polarizing screen can have little or no effect on them.
It helps if you can throw the reflections out of focus. This should be easy because you are likely to be working at a wide aperture anyway,

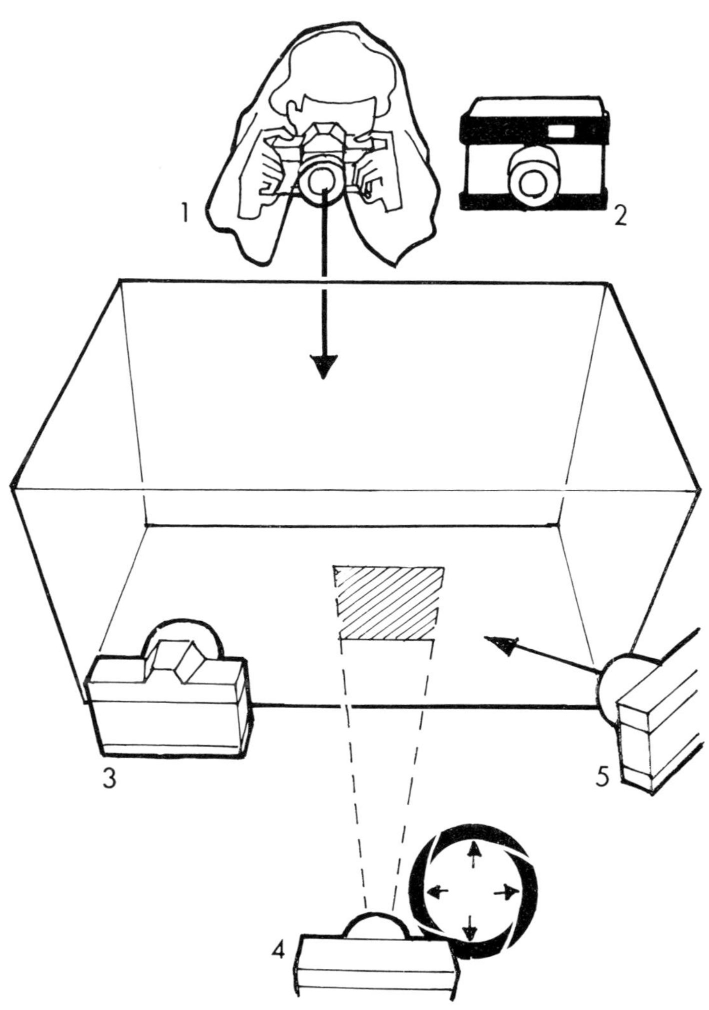

Objects behind glass. (1) Reduce reflection by placing a black cloth over the camera and your head if necessary or (2) black tape over chrome parts of camera. (3) Place the camera against the glass and use a rear focusing device or macro lens. (4) Select a wide aperture to limit the depth of field and reduce smaller reflections by throwing them out of focus. (5) Angle the camera away from the glass surface, if not in contact.

which gives less field depth. So, when taking pictures of paintings and engravings, use a fairly wide aperture (not maximum, where the performance begins to fall off) and a short enough shutter speed to hand hold if you have to. A tripod is the ideal assistant in taking gallery or museum pictures but many galleries do not allow you to use one. It is far more likely that you will have to hand hold your shots.

A few galleries and many country houses do not allow you to take pictures at all. At all events it is better to ascertain beforehand what is or is not allowed and to obtain any written permission necessary prior to going along with your camera and tripod.

Showcase and other exhibits

Museum exhibits and sculpture galleries often have specially arranged lighting to suit an object being displayed. Sometimes it may show well-calculated positioning in relation to light from a window. It may be only a piece of striplighting built in to a showcase or it might be carefully arranged spotlighting. The lighting is, of course, set up to give the best effect visually. It could be rather contrasty for the best effect photographically. There is now a much greater tendency for dramatic lighting to be used in exhibition and museum showcases. The days of the bleak case with a striplight seem to be coming to an end. In a way the newer method makes it more difficult to get good results using the existing light only. It is a good idea to take a small roll of paper along to use as a reflector if you are photographing small objects in a place that allows the use of tripods. Even that cannot help however, if the exhibit uses well shielded lights and does not reflect enough light itself for you to pick some up to reflect back. With all showcase exhibits, aquaria, etc, you must of course watch out for reflections off the glass. Chrome or shiny parts of the camera are certain to reflect if you shoot square on to the glass so you must mask them with black tape or dark cloth. It is better to shoot from an angle if possible. You then avoid reflections from the camera and may be able to suppress others with a polarizing filter.

Some museums have elaborate displays with pictorial backgrounds which, if rendered slightly out of focus, can look quite realistic. The exhibit may combine real objects, costumes and furniture, for example, with a mock up or real room interior and a mock scene through a window. Natural history exhibits are often seen surrounded by real dried grasses and rocks, with a painted backdrop behind. If you work at a fairly wide aperture when shooting in museums it helps you to play down background objects that you cannot remove by any other means.

When you are photographing pictures, maps, manuscripts or other items hanging in frames, keep the camera square-on to the surface of the subject. If you have to point it upwards to a picture hanging on the wall you may get a "keystoning" effect where, instead of being rectangular the top of the picture appears narrower than the bottom because it is slightly further away from the lens. Often it is impossible to get enough height to be level with the centre of the picture. In that case move further away and use a lens of longer focus.

If you are using colour transparency film, choose the film to suit the light source. Most showcase or set piece displays are lit with tungsten lamps and a high speed artificial light film would do for these. In all other instances use daylight material if you want the most accurate colour rendering.

You may wish to take candid pictures of people in museums or galleries. There are no special problems here. No one is likely to be moving very rapidly. It is mainly a case of remaining fairly inconspicuous to avoid getting self-conscious expressions or indeed causing annoyance to other people. You can often slip behind showcases or shoot through them. You can pretend to be photographing some exhibit. If the object is to photograph people and not exhibits you are often better off using a wide angle lens.

Church interiors

Churches and halls may be hunting grounds for inanimate subject matter or pictures of people. You may, indeed, be asked to take pictures of a ceremony.

If it is the church interior you are interested in, the main obstacle will probably be the question of light level. Many churches, particularly those with extensive stained glass, tend to be rather dark. Some Victorian gothic interiors must be among the darkest ever created. Other churches and cathedrals, even very ancient ones, can be relatively light. Most church interior photography has to be by daylight. Few churches could equip themselves with the lighting necessary to illuminate the whole interior fabric, and the strongest illumination tends to be concentrated on certain areas of interest. The altar is invariably provided with strong lighting and special lights are often installed to illuminate a particular wall or roof painting, fresco or some object of curiosity in the church. The most atmospheric church interiors are taken by daylight coming through windows – and we are talking here of a subject where the atmosphere is of prime importance.

The best church interior pictures are obtained by traditional techniques using time exposures. Preferably you should have permission to use a tripod. Otherwise you may have to resort to propping the camera up on an altar rail or a pew end to have it steady enough for a time exposure. Permission sometimes involves paying a small fee. If no fee is asked, some recognition to the verger will not go amiss.

Ideally, to take pictures in a church you need relaxation and a whole day at your disposal. Churches have windows on all sides and the appearance of the interior alters significantly as the sun moves round during the day. At a certain time it may fall on a window and throw light across a tomb or cast a pattern in light on the floor. Some parts of the building will light up properly only at particular times and the modelling of piers, vaults and carvings may be stronger when the light comes from that direction. As you walk about you have to watch your building and choose your times carefully. You also have to take account of any services that might be arranged to take place at intervals and the presence of visitors and others.

The average church interior represents a subject of enormous contrast range. You cannot hope to accommodate in a straight picture the detail in the darkest corners, the figure in a stained glass window and all the intermediate tones between these two extremes. One or other has to take precedence. If the window area in the picture is small then it is best to concentrate on the general scene. Only if the windows form the main part of the subject interest do you have to arrange your exposure in their favour.

Stained glass windows

To photograph a stained glass window you take your exposure reading straight off the glass, excluding as much as possible of the

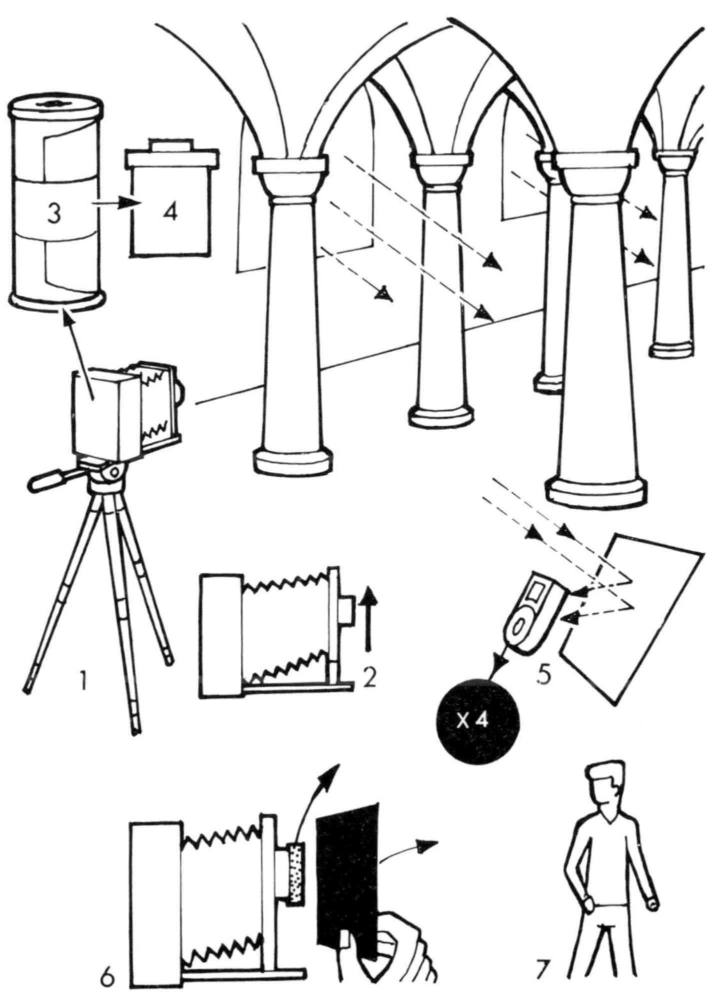

Success with church interiors. (1) Put the camera on a tripod (most conveniently with two legs at the back) make sure it is level. (2) Use a wide angle lens and if you have the ideal – a camera with movements – frame the subject with the rising front, keeping back and front parallel. (3) You can use a slow film for fine grain but (4) use a soft working developer to reduce contrast. (5) Take a white card reading and multiply by four. (6) Stop down to small aperture and expose in stages, shading if necessary. (7) People on the move may not register.

surrounding area. If you cannot get very close you must reduce the recommended aperture by one stop or more to allow for the effect of the dark walls. Do not take pictures of stained glass with the sun shining directly through. That is asking too much of the film, and leads to uneven lighting as well as a loss of colour or detail in the glass itself. So wait until the sun has moved round off the window before shooting. The ideal background for a stained glass window is the diffusion of an overcast sky. Medieval church builders used to build their own diffusers into the glass by giving the outside surface a white roughened finish. This scattered the light before it penetrated the glass and so increased its luminosity. If you work purely by available light the surroundings of a church window will come out very dark. You would need a flashgun to put some detail in here, but there are often restrictions on the use of flashguns in churches.

Advantages of time exposures

If you are taking general views of the inside of the building, the best method is to set up the camera, level if possible, on a tripod and stop the lens down to give a lengthy time exposure. You assess the exposure from a white card reading (see page 40).

The time exposure gives you an opportunity to increase the exposure in the upper part of the picture in relation to the rest of it. The upper portion is usually vaulting or roof interior and this is certain to be rather shadowy. Holding a piece of black card over the lens, you open the shutter and wait until vibration has subsided. Start the exposure by taking the card away and count off the seconds. Dodge in the upper part by shielding the lower part of the picture with the black card held closely in front of the lens. If anyone walks into your picture they probably will not register if they keep moving. If they stop, just cover the lens and wait until they have moved on. You don't have to use a fast film for this technique, therefore you have an opportunity to get the finest-grain image, though you have to weigh against this the fact that a slow film is more contrasty. If you are shooting on negative film, you can extend the correction for shadows when you come to make the print, evening up the whole picture to show detail everywhere. Do not overdo it though. You should retain the character of the lighting.

The aim is only to accommodate that on the print. Another dodge is to print in the window area separately so that you also get detail there. The "old master" photographers who took marvellous pictures of church interiors used to employ soft working developers and a little hand abrasion of the dense window areas on the negative, and then make final small adjustments in printing. The perfectionist can do this today, but you need a larger format camera which gives a big enough negative for handwork. Also, having a rising front, this type of camera allows you to include more ceiling and less floor foreground without getting converging verticals caused by pointing the camera upwards.

If you are photographing individual objects, again watch the lighting closely. The "dark light" in a hall or church is still light. It can model objects and create highlights and shadows as effectively as any other lighting; light is directly related to exposure. Also watch the background. If you are shooting in a dimly lit place you tend to overlook it because it may be relatively shadowy to the eye. But a time exposure discounts all that. A greyish object may come out obstinately white and spoil or confuse the outline of the object you are interested in.

After a while you get a feeling of how things are likely to come out in a picture. For this reason it is a good practice to make a habit of using the same materials and standardized processing.

When photographing groups of people in a church or hall time exposures are rarely practicable. Use fast film and, if necessary, pushed processing (see page 206). You need as much light as you can get, so if there is any supplementary lighting, arrange for it to be switched on. This may give you a mixture of colour quality if the main source is daylight but the effect should not be too pronounced. The predominant source should dictate the kind of film used. If the group is lit from lamps near at hand it would be better to move them as far away as practicable to avoid unevenness of lighting. The film exaggerates such differences even if they seem insignificant to the eye. You should choose a higher viewpoint than normal (standing on a chair, perhaps) so that you can include everyone in the shot and exclude the windows. Their appearance in the picture generally contributes nothing except possible trouble. Do not go too high or the subjects' faces will be unrecognizable from such an oblique angle. Another method of getting everyone in the picture is to arrange them at different levels standing on steps, or some standing and some sitting. With informal groups you have to take more of a chance on including everyone satisfactorily in the picture.

Clubs and pubs

Here the lighting can range from anything between quite reasonable – as good as the average domestic interior – to very dim indeed. In some places of entertainment the lighting is deliberately set to a very low level – the equivalent of using a 15 watt lamp in an average sized living room. Dark furnishings may also be chosen to match the lighting. In such cases you have real problems. The brightest reflecting surfaces may be the customers' faces but they are surrounded by darkness and in the final picture may just appear to be suspended in space. In such a context, assuming that you can take the pictures at all, you have to consciously aim to fill the picture space with any light-emitting or reflecting objects you can find, simply to suggest the location or provide some atmosphere.

Exposure at exceptionally low levels can really only be based on readings taken from a white card (see page 40) or the best reflecting main area of the picture, in this case faces, unless you have an exceptionally sensitive exposure meter. You will almost certainly be limited to areas of inactivity and so you have to look for stationary but nevertheless interesting situations.

The existing light you find will probably be highly diffused generally but you can still look for light pools under lamps, etc.

In a club or pub with a band or floorshow, the general lighting level is much higher in the audience area by reflection from the stage. It is also fairly directional, and this is exaggerated by the film. The atmosphere, and detail of faces in the audience is far better but you must take care to differentiate between the exposure level for the audience and that for the stage, which is far higher. If you expose for faces in the audience, the stage is considerably over exposed. If you base exposure on the stage only, a few faces in the front row are clearly defined, but the remainder quickly fade into the darkness.

The stage lighting in clubs is often bright enough to permit shooting moving subjects at precise moments of rest. These are often anyway the best parts of a dance to put on film and you have a much better idea of what you are getting than shooting the movements in an intermediate position. Colourful lighting provides the interesting possibility of deliberately setting slow shutter speeds ($^1/_4$–1 sec) to give long coloured streaking effects or patterns on the film. Intermediate speeds ($^1/_8$ –$^1/_{15}$) may give enough blur to impart a sense of movement, but not so much as to make the subjects indistinguishable individually. A pop group moves sufficiently to blur on such an exposure time yet still retain some outline to suggest what it is. Intentional blur pictures are generally far more successful if the background is completely dark. You need an even, neutral ground for the blur to be distinguishable. A pop group has the advantage of being at roughly the same distance from the camera for most of the time. Dancers and cabaret artists often move about as part of their act. You have to follow with the focus fairly carefully. With the band, on the other hand, you can afford to select a wider aperture and still keep the subjects reasonably sharp all the time. If you are not allowed to move about during the show you may have to shoot from exactly the same spot throughout. Subjects such as dancers who themselves constantly form new compositions would seem more promising material than subjects whose act is less mobile or tends to repeat itself.

Many, perhaps most, clubs do not permit photographs to be taken, but you might be able to obtain special permission. It can help if you suggest that the management may use some of your pictures for publicity purposes. If you undertake to supply pictures to someone, do not fail to do so, if only for the sake of other photographers who may follow you.

If you are taking candid pictures in a pub or social club it is a good idea to base your shooting on a definite centre of interest such as a dartboard, billiard table or pinball machine. Here you should get a variety of faces and good expressions. Also the situation is more controllable from your viewpoint as you are shooting from more or less standard distances. Working by available light only should help you to remain unnoticed for some considerable time if you are subtle about it. Also if people's attention is directed towards a game it is less likely that they will pay much attention to you. You might manage a slow speed exposure in very poor light by putting the camera on a table or bar counter and nonchalantly pressing the button to get your victim. But one advantage of pub or club games is that the participants have to have enough light to play by. Base the exposures on faces and add to that what you can. You can take a reading off the palm of your hand to find the basic figure. Do not balk at putting a light in the picture area. This can work wonders for the atmosphere conveyed by your results. Go for close ups of faces with expression. Heated conversation, businessmen's cabals and boy meets girl situations are typical of the endless human interest that is available to you. Chance the occasional unusual angle such as billiard table with huge balls in the foreground and a miniature player on the far end of a cue, with light streaming down from a shaded lamp above. Card tables and roulette wheels are other such centres of interest where the light, though shielded, is strong and the place is rife with an atmosphere which may be actually visible in the form of cigarette smoke!

Sport and shows under artificial light

Few professional theatrical producers grant permission to take photographs of a show. Your activity in this direction is likely to be largely confined to amateur dramatics. Most indoor entertainments operate the same restriction. Outdoor floodlit sports fixtures are conducted under less stringent conditions and usually no questions of "copyright of a work of art" apply.

Assuming that you have obtained permission to take photographs on the premises, stadium, etc, if necessary, your next problem is to make sure that you are situated in a convenient position for all the best shots. There are preferred positions for certain sports, normally places where the action is decisive in the game.

For football, a position among the spectators looking into the goal mouth or a position on the goal line is the best. With tennis and badminton a position at either end of the net allows you to cover action at both sides. Unless you shoot from a high angle, in shots from the end the far player may be almost invisible. Boxing requires a ringside or gallery seat for general views or close ups through a telephoto lens. Athletics must be covered from a position where the athlete shows up clearly against the background, but not from so low a viewpoint as to be shooting directly into the lights. Domestic games such as table

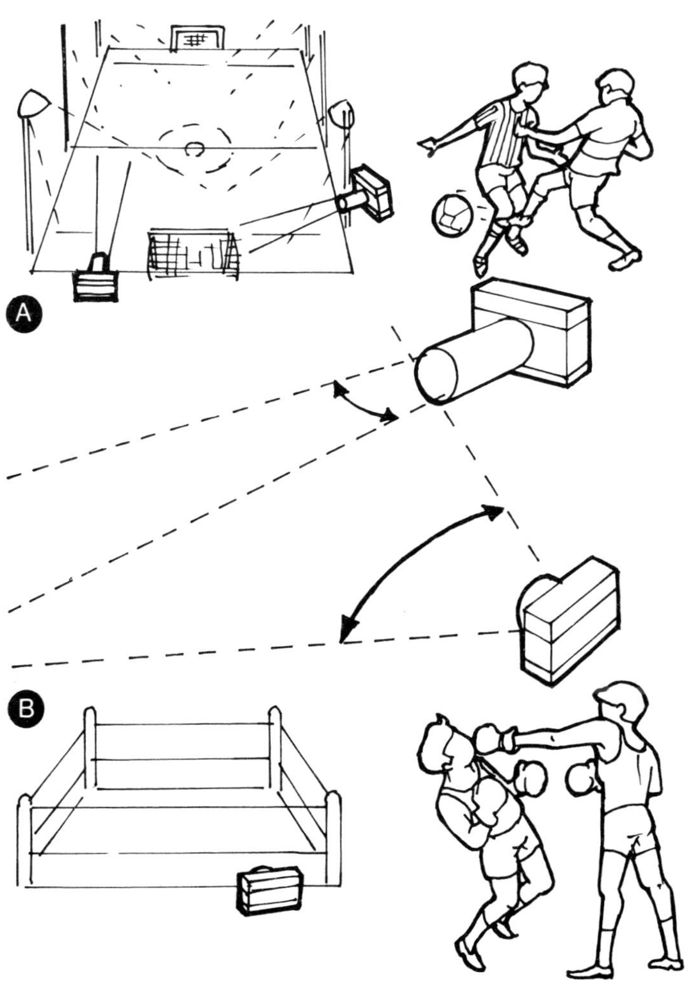

Sport and action. A. Football. Good positions to shoot from are beside the goal or in to it. Use a long focus lens if necessary to obtain reasonable shots, but its maximum aperture may not be wide enough. B. Boxing. A ringside seat is best, using a normal or wide angle lens.

tennis do not permit you to move very far away from the point of action; you could easily get in the way of one or both players. You are safer shooting from the centre of the table, or one player may block your view of the other.

You must select a location near enough to include as much of the action as possible without needing lenses of too long focal length because these lenses have a smaller maximum aperture and you will almost certainly find this a disadvantage. On the whole you have an easier task if you aim for general views rather than close shots of individual players or athletes in these conditions. A general view can be taken with a lens of shorter focal length, allowing more depth of field, than a long lens which would have to be very quickly and accurately focused for every shot, as you would probably be working at or near the maximum aperture for the lens in use. General views are usually more effective from a higher viewpoint than from ground level.

You cannot hope to arrest the rapid movement of the average sport in the way that you can in daylight unless the lighting is very bright or not far from the subject, you have a wide aperture lens, and you use the fastest film. It is easier to take such pictures in black and white because you have at your disposal the ultra high speed film materials.

Some sports, however, are not really very fast moving for much of the time. Wrestling, boxing, gymnastics, archery are cases in point. You could get away with quite slow shutter speeds for these, 1/30 sec or less.

Sports activities and other shows may be lit by carbon arcs. For these you need daylight film. Some, in institutional buildings, for example, often use fluorescent lighting. This suits dahlight film also. Most theatrical productions however, use tungsten illumination. At circuses, ice shows and tattoos where much larger areas are lit you may encounter either tungsten or carbon arc lighting.

For most of these situations, if well lit, you could expect the exposure to be around 1/30 sec at *f*2.8 with a medium speed film. If the action required a faster shutter speed you could load with a high speed material or push-processed colour and use 1/125 sec at the same aperture. These recommendations are, however, generalized, and should be used only as a basis for selecting a suitable film, or for exposure where no reading can be taken.

Circus lighting tends to be concentrated in the central area and mostly comes from overhead but with an occasional spotlight added from the side. Circus lighting should be fairly consistent in strength through an evening's performance.

Despite the circular arena, there does tend to be a "front" to the performance and it is as well to be on or near that side. Probably the best position would be on a gangway (no heads and clear foreground) to the right or left of the frontal area, and not too close if you want to take everything in. A ringside seat is, however, good for close-ups.

Theatre pictures these days are mostly taken at dress rehearsals unless there is a special photo call. In amateur productions this is by far the best solution and for these you may gain permission to shoot on stage.

Off stage, the best positions are usually centre stalls for individual groupings or the front row of the dress circle for a general view. In theatres with wide stages you sometimes have to retreat in to the rear stalls to include the whole acting area. The lower boxes or side circle seats are a good position for close-ups of individual actors but wider views from this position tend to overshoot the stage.

Exposure with a normal stage show with full lighting might be 1/30 sec *f*4 with a medium speed film. But the light level may alter from one part of the production to the next. Also, with musical or variety performances coloured lights are often brought in for effect. It would be advisable to increase exposure by one stop over that for the full stage lighting to take account of the drop in light level for coloured lights.

Shooting the TV screen

An important event, a favourite actress or a person you know can be photographed as they appear on the television screen. There is no particular problem with shooting it in colour or black and white. The camera should be rigidly supported and lined up so that the screen fills the image area to get the maximum sized picture on the film, taking care to correct for parallax error if necessary. Readjust the set so that the contrast is lower than you normally have for viewing and turn up the brightness to bring out as much detail in the picture as possible. Set the colour balance controls to get as good a rendering as you can achieve and set the camera shutter on a speed of 1/30 sec or less. Each complete picture is formed every $1/25$ sec ($1/30$ sec in US) so with shorter exposures than these there is a risk of losing part of the screen image. Leaf shutter cameras are more reliable in this context because with them the whole image area is exposed simultaneously, owing to the very short opening time of the shutter. The blind of a focal plane shutter, on the other hand, moves relatively slowly and can fail to synchronize with the linear movement of the television scanner. The result is diagonal darker bars across the picture.

A medium speed film should allow an aperture of about *f*4 but it is a good idea to take a series of test exposures at different apertures. Exposure meter readings directly from the screen are reasonably reliable but lighting levels vary considerably in some productions and the needle may swing violently. You have to estimate an average reading. You will probably obtain the most successful pictures by catching moments on the screen when the activity is not too violent. It is advisable to switch off all lamps in the room and draw the curtains to avoid picking up strong highlights reflected off the front of the screen. The television image is projected on to a curved surface so do not expect to achieve completely distortion free results. Television pictures are normally the copyright of the television company concerned though many companies would not object to your taking them unless the pictures were to be reproduced commercially.

How
Processing
Can Help

When shooting by existing light, even with present day equipment and materials, you can still have problems in getting enough image density on the film to make an adequate picture. The exposure given to the film is of course only a part of the story. Photography is a two-part process and exposure and development go hand in hand. The latent image put on the film by exposure to light is dependent on the right development to make it suitable for viewing (in colour) or printing in colour or black and white.

Film is designed for exposure at a given ASA speed. This speed is calculated on the basis of average working conditions with certain processing chemicals, time and temperatures. If the chemical content of the processing solution, the temperature or the development time is modified in any way, then the effective speed of the film too, is affected.

As a general rule, you do not modify the recommended process because it is designed to give optimum quality for the material concerned. But if you want to extend its performance you can do this in a number of ways, provided that you can accept that results may not show the finest image quality in all respects.

Colour

You can increase the effective speed of a film by using prolonged development times or special high energy developer. With colour film, which is often handed over by the customer for processing at a commercial laboratory, you can have the sensitivity increased by the same means. High Speed Ektachrome, for example, can be increased to $2\frac{1}{2}$ times its normally rated ASA speed by being specially processed. This would give it an effective speed in daylight of 400 ASA and in tungsten light of 320 ASA. That offers you a great advantage for hand-held existing light pictures. When you combine it with the widest aperture setting it brings most subjects and situations within your reach. It also means that in brighter conditions you can stop the lens down to smaller apertures than would normally be needed and so gain depth of field. Alternatively, you can use a higher shutter speed which might be useful for action pictures by existing light.

If you use a laboratory to process your colour transparencies you must give them very clear instructions as to how you want them processed, stating at what rated speed the film has been exposed and that you want it "force processed" or "push processd" to compensate.

In the case of Ektachrome films processed in the US a special processing bag is available which is coded to indicate to the Kodak laboratory what type of processing is required. You indicate this on the outside of the envelope.

For special processing of this film in the UK and continental Europe, the film must be handled by an independent laboratory, because Kodak do not provide the service themselves. In that case you give the instructions to the dealer or laboratory.

Get your film processed as soon as possible after exposure to avoid deterioration from the effects of latent image failure (where the undeveloped image gradually fades after exposure, affecting the density of the image or colour balance).

Some colour films can be processed by yourself at home using kits supplied by the photo dealer. Colour transparency processing is not as straightforward as colour or black and white negative work for either of which you can use simple two-bath methods.

The main stages in processing colour transparencies are:

1 First development to obtain negative image.
2 Re-exposure to produce reversed (positive) latent image.
3 Colour development to give positive image in dye and silver.
4 Bleaching of silver images to leave an image consisting of dye only.
5 Fixing of image.
6 Washing.
7 Drying.

Temperature control at the development stages must be fairly precise, particularly for the first development, which controls the film speed.

To increase the effective sensitivity of the film the standard development time can be extended. Below is a table for push-processing films by the Ektachrome E4 process:

PROCESSING TIMES FOR INCREASED FILM SPEED

Ektachrome X	High Speed Ektachrome Daylight	High Speed Ektachrome Tungsten	Multiply the time in the first developer by:
ASA	ASA	ASA	
250	640	500	1.75
160	400	320	1.50
125	320	250	1.35

There is no special economic advantage in processing your own colour reversal films unless you can obtain the film at lower cost in bulk lengths.

The image quality of push-processed colour transparencies is not quite as good as normal. There is an increase in contrast and grain, in proportion as you extend the development time. Grain becomes a little pronounced on high speed film pushed to two stops or more. Pushing film beyond the recommended maximum affects not only grain but colour renderings. Within the recommended maximum, colour rendition should be good.

It is not recommended to push-process colour negative films. In fact, as far as existing light photography is concerned, there is no special reason for processing your own colour negative film (unless you are also colour printing and using a kit whose chemicals are suitable for print *and* film processing). Colour printing, on the other hand, has some advantages in as much as you may wish to make adjustments in colour balance to the pictures you have taken in varying lighting conditions.

Many people who print their colour also process their own film. The processing of a colour negative film resembles that of black and white but by most available methods it involves more separate stages and takes longer. The control of temperature and processing time, however, must be more rigid and greater care is needed in handling to avoid physical damage of the soft emulsion. Two-bath procedures are becoming available, but the main stages in many processes are: develop, stop and harden, wash, bleach, wash again, fix, wash, rinse, dry. These stages, added together, can take the best part of an hour, without drying, and assuming that you have previously prepared all the solutions and raised or lowered them to the working temperature. So it can be quite a time-consuming operation.

Full working details of processing and printing with colour materials is supplied with the kits made for them. Other details in connection with handling the materials in the darkroom are covered by three other books in this series: *Photoguide to Home Processing* by R. E. Jacobson, *Photoguide to Enlarging* by Günter Spitzing, and *Photoguide to Colour Prints* by J. H. Coote.

Black and white

One of the advantages of black and white photography is the great flexibility in handling it offers in exposing, printing and enlarging the picture. This is especially true with existing light work where you may be making demands on the film which it was not originally designed to accommodate.

Present day monochrome films even with quite high speed ratings such as 320 or 400 ASA when processed according to recommended time and temperature in a suitable developer produce a surprisingly grain free image and good definition. The higher speed films tend in any case to be of lower contrast than normal. Often it is difficult to distinguish between the grain structure of an enlargement taken from a standard speed film and that from a fast film when correctly processed.

As the faster films can cover virtually all available light situations, even with a hand-held camera it is less likely that you will want to push-process them, though this too is possible and usually gives fewer problems than is the case with colour, for there is less to go wrong.

Black and white films are available in a much wider range of speeds than colour. At the upper end of the speed range there are the super speed emulsions far beyond the maximum speed of colour materials even with push-processing. The exposure latitude is also greater and these films are tolerant of a wide margin of error compared with colour transparency materials. This means that you can still obtain quite a good quality print from a negative which has been under- or overexposed, particularly the latter. It is even possible to underexpose deliberately by a stop or so in order to "get the picture" in difficult lighting conditions, yet still achieve an excellent negative with standard processing. Much depends on the contrast range of the scene you are shooting, however, and the kind of result you want. If the scene is full of light tones or of low contrast, generally you can afford to cut exposure. If you want to have a picture full of shadows you can also afford to give less exposure than that normally demanded. When underexposing you lose detail in the shadow areas first. Mid tones and highlights are not greatly affected.

Contrast in a negative is related to the processing time and normally, you should process your black and white films for the times recommended. If you increase the development time you will increase the image contrast because the developer works more vigorously in the areas where there is an image already than in the areas where there is little or nothing to increase on. So the highlights become "blocked up", and lacking in detail. If you decrease the development time the reverse happens; the highlight areas are less blackened than they should be, and there is little detail in the shadows. The differential in density between highlights and shadows is insufficient to give a print that uses the full contrast range of the paper. The result is a "flat" print, which is also generally rather dark or muddy. Detail, as such, is confined to highlight areas; the shadows are often just empty spaces.

Because so many existing light situations tend to contain excessive contrast between highlight and shadow areas it is quite useful to have a method of reducing contrast in the negative. With conventional photography a normal method to reduce contrast is to underdevelop the negative, having made up for the loss in image density by overexposing while taking the picture. The problem here is that in most existing light situations you do not have the scope for much overexposure. Overexposure does also tend to increase the grain size. Marginal overexposure may be obtained by using a faster film but this also depends on the particular working conditions. A better approach is to adopt a developer that is designed to give low contrast within known limits.

The most commonly used low contrast developer is an MQ type with an extra concentration of metol and no hydroquinone (which is the main ingredient for high contrast). The percentage of sodium sulphite (preservative) can be reduced because of the relative stability of metol in solution. Various proprietary brands of low contrast developer are available.

Another approach to obtain low contrast is to use a low energy "fine grain" type of developer. The main problem attendant upon these developers is loss of film speed, although this has become less evident in more recent products. Two developers are suggested below in case you wish to make up your own solutions.

Low contrast

Metol	5 gm
Sodium sulphite (anhyd)	25 gm
Sodium carbonate (anhyd)	37 gm
Potassium bromide	1 gm
Water to make	1 litre

Dilute 1 + 3. Dev. time 10 min.

Low contrast "fine grain"

Sodium sulphite (anhyd)	100 gm
Hydroquinone	5 gm
Borax	3 gm
Boric acid	3.5 gm
Potassium bromide	1 gm
Phenidone	0.2 gm
Water to make	1 litre

Generally speaking, lower contrast is obtained by employing developer in greater dilution than normal. The use of "compensating" development increases exposure latitude and compresses the tone scale thereby making it very suitable for high contrast subjects.

Push-processing black and white

It is possible to increase the effective speed rating of a film by selecting a developer designed for that purpose, by increasing the development time or by stepping up the concentration of developer when making up the dilution from stock solutions. With all these methods there is, however, a deterioration of image quality, mainly a loss of detail in shadow areas.

By uprating a film from, say, 160 ASA to 320 ASA, what you are in fact doing is underexposing the same film by one stop. This results in a loss of detail in shadow areas. No amount of push-processing or other remedies will restore an image that has not been allowed to register as a latent image. Push-processing or the use of developers in stronger concentration increases the density of the areas already containing an image (ie *not* the shadows). But there is a loss of quality to the image due to an increase in both grain and contrast. Push-processing should therefore not be regarded as a regular technique but as an emergency measure, unless image quality is unimportant to you.

Much depends on the contrast range in the original scene. If you are shooting a scene with high contrast range a greater loss of detail is evident than if the scene is evenly lit though at a low enough light level to be photographed at the normal speed rating. It is best to avoid the technique with high contrast scenes because the resulting negative may have such an excessive contrast range that it cannot be printed and one side of a face, for example, may be in such deep shade that the person is scarcely recognizable.

There can be no rigid recommendation for push-processing; it must vary with every film and developer combination. But as a rule of thumb an increase in concentration of developer to double the normal strength might be expected to produce an increase in speed capable of compensating for underexposure by one full stop. An extension in development by half as much again as the basic recommended time would have something like the same effect. This is about the limit before image quality begins to be seriously impaired.

You may, of course, wish to emphasize the contrast or restrict the tonal range of the image for effect, and in that case there is nothing to prevent you from using the technique in any scene and extending it to cover even greater degrees of underexposure.

Printing

The main difference between printing existing light pictures and ordinary negatives is the greater contrast range and the lack of detail in shadow areas.

Good technique in printing has always been thought of as utilizing the full range of tonal contrasts of which the printing paper is capable. This range, as with film, is very limited compared with what we see in real life. In fact, you have to "fit" a range of contrasts on the negative in to an even more restricted range on the paper. There is, therefore, all the more reason for using the whole of it.

Try to use a paper which will give you both a full black in at least one or two areas of the picture and a full or near-full white in another. If you do not, the print may look rather poor.

With many negatives of high contrast subjects (such as those taken by window light) you will find that normal paper grades (2 or 3) give too high contrast to separate or even register the intermediate tones. If these are important try grade 1. This often gives what you want. You may not need to print every detail visible in the negative – this depends on the effect you are after. But you should avoid choosing a grade of paper so soft that it shows the shadows as grey areas without detail, although the gradation in the highlights is satisfactory. This type of print is characteristic of a negative that has been underexposed.

Deciding the best contrast for printing existing light pictures can be a little tricky: you must not show up the limitations of the negative in the printing. If the original negative has been underexposed and lacks sufficient density in the highlights to give enough contrast for the normal printing papers, you have to use a higher contrast paper even at the cost of a high-contrast print that makes the scene look darker.

There are methods of intensification to increase the density of existing images but they work most effectively with negatives which have been underdeveloped rather than underexposed. There is also a method of re-photographing a very thin negative placing it against a dark background and obliquely lighting the surface of the silver image. But these rescue operations are difficult to manipulate and rarely produce a worthwhile result. Nothing can really compensate for poor technique in the first instance.

Adding Light

The many advantages of taking pictures by existing light do not preclude its combination with special photographic lighting – lamps or flash in either a supportive role or as the main source.
Anyone who values the quality of existing light for any of the reasons discussed in previous chapters would probably use photo lamps or flash only as a last resort. A single flash head with a short lead (or no lead) is severely limiting as a primary source for photography. Moreover, it has several distinct disadvantages which rule it out almost completely for serious work where the artistic quality of the lighting is of any importance.
The built-in or camera-shoe-fitting flash method gives some of the most unpleasant lighting that it is possible to achieve by any means. There is absolutely minimal modelling on the subject, often a fringe of hard shadow appears around parts of the subject's outline, and the reflection of the flash off the back of the eyes makes them glow red like something out of a horror film.
Manufacturers place the flash gun on the camera purely for the physical convenience of doing so. Often the flash unit cannot even be directed away from the line of sight so it is impossible to bounce the light off any other surface and, via that, on to the subject to give a softer effect. The bounced-light technique is the basis of existing light plus flash, where the existing light is the main source and you use the flash gun to add a little detail to shadow areas. This is probably the best use for flash in the context of existing light work.

Existing light plus flash

Where your subject is lit by existing light a flash gun can be used directly for reducing the general level of contrast or supplying light from a direction which would otherwise be in total shade, such as the room side of a subject seated at a window. If the general contrast level is to be reduced, the flash can be positioned frontally, coming from the camera position or close to it. This adds light to both highlight and shadow areas but the greatest effect is in the areas of shade. So the whole picture is reduced in contrast and surroundings that are not too distant from the camera yield greater detail. Foreground objects might appear overexposed or as distracting

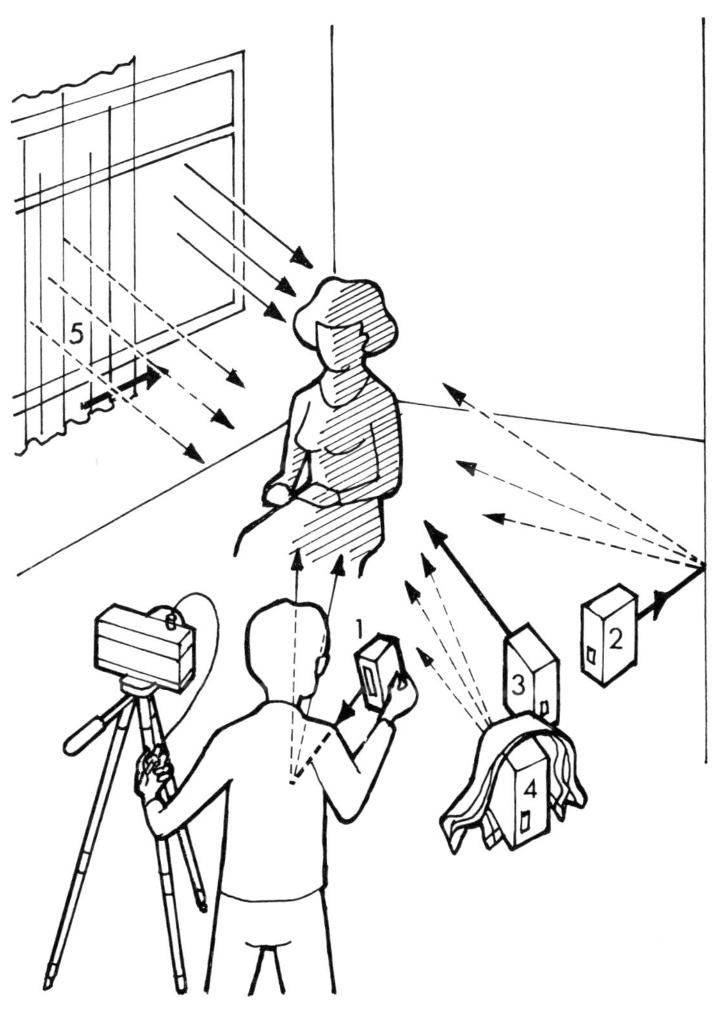

Existing light plus flash. With window light as the main source, to fill shadows you can (1) bounce the flash off your own body (2) off the wall (3) use it direct (4) diffuse it with two folds of handkerchief or (5) adjust the strength of the window light with a blind.

highlights, so you should remove any object that might offend in this way.

Fill in flash from an open (undiffused) unit, however restrained, has an unfortunate habit of appearing artificial. The small bright flash tube is inescapably reflected in the subject and perhaps elsewhere as a pinpoint or pencil line highlight, or on skin as a small "greasy" patch. To obviate this, try diffusing the flash with several folds of white cloth or paper handkerchief. Another method is to turn the flash head round and bounce if off your body. For this purpose it helps if you are not wearing a brightly coloured shirt or blouse, for instance, or the bounced light will throw a cast of that colour on to the subject. You could bounce the flash off a sheet of white paper placed near to the camera, but take care not to let any light spill in to the lens.

Sometimes you may wish to fill the shadow area of the subject from an angle away from the camera viewpoint. This is particularly appropriate if half the subjct is in shade. But the lighting should preferably be quite restrained and diffused to avoid cross shadows, and the secondary shadow of the subject should be arranged to fall out of the picture. The shade side of the subject can be filled by bouncing the flash off a wall, such as the wall facing the window. This way, the fill light appears most natural in its origin, merely making amends for the exaggerated contrast effect of the film.

Precise exposure control for fill in flash is important as the fill light must not overpower the main source, which provides the key lighting and modelling. The fill light should preferably appear to be the result of natural reflection in the scene rather than a secondary source.

You can calculate the strength of the flash on the subject by a simple method. The aperture set for the key light (the existing light) provides the basis for this. You divide the guide number for the particular flash gun or bulb by the *f* number and that gives you the range, in feet, at which the flash gun should be set to give lighting equal to the key. You then reduce it proportionally to obtain the right balance, either by moving the unit further away (twice the distance for a quarter of the light), by heavy diffusion or by bouncing if off an intermediate surface. For the latter purpose you calculate the distance by adding that from the gun to the surface to that from the surface to the subject plus any absorption factor for a wall that is not a good reflector.

It is difficult to determine the exact amount of fill-in flash required by

calculation alone, and it would be wise to take more than one shot at different flash distances, or with different degrees of diffusion and pick the best result. A reasonable starting point is to set the fill light at one quarter of the power of the main light.
Flash can be used in conjunction with existing light to provide an effect. It might be a highlight in the hair, rim lighting to one side of the head to separate it more distinctly from the background, or light on the background itself to separate *that* in tone from the subject. In any of these roles it is not the major light source, but in each case the power of the flash must be calculated in relation to the known aperture determined by the main existing source.

Flash plus existing light

In some conditions where the existing light is simply not strong enough to provide an effective key, the flash can take over the role of modelling and the existing light serve as fill in or effect light. The balance of the relative power of flash and existing light must be just as accurately controlled but in this case your aperture and shutter speed are set to the values at which the existing light provides sufficient fill, ie about one quarter of a full exposure. The flash distance is calculated in the normal way, by dividing the guide number for the unit or bulb by the *f* number set.
As with the previous technique, a flash providing the key light can be adjusted for distance in various test shots until you achieve the most desirable balance with the existing light. The flash must, of course, be positioned as if it is the key light in the scene.
If you have a flash gun of the automatic or "computerized" type it is best to set it on manual operation when using it in conjunction with existing sources. Automatic flash does not offer you sufficient control over the situation because from the outset the flash is governing the aperture you must use. Some automatic flash units require you to set only one particular aperture for film of a given speed. Others allow a choice of two or three apertures for each film speed, automatically cutting the flash off at a point when the sensor on the gun measures sufficient flash light reflected off the subject. This, of course, varies with the distance, so that in each case the amount of flash permitted

to fall on to the subject is tailored to fit the operating distance at the known aperture set. The flash unit is always used from the camera position and in most cases cannot be used for bounced illumination but only direct with the light sensor's line of sight corresponding to that of the flash itself.

The main advantage of an automatic flash unit is that it allows you to move the camera and gun towards or away from the subject, yet the flash remains correctly adjusted for the distance. It works well enough in average conditions but can nevertheless be misled in the same way as an exposure meter, by isolated areas with excessive light or dark reflections.

The arbitrary aperture of, say, *f*5.6 or *f*11 that the flash gun requires you to set for a given film speed is unlikely to correspond with that needed for the non-adjustable existing light situation whether you are using the flash as the key source or as fill in. You could set a smaller aperture on the camera than that indicated for the film speed if you were using the flash as a quarter-strength fill in. You would, however, also have to make a compensatory adjustment to the shutter speed to keep the exposure correct for the existing light. The problem here could be that some cameras do not allow flash synchronization at many shutter speeds and if the required speed was quite low, as it would be in many existing light situations, there might be trouble with movement during the exposure.

Unless things just happen to work out right, on the whole it is best to avoid using a flash gun on automatic for this type of work.

Flash with daylight and indoor lighting

The ratio of brightness between the light from the flashgun used as a fill in and the main source, whether it be daylight or artificial light has been stated hitherto as 4:1, that is, two stops. It has been assumed that you do not wish fill in flash to serve any function beyond giving marginal fill to the shadow areas, so that the basic character of the existing light can be maintained. Indoors, where there are probably many reflecting surfaces around – walls, floor, ceiling, etc – this ratio may hold true. Outdoors, even where the flash is being used in dim light, its effect is further reduced quite often by the absence of any nearby reflecting surfaces. A proportional increase of, say, half a stop, or equivalent shortening of flash-to-subject distance would be called for to gain the same ratio as that for an indoor picture. If you want the full effect of fill-in flash the difference in brightness between flash and main light need be only one stop. In that case you could move the flash gun by roughly half as much again as the calculated distance for the flash as a main source. Used in this way, the presence of flash is very obvious, and you do not have, in the accepted sense, a picture by existing light. In particular circumstances, however, that may be the only way you can get a printable shot.

There are no particular problems with mixing flash and daylight whether outdoors or through a window. Using daylight film, the colour balance of these two sources is close enough in most cases, provided you use the blue bulbs (which almost all are these days) or electronic flash, whose light quality is equally suitable to mix with daylight. Naturally, there will be differences in colour quality if it is evening or early morning and the daylight is consequently much warmer in hue. You could filter the flash but it is probably hardly worth the trouble. It is possible to remove the blue coating from bulbs to give much warmer tones but this makes them more liable to explode on firing, and could be dangerous without a shield.

The real problem arises when you want to use flash combined with artificial light using colour materials. If you use daylight film, the artificial light appears very orange or red and the flash by comparison slightly cold and blue although it is, in fact, correct for the film. If you use artificial light film, on the other hand, the artificial light appears a little warm but the flash very cold indeed. (Fluorescent tubes vary between these extremes according to the colour of the particular tubes.) On the face of it, clear (uncoated) flash bulbs would seem to provide an answer, but they are not generally available and the only remedies are to remove the coating (risky), filter the flash, or bounce it off some warm-toned reflector such as a pink shirt or red/orange reflector. A suitable filter is an R12 or 85B over the flashgun. Gelatin or acetate sheet filters are suitable for this purpose. If the flash is intended as a very restrained fill, bouncing it from warm-toned surroundings might be sufficient to correct the balance to acceptable levels. What is acceptable in this context is largely a matter of subjective judgment.

Further technical details on the use of flash both on its own and combined with other light sources are in the *Photoguide to Flash* by Gunter Spitzing.

Flash at night

You can use flash at night, either as the main source to illuminate the subject or as shadow fill-in to a picture which attempts to preserve some of the mood of a night scene. In neither case is the result likely to be particularly pleasing.

Light from a flash gun outdoors falls off in brightness very rapidly because of the lack of reflecting surfaces around the subject to carry the effect further in to the field. Consequently, unless the background is very close to the subject it is certain to come out very dark, or at least be almost untouched by the flash. In such circumstances the light from the flash conforms very closely to the inverse square law. Visually, flash lit night pictures are almost always very unappealing. The flash from the camera position gives very flat lighting, no modelling in the subject, and a feeling of unreality. It is difficult to account for the light source psychologically and consequently one does not associate it with anything real. The subject in fact often looks like a cardboard cut-out against an artificial background (if indeed a background is visible).

You can combine flash with existing light in the evening or night by using a time exposure and the open flash technique. You set the shutter on B, open it, give the time exposure required for the background or other features to register on the film, and then fire the flash independently of the camera and finally close the shutter. The camera must be on a tripod and the subject must not move during the exposure or there is a risk of recording a double image on the film. If you are taking a flash picture against a sunset, you base your exposure on a direct meter reading of the sunset, giving half the exposure time indicated, in order to preserve the colours in the sunset at their full intensity. You then make the exposure and flash during that exposure, using the manual "open flash" trigger on the flash unit.

If you are actually using the flash as the main source at night, you could try taking a few shots with the unit placed at an angle away from the camera viewpoint, giving some modelling. The shadows will probably be very black, but unless there happens to be a convenient reflecting surface nearby, such as a wall, the result may be just a little less unpleasant than a direct head-on flash into the subject. You could also try bouncing the flash off your own body so that at least the subject is lit by diffused light and the shadows are less hard-edged.

There are various other techniques involving flash which, though they might in some circumstances be combined with existing light, do not have any particular relevance to it. These include lighting set ups employing more than one flash head, in the role of key and fill light perhaps with existing light acting as an effect or some other arrangement of these three functions involving existing light as one. Or there is the technique of using time exposures with more than one flash.

Existing light and lamps

The great advantage of photo lamps and an advantage that makes them infinitely superior to the average flash gun is that they allow you to see what you are doing. You can see what effect your lighting has on the subject before you take the picture. With flash you can do this only if the units include special modelling lights, and these are usually fitted only to the fairly elaborate studio type flash sets. With ordinary electronic flash units your lighting is the result of a calculation and not a visual inspection. Some people consider photolamps essential for portraiture, for example. Being able to see the light, you can control it exactly and make the kind of subtle adjustments necessary.

Another advantage of photo lamps is that their colour quality blends more easily with that of existing artificial light without the difference in warmth being too obvious. Artificial light film is made in two forms balanced for use with light sources that differ slightly from one another in warmth.

Artificial light film such as Kodachrome Type A, is balanced for use with photoflood lamps (3400 K). They have a filament designed to be overrun so as to give a far higher light output than their rated wattage indicates. The No 1 photoflood, rated at 275 watts, has an effective output of 750 watts and the more powerful No 2, rated at 500 watts has an effective output of about 1600 watts. Overrun lamps have a short working life: 2–3 hours for No 1 and 6–10 hours for No 2 lamps. Artificial light films such as Agfachrome 50L (3100K) and Ektachrome Type B (3200 K) are balanced for use with photopearl or studio lamps. These high output non-overrun lamps are available in 500 and 1000 watt versions. They have an operational life of about 100 hours. Colour films designed for use with such lamps are also corrected to work well with longer exposure times than normal, yet retain good colour quality.

Photoflood lamps can be used to substitute ordinary dometic bulbs by inserting in the same table lamp or overhead fitting provided that you do not run them for long enough to burn the shade. You can switch them on just before the exposure and off again immediately afterwards. It would be far safer to remove the shade altogether.

Photofloods, and indeed photo lamps in general are so powerful that they easily overpower most existing artificial light. They can be used as the main source or, heavily shielded, as a fill in for the subject or a large scale background if the subject is either very close to the existing artificial light or is basically lit by daylight.

Photoflood lamps (3400 K) do not balance well with daylight. Unlike flash, their colour quality is far warmer than the nominal colour temperature for daylight films (5500 K). Whether the effect is acceptable or not depends on how it works out in specific pictures and is also a matter of personal opinion.

The colour bias of a colour negative film can be corrected in printing. But with no colour film can you correct for the differences between two different-quality light sources used in the same picture. The bias must be either towards one or the other. In principle then it is best to bring them together as much as possible at the time of shooting. But as we have seen, existing light photography normally precludes the use of filters. Usually you have to accept some inequality so it is best to restrict the less tolerable colour to a small area of the picture. Lighting methods with one or more lamps in supporting or substituting roles in existing light apply in just the same way as those using other forms of tungsten illumination outlined in previous chapters. In most cases these days you will find it is not too difficult to avoid the use of substitute lighting altogether, and thus retain the beauty and versatility of existing light.

Long Exposure Compensation

The effective sensitivity of colour and black and white films is reduced when exposures of one second or longer are given, due to reciprocity law failure. If this is not taken in to account and exposure is based on the nominal reading or calculation obtained, the resulting negatives or transparencies can be between ½ and 2 full stops underexposed. Figures for exposure compensation with individual films are quoted by most film manufacturers, but generally the faster the film emulsion and the longer the exposure, the more compensation is needed.

With colour film, longer exposures also result in a shift of colour balance. This, though not serious, can be adjusted with a colour correction filter.

It is not recommended that colour film be exposed for periods longer than 100 sec. if a natural colour balance is desired.

Film	ASA (Daylight)	Sec.	(Add Sec.)	8 Sec. (Add)
Slow speed	25–50	+½	(or ½ stop)	8 (1 stop)
Medium speed	64–125	+1	(or 1 stop)	8 (1 stop)
Fast speed	160–320	+1	(or 1 stop)	12 (1½ stop)

Kodak issue data for the colour compensating (CC) filter required with each of their colour film emulsions.

Agfachrome colour slide film is available in two versions, CS & CL, for short and long exposures.

Fluorescent light filtering and exposure increase

Lamp	Daylight film	Tungsten film
Daylight	Filters: 40M + 30Y Add: 1 stop	85b + 30M + 10Y Add: 1 stop
Cold White	Filters: 30C + 20M Add: 1 stop	10M + 30Y Add: 1 stop
Warm White	Filters: 40C + 40M Add: 1 stop	30M + 20Y Add: 1 stop

Recommended exposures for low light photography

Indoor Subjects artificial light	Slow Speed sec.	fno.	Med. Speed Film sec.	fno.	Fast Film sec.	fno.
Bright areas	1/15	2	1/15	2.8	1/30	4
Medium bright	1/4	2–2.8	1/8	2–2.8	1/30	2–2.8
Poor light	1	2.8	1/2	2–2.8	1/2	1.4–2
Firelight, candlelight, small lamps	1	2–2.8	1/4	2–2.8	1/15	2
Stagelighting, circus, shows	1/30 1/60	2–2.8	1/30– 1/60	2.8–4	1/60	2.8–4
Sports, stadia	1/30	2.8	1/60– 1/125	2–2.8	1/125	2.8–4
Church halls, amateur stages, swimming pool	1/15	2	1/15	2–2.8	1/30	2–4
Church interior (Hand-held)	1	—	1/8	2	1/15	2–2.8
Church interior (Viewcameras)	1 30	2.8–4 11	1 15	5.6–8 11	1 15	8–11 11–16
Daylight and Night Scenes						
Street at night	1/15	2	1/15– 1/30	2.8	1/30– 1/60	2.8–4
Lights only	1/30	2.8	1/60	4	1/60	4
City centres	1/30	2.8	1/30	4	1/30	5.6
Shop windows	1/30	2.8	1/30	4	1/125	4
Floodlit bldgs.	1	2–2.8	1	4	1/15	2
Fairgrounds	1/15	2	1/30	2	1/60	2.8
Fireworks	13	8	13	11	13	16
Bonfire	1/30	2.8	1/30	4	1/60	4
Lightning	8	5.6	13	8	13	11
Window light bright	1/30	4	1/30	5.6	1/30	11
Window light medium	1/15	3.5	1/30	3.5	1/30	5.6
Window light dull	1/15	2.8	1/30	2.8	1/30	4
TV Screen	1/30	2	1/30	4	1/30	5.6–8
Moonlight	—	—	45	2	15	2
The Moon	1/15	2.8	1/15	5.6	1/30	5.6

Index